Boy Meets Horn

The Michigan American Music Series

Richard Crawford, Series General Editor

The Michigan American Music Series focuses on leading figures of American jazz and popular music, assessing both the uniqueness of their work and its place in the context of American musical tradition.

BOY MEETS HORN

by

REX STEWART

edited by

Claire P. Gordon

Ann Arbor
The University of Michigan Press

Copyright © 1991 the estate of the late Rex Stewart, and Claire P. Gordon

Published 1991 by the University of Michigan Press

1993   1992   3   2

This edition not for sale outside the United States of America and Canada

Library of Congress Cataloging-in-Publication Data

Stewart, Rex William, 1907–1967.
    Boy meets horn / by Rex Stewart ; edited by Claire P. Gordon.
        p.   cm.
    Includes bibliographical references and index.
    ISBN 0-472-10213-3 (alk. paper)
    1. Stewart, Rex William.   1907–1967.   2. Jazz musicians—United
States—Biography.   I. Gordon, Claire.   II. Title.
    ML419.S767A3   1991
    788.9'6165'092—dc20
    [B]   90-26950
                                                                                      CIP

Typeset by Opus, Oxford
Printed in the United States of America

Contents

REX STEWART
by
Elmer Snowden

    I have been asked before to write a few words about "REX"
but I never did, because I am not a writer, and I felt that it would
be better for both Rex and me if I just told what I knew to some writer.
Well, after reading some of the things that I am supposed to have said,
I am going to try and set the record straight for once and for all time.

    I first knew Rex in Washington, D.C. that was back in 1920, and
I had just about the most popular band in town, in my band was Otto-
Hardwick, Art Whetsel, Eddie Ellington, who became known as
"Duke Ellington", later. We played all of the Dance Halls and worked
almost every night. One night we were playing Murrays Casino and a
band of younger fellows came in to audition or try out for some dates.
that was a crazy bunch of kids led by a piano player named Ollie -
Blackwell. They called themselves the "Clowns Band" and sat on the
Floor or jumped up on the piano while playing. We did not think much
of them, but we did notice Bernard Addison the Band-Man, and the kid
in whort pants, who did not blow good, but he sure was loud!!!!
Well the years passed and the next time I saw Rex, we both were in
N.Y. There had been the split up of my original Washingtonians and I
was playing at a Ballroom named the "BALCONADES," in my band I had
Jimmie Harrison on trombone, and he told me how good "Rex", was
playing, I couldn't beleive it, but Jimmie insisted so often that
I told him to bring Rex down and let me hear him. That was in 1923,
and when the boy came down he was hired, and stayed with me until 1926,
when I made him join "Fletcher Hendersons Orchestra". Now when I
say that I made him go with Fletcher-I mean just that. Rex was loyal
to me, so loyal that he did not want to leave me even for more money,
and the prestige of taking "Louis Armstrong's place in the Greatest
B ig Band, of that time. Looking back over the years I realize now
that Rex always had something to offer, when he was with me, he
developed amazing technique that was the foundation of Roy, Dizzy,
Clifford B rown , and others. Then I watched him grow into a High Noter
with Fletcher Henderson, influenced of course by Louie. And DOGGONE,,
if he did not come up with still another style when he went with "
"Duke", because I never heard anybody else play entire melodies using
half-valves! I haven't heard Rex for years except on records, but I
wouldn't be surprised, if he did not come up with something new again.
    In closing, I would like to say that it is a pleasure to write
about a good friend, a great musician , like Rex Stewart.

                Sincerely
                Elmer Snowden

A Few Words from the Editor

Many will wonder how this book came to be written. How is it possible to publish the autobiography of a musician who has been dead for over 20 years? These are the facts. During the last decade or so of his life, Rex Stewart spent a great deal of time writing. Since his typing was of the hunt and peck variety, loaded with typos, and his spelling was entirely original, I was his willing assistant, collaborator and associate for most of his published works. He and I had worked on about ten chapters of the autobiography before his death. These pages I had typed and edited from his hand-written manuscript and he had then revised. The remainder was on many legal pads, plus scraps of paper, scribbled notes on envelopes and so on. In his will, he left me all his writing and I knew he counted on me to finish the autobiography.

After his death, I farmed out the remaining hand-written pages to be typed and tried to induce a writer friend of his to tackle the autobiography. It really was an insuperable task. The material was shipped back to me, some having meanwhile been xeroxed by another would-be compiler, and now the pages were in haphazard order, a jumble of hand-written, typed and copied pages.

The box full of his writings sat on a high shelf in my closet for several years, waiting for the word processor to be invented as well as for me to have the time to plow through these thousands of words of notes, put them into appropriate time-frames, and select the best writing (at least 10,000 words do not appear in the book as they are in some way a duplication of other material or not relevant). This is an appropriate time to give much deserved credit to my friend and Ellington expert Steven Lasker. It was he who inspected the contents of the "Rex" box and persuaded me to begin work on the book.

Subsequently, he researched dates, spelling of artists' names, etc. For his invaluable input and encouragement, my wholehearted thanks.

Incidentally, I have been asked why the reminiscences only go up to 1948. That is because Rex believed that the events in his life and the music business both underwent a significant change at that time. His intention was to write a sequel incorporating the later years. For the reader's information, in spite of ill-health (high blood pressure and diabetes) these later years were a busy time for him. Most likely, he would have written about having had a small (unsuccessful) food operation in upstate New York, being music director for a New York radio station and playing dixieland music with Eddie Condon before moving to California in 1960. On the West Coast, he contributed jazz reviews regularly to the *Los Angeles Times*, was a disc jockey on local Los Angeles radio, played an occasional gig (many with Stuff Smith), wrote several articles for *Downbeat* (most of which were compiled as *Jazz Masters of the Thirties*), lectured at colleges, did some fancy food catering, composed music, was involved in an oral history project and coached a few advanced cornet pupils. His notes say that he wrote articles for the American magazines *Esquire*, *Jet* and *Downbeat* as well as for *Melody Maker* (England), *Le Jazz hot* (France) and *Estrad* (Sweden). He died suddenly on 7 September 1967, not having started work on the proposed sequel.

In this entire autobiography, only about 500 words were not written by Rex. These consist of further explanations, connecting sentences and such. Basically, this is a book by and about Rex Stewart. I hope the reader will enjoy reading it as much as I did while putting it together.

Claire Gordon
Los Angeles, California, July 1990

Prologue

A book is a printed work on sheets of paper bound together, usually between hard covers. I cannot guarantee that this alleged book will be bound together but I can assure you, dear reader, the work is harder than the covers that I hope the book will be bound with. Possessing no starry-eyed illusions as to the magnitude of this self-imposed task, still I labored under the compulsion to add my thoughts, experiences and recollections. Dealing mainly with segments of a musico's life, I trust this work will prove amusing, informative and even thought-provoking. And before continuing I do want to point out that this account is factual. And although some of the incidents border on the fantastic, they actually happened – and to me.

Yes, my little book is a sort of catharsis and at the same time it proved to be a tenuous thing in substance as it evolved. And I felt a rosy glow of relief, plus a sense of great accomplishment after finding my way out of the maze of memories, despite the obstacles of trying to talk like a third trumpet player and at the same time like a writer. I can go no further without thanking the following enemies and friends, associates, tutors and mentors. And if the above is not quite explicit, let me put it this way: I consider my scope is enlarged by each contact with humanity, whether friend or enemy. As long experience has taught me, the roles are interchangeable and varying from time to time. But they all have been my inspiration and I hereby dedicate this book to Fletcher Henderson, Louis Armstrong, Douglass Gorseline, Happy Caldwell, Paul Whiteman, Duke Ellington, Boris Via, André Hodeir, John Norris, Francis Thorne, Richard C. Green, Ted Stromin, Billie Holiday, Claire Gordon, Margie Stewart, Paul Draper, George Simon, Hugues Panassié, Salvadore Nepus, Benny Carter, Budd Schulberg, Eddie

Condon, Joe Glaser, Elmer Snowden and, with special thanks, Henry Felsen. These names represent a fair cross-section of my friends (and enemies) and I want to thank them collectively for the privilege of having known them.

These thoughts, these dreams, have been built into a marvelous montage which emerges from my consciousness in such torrents that I pause and wonder how could all this have happened to me? Yet, the ten thousand or more one-nighters, as I recall them, kept step with the days – the hungry days, the well-fed days. Nor can I slight the mountains of triumph or the valleys of despair, the glorious acceptances mingled with the humiliating rejections. Separable? Oh no, they are joined, as twins, side by side in the kaleidoscope of my life as a musician, which has been truly a pot-pourri of mirth, madness and melody.

How unfortunate that most musicians get so worn out from the constant struggle to earn a living that they become inarticulate, their memories beclouded and all illusions lost. But, as I mentioned before, I have nothing to lose. I am not on any way-out kick nor am I an alcoholic. And although I do not consider myself a writer, I feel that I can spell out these pertinent thoughts just for the record. One truth I have discovered: it's much easier to blow a horn than to write about when, why and how. Which is why I hasten to disavow usage of the word. And while I am being humble (for the moment) I might as well beg your indulgence for any unavoidable lapses into the vernacular of my trade. No doubt most laymen are aware that musicos have a private language of their own. Anyway, it is my sincere hope that this self-imposed catharsis will be accepted in the spirit of informative fun or something.

THE RAJAH'S establishment was perhaps the most bizarre, of all of the places of that type that I have ever known. And I only became exposed to his operation, by chance, as he ~~only~~ catered strictly to those with beau coupe bucks. One morning about 4 or so a party of 6 people decended upon the club where I was working. And we were damn sorry to see them fall in, (as in those days, the band played on until every last customer, left.) But, Dago Frank was the epitome of obsequiousness, the head waiter when they ordered wine, so we began playing, in between our yawns, a bunch of Broadway showtune crap. But we might as well been the furniture, for all of the attention that the party paid us. Until one of the women called out, to hell with that ~~corn~~ corn, get the lead outa your a———, play us some blues, don't cha know the blues). We segued into some down to earth blues, and the party got groovy, especially after one of the fellows put a hundred dollar bill on the piano. On and on, we played the blues and the piano became increasingly decorated with bills – 10's, – 20's, – 50's – we didn't even care when we quit. This was a bonanza night, based on the blues, Happy Caldwell, turned to Herb Gregory, our trombone man, saying man, come on wake up. N' play some more blues, keyhole blues, old blues, new blues, dirty red blues — with all of this dough in front of us, we're gonna play them blues, until — until — ah sheet, until, no – not – one. The party finally broke up, and one guy said to his woman, honey, why don't we go by the Rajah's, we'll go, and take this horn man. She agreed, and off, we went, little did I know what I was getting into. And I didn't care, not with all of that mola floating around.

Part of Rex Stewart's draft of the story that appears on pages 74–5

1

Go-Get-It

To paraphrase Aesop's fable which said the race goes not to the swift but to the one who endures, I figure to qualify as an endurer. Going back to 1921, when I was one of the seven young members of Ollie Blackwell's Clowns, I stayed in music all my life.

1921 was a momentous year for us members of Ollie Blackwell's Ragtime Clowns because we were actually part of a show! The group ranged in ages from 21 down to 14. Blackwell was 21 – and I was 14. Yes sir, to a man we felt that we were knocking at the door of destiny. We saw *Go-Get-It* shimmering in bright lights over the marquee of the Howard Theater. This theater, in Washington, DC, was named after General Howard, an abolitionist hero of the negro people. I will always remember that fateful day. Although you could not have found our names among those shimmering lights that spelt *Go-Get-It*, still, in the lower left-hand corner of the program, there it was! "Ollie Blackwell's Ragtime Clowns." That was us and we felt about ten feet tall. After all, we had been selected to do the show over all the professional musicians around town.

I'll admit that I was mystified when we youngsters latched on to the *Go-Get-It* show over all the well-known bands and entertainers of the time. I figure we must have been hired because we were the cheapest, because we sure weren't very good – just a group of green, inexperienced kids. Maybe our naivete was refreshing, and the fact is we *had* to be kids to have the nerve to play dance music all dressed up in clown suits. Come to think about it, though, it was a pretty good gimmick.

Anything went as part of the act, including bad notes, of which there were a-plenty.

Naturally, we were overjoyed at the chance of earning all of that money, 15 whole dollars a week! And there would be no more getting run out of the hall, which often happened when we dared to ask for the $1.50 that we earned on most jobs. Everything looked great, but I was a bit worried because, with the exception of Perry Smith our violinist, none of us could read music. Not only that, we only played in B flat, E flat and A flat – some keys for singers. This was because Ollie, our leader, was self-taught and couldn't read. But it turned out all right. There was little written music. We woodshedded our way through with many rehearsals and were off to a flying start. The group was piano, drums, banjo, violin, C-melody sax and cornet. The most important man in the group was the violinist Perry Smith, who was 18 at the time. This beloved compatriot deserves much more credit than he has ever received, and I, for one, propose thanking him in print. Perry taught us the melodies, the correct harmonies and directed the group. If it had not been for his help on the music, I guess I would still be in Washington. What a drag to think how constricted my life would have been without the broadening influences of my travels and the people I've met and the things I've seen.

The other fellows in the band were Ernest Hall, our 19-year-old clarinetist from Pops Johnson's band, the same kid group where I had started learning to play; Bernard Addison, who played banjo quite well for his 18 years and later became well known; Ollie, our leader, who played piano and was the oldest at 21. I was the cornet player. There was Tommy Edlin, aged 19, a horn player, and Jim Blair, a triple-talented man whose first instrument was kazoo, a sort of musical gadget with a sound like blowing on a comb with tissue paper. Jim's home town was La Plata, Maryland. He had several talents. One was consuming great quantities of corn liquor, and besides kazoo his other instruments were violin and trombone, which he played quite badly even by our standards. Despite his playing several instruments, nevertheless he was eased out of the band.

Luck was with us all the way during that period. Our

drummer, Tommy Wood, had recently married and was not planning to make the tour with us. We were worrying about this one day when Tommy was late for rehearsal. Just then, the candy butcher, whom we all knew as String Beans, wandered in, sat at Tommy's drums and said, "You are looking at the world's greatest show drummer. I'll take this deal down for you." We liked his work and know-how so much that we all agreed to chip in so he would have the salary he demanded of $35 a week, and prevailed on String Beans to come along.

It was intended that *Go-Get-It* start with two weeks at our local DC playhouse, the Howard Theater. This theater usually featured revues with casts of 40 to 60 people and was the starting point of a chain of theaters. We were scheduled to follow the usual route, going on to two weeks at the Royal in Baltimore, followed by one week at the Crispus Attucks in Norfolk. Then we would settle in for a long run at the Gibson in Philadelphia and wind up the East Coast tour with two months at the Lincoln, New York City. After that the show was to go west, all the way to Chicago. At least that was what Mr John Mason and Mr Slim Henderson (our bosses) told us.

John Mason's claim to fame is that he is the person who created the comedy routine *Open the Door, Richard*, which later was a song hit for Dusty Fletcher. Anyway, while they sat in the dressing room with us, these two gentlemen told us youngsters all about our potential careers, starting with the musical opus *Go-Get-It*. We were in seventh heaven as we listened to the great showman explain how the colored people were ripe to break away from the traditional vaudeville-type show. Mr Mason and Mr Henderson were sure this experiment was bound to wow the public who were tired of the same old TOBA stuff, which usually consisted of loosely strung together skits and songs. On the other hand, *Go-Get-It* was a revue held together by a plot. It had a story line about two crooks trying to get rich.

To explain about TOBA, these initials stood for Theater Owners' Booking Association and there were about 20 or so members all over the country. Started by S. H. Dudley, this was a loose-knit organization of negro theater-owners, reflecting the growing awareness of entertainment as a release from everyday life. They were able to book acts for 20 consecutive weeks, often beating down the price of good talent because, if an act wouldn't work for less money than they could get from the white theaters, they couldn't have the 20 weeks. This was standard business practice and poison for some of the fine talent of the time.

This reminds me that it is strange that there's never been any historical mention about the East Coast and its being the center of musical activity. That is a pity because there were so many dance halls, oyster houses, honky-tonks, beer halls and so on which provided employment for them.

I still remember some of the outstanding acts. There was Boots Hope, who was a truly original ventriloquist. He worked in Chinese make-up speaking pidgin English. Then there was Wilton Crawley, who was famous for dancing with a lighted coal oil lamp on his head. And that's not all – he played the clarinet at the same time! Another personality was Jack Wiggins, "the fastest tap-dancer in the world," as he billed himself. He would open his performance by having a pretty girl come on stage holding out this 100-dollar bill. He bet the money every show that nobody could dance faster than he did. And there were never any takers. I'm sure you've never heard of all the talented people but they were there, spreading joy, as the saying went.

There was a lot of music and bands around Washington at that time. Some of the better known were Doc Perry (whose piano man was Eddie Ellington – before he was called Duke), Elmer Snowden, Sam Taylor and Gertie Wells. Professor Miller had the best doggone military band in town outside of the US Marine band. Then there was Cliff Jackson, Emory Lucas, the Eglin Brothers, Tommy Miles, Jim Blair and Caroline Thornton, to name a few more people you probably never heard of. Only a few old-timers will recall Marie Lucas, who had the greatest ladies' band with at least one male member. Juan Tizol, who later played trombone with Ellington, was with this band. There was a trumpet player, Dan Johnson, nicknamed Georgetown, who was so great that every band wanted him when they heard that horn. Nor shall I ever forget the

Washington Bell Hops. Mose Duncan's Blue Flame Syncopators and Ike Dixon were out of Baltimore. There were the Hardy Boys from Richmond, Virginia. Pike Davis was a wonderful trumpet player and "Baltimore" was a great show drummer; Allie Ross was a violin prodigy and Catherine Perry was another violin great. I couldn't help wondering why we had been chosen over all these accomplished professionals to play this extravaganza *Go-Get-It*. We had a right to feel pretty cocky. Our salary of $15 a week was big money. Why, at that time grown men were raising their families on far less!

It was all new to me. I was due to start high school that same fall. I had started playing hooky from school to take some of the engagements Ollie Blackwell got for the group. Gradually our price went up and I was earning a dollar and a half. I used to proudly give Mother the dollar and bought myself oysters and pie and cake at school. And I began to feel my oats as I stood on the corner and said, with great nonchalance, "Well, I'll see you fellows when I get back from La Plata or Indian Head." The kids would gape. Some envious youngster would ask, "But won't you be in school tomorrow?" And I would retort with scorn, "School! I haven't got time for school when I can make three dollars for two nights. I can go to school anytime." But I was never so wrong. My school days were just about over and I never did return for any length of time. At that time, I was overwhelmed with the feeling of being a man and almost independent, coupled with the knowledge that in two nights of playing music I could make as much as my mother did at the theater! She played piano at the Blue Mouse, the neighborhood stage and movie house theater, and earned, as I recall, about two dollars a week. And actually that was a fair salary back at that time.

My mother could understand my wanting to be a musician because she and all the rest of the family were so musical. There was always music in our home. One way and another, I had always been exposed. I've read of kids having early recollections of being in a theater trunk. My first memory was hearing organ music. It was nice and warm where I was and I heard beautiful sounds all around me. The memory persisted for years, so I asked my mother about it. She told me that I was two years old when I attended my first concert – in a box behind the organ! Every member of the Johnson family played instruments and, along with other talented people, were in demand for concerts. My grandmother, grandfather, Aunt Dora, Uncle Fred and mother were all musicians. Grandpa, Grandma and Mother played organ; the others were accomplished on one or more instruments, too. That night they were all performing and, as this was in the days before baby sitters, they had to take me along.

My Uncle Fred was the first person I ever heard playing ragtime. Although my grandmother frowned on what she called the "Devil's music," Uncle Fred would play for me as much as he dared. One of his favorites was a tune called *The Preacher and the Bear*, which turned up again 45 years later in jazz music, and it seems strange to me that during those intervening years the bear got lost! The first ragtime piece that I learned to play from reading the notes was *Cuban Moon*. The rest of the tunes came easy, especially since I could learn by ear, and later Mother helped me by teaching me from her sheet music. At the theater she played tunes like *K-K-K-Katy*, *When You Wore a Tulip*, *Walking the Dog*, *Hello, Ma*, *Zip, Zip, Zip* and other popular songs of the day. She alternated these with semi-classical music, Viennese waltzes, the *Poet and Peasant* Overture, some Bach, etc. As a result of her well-rounded musical background, Mother Jane was considered one of the best piano players in town, which was something to brag about because there were many movie theaters and, although each had a good piano player, needless to say, the others were mostly men.

After I had been with Ollie Blackwell for a while, we had a Saturday night job playing a dance at the Eye Street Hall, which was located in the red-light district of Southwest Washington. This was a lowdown district, even lower than Foggy Bottom. All of the pimps and whores were out for a good time. And all of the hod carriers, washerwomen, cooks and housemaids were there forgetting their cares and woes for a while.

"I'm stomping off, let's go," Ollie shouted. We played "Get way back and snap your fingers, get over Sal and don't you linger, one step, two step all round the hall." These were the words to a popular ragtime tune. Ollie Blackwell's Clowns were popular along with the song that night at Eye Street Hall. I was happy about that and even happier to know that, when we got paid, I'd have plenty of money. I intended to buy a lot of fried oysters, ice-cream sodas, ginger bread and hot dogs – all of the favorites of a growing 14-year-old. Yes, the truth of the matter is that most of my earnings went into food. Nevertheless, I was a skinny kid then, with pipe-stem legs, and I have the snapshots to prove it. But I had already nearly attained my full height of 5 feet 6 inches, and weighed about 125 pounds. Even though I've never grown any taller I've expanded considerably in girth over the years. Mostly, I've weighed 100 pounds more!

As a growing lad, I was bicycle mad. For a short time, when we lived away from Georgetown, there was a neighborhood grocery store owned by Mr Parks, an Irishman. I talked him into hiring me as a delivery boy and buying me a bike. But then, when we moved back to Georgetown, no more bicycle. I had pleaded and begged but I see now that this was a stupid, unrealistic demand because there was not bicycle money in our house. Besides, my mother was afraid I'd get hurt and my Grandpa wouldn't go against her wishes. Although the music bug had certainly bitten me at that time, nevertheless for a few years I would have sold my soul for a bicycle.

It must have been fate that sent Danny Doy asking me to play cornet in his seven-piece band at that time. As chance would have it, Doy had a cycle that he could lend the cornet player who lived in Georgetown so he could get to rehearsal way over in the northeast. So that's how I got a bike again. Later, when Danny turned his group over to Ollie, I kept the bike to go to the Clowns' rehearsals in Southwest Washington. This was a wild area. There'd be all kinds of interruptions during rehearsals, like a brawl or some woman screaming "He's going to kill me." Once the police shot it out with bootleggers, right across the street from Ollie's house! It was the closest thing to New Orleans's Storyville at that time.

As for Georgetown, these days it is a swank section of our nation's capitol, but the time I write about, 1921, Georgetown had been written off by the people of quality and was no longer a fashionable area of the city. For the gang who hung around 29th and Dunbarton avenues, Georgetown was wonderful. In fact, life at that time was a bowl of cherries, and I don't mean just the cherries we stole off Mrs Worthy's tree in season. There were also the pear trees, grapes, and apple orchards that we raided whenever possible. The group of boys I played with had an athletic team which was called the Georgetown Quicksteps. On the baseball team I was the spare outfield and on the basketball team I was the one who only got to play if everyone else was out sick. I had, however, managed to gain a bit of popularity with the key players by taking the fellows to the Blue Mouse Theater. My mother playing there gave me free entree and I could sneak in a friend or two. The group had equipment donated by a coach at Georgetown University, so this team was the envy of all the other neighborhood groups for football, basketball, baseball, etc. I wonder if anyone still remembers the time we played the team in Foggy Bottom?

That particular autumn afternoon the game was football. Ralph Dorsey, neighborhood star of all the sports and leading player of the Georgetown Quicksteps, was playing at left half back so he could stem the tide of those tough guys from the Bottom. I started the game at guard, as I was a brave kid and didn't mind getting knocked down and trampled in scrimmage. But this day I became a hero. We were playing on the Monument grounds and those other guys were murder, beating us so badly that coach had used up all of the reserves, even the water boy! These fellows had made mincemeat of our entire line, plus shaking up our backfield to a fare-thee-well. I had been in and out of the game twice, but then coach Steele called me into the huddle and said, "Stewardie, we're going to try something new and I'm putting you in at backfield."

I perked up at this honor and thought to myself that I would finally have a chance to show them. I trotted afield with mixed emotions because I wanted the Quicksteps to step out and win, but at the same time I realized that today wasn't the day for us. When Dorsey said, "We'll try number 93," I really wished I was somewhere else. You see, 93 was a trick play and it meant

Stewardie (that's me) was to go backward from the line of scrimmage, grab the ball from our quarterback, Frankie Gibbs, and tear out across the goal – if there was a hole for me to go through. Now, if you haven't gotten the picture, the fact is that I was the worst player on the team and they only gave me the ball for two reasons. First, I had not carried it at any time that afternoon, so the strategy was supposed to surprise the opponents. Also, Dorsey knew that if I could get a two- or three-yard head start, they would never catch me (as I was one of the fastest runners in the neighborhood).

We lined up. Signals! 26-36-76-hunph-86-93! 93! 93! Honest, I don't know what happened but I did wonder why Frank didn't stop saying 93. I guess I pulled a blank. Later I came to myself, because somebody was dousing me with water and covering me with a blanket. I realized that the play was over and so was I. Yep, I had finally caught on and made the play. I had gained almost ten yards before I was tackled by two big fellows and somebody kicked me in the head. To be kicked is embarrassing enough, but I had to go get knocked out, too! However, my act of bravery and my wearing a red jersey that fateful day won me the nickname "Devil."

After all that action and acclaim on the football field, it was pretty hard to reconcile myself to being just "Stewardie," the young kid in Ollie's band. I desperately wanted to show these older guys that I was game for anything, including running away from home to stay with the group, if that's what it took.

Looking back over all these years, if I had the chance to do it all over again, I would do it the same way, as I have no regrets. Who in their right mind would miss a chance to see the world at 14, getting paid real money and blowing their beloved horn at the same time? But, to be honest, it was hard to leave home.

2

The Family

When I was growing up, it was not uncommon for a boy to quit school and go to work to help with the family finances. But my family, the Johnson family, was different. They would not take the news about my running away calmly. They believed in education. And then there was the unfortunate case of Uncle Jacob – more about him shortly.

The Johnsons were a colorful clan and I couldn't have picked a family more to my taste. They were talented, literary and musical, ruled with an iron hand in a velvet glove by Angelina Fawcett Denby Johnson, my Grandma. She was the only child of Edwin Denby and Angelina Ricketts, whose Indian name was Ome-A-Was-O. I was told the name meant "Sweet Song of the Morning Sun." Great Grandma was considered gifted in her tribe, which she forsook after she married Denby. Ome-A-Was-O was among the first girls to attend a Quaker school and she had a flair for poetry and recitation. She was also well known as a mystic by both Indians and Whites, perhaps due to her being born with a caul (afterbirth). The Indians attach great significance to this phenomenon.

Grandma's name was also Angelina and she was an invalid in a wheelchair when I appeared on the scene. Although I loved her, I do remember wondering if Grandma was sour because she was sick or whether she was sick because she was sour. Anyway, to me she seemed unpleasant most of the time. It was Grandma who first attracted my attention to race and class distinctions. I guess I must have been four or five years old. I was playing on the lawn of the big gray house which sat on a hill opposite the large red weather observatory. Some man that

I did not pay any attention to passed up the steps. In a few seconds I heard Grandma yell, "Scat, white man." Then she gave the Indian war whoop. That really scared me, never having heard anything like it before. Years later, to my surprise, when I heard the "rebel yell" it was that very same sound! Grandma kept yelling and then she would punctuate her yells with remarks like "dirty white renegade" and "whoo, stinking thief – white trash." I did not know what the man had said or done to rile Grandma, but I'll never forget that scene.

That was one side of Angelina Johnson. The other and more attractive facets were her poetry and organ playing. To my ears, she played beautiful organ but, after I had pumped for her for a while, I longed for her to stop as I grew tired quickly. Then I would beg her to read me a poem – one of her own. That would please her and then I could rest. Besides, later on she would tell Mother or Grandfather to give the boy some more of some delicacy or sweet.

On reflection, Grannie always called me "Boy," never by my name. I guess she never accepted her Jane's being married to Rex and that perhaps explains why she never had anything good to say about my Pop, whom I scarcely knew until I was 16 years old. To Grannie, the only worthwhile people were the Indian people – and only a few of *them*. She had two old lady cronies, and the three of them would sit on the back porch conversing in grunts and giggles while they dipped snuff. Once in a while they would smoke real cigars, kind of sneaking. Once, when I saw them, Grannie really furthered my education in race relations by yelling "Scat, black boy. You are black, your pop is black and you will never amount to anything." Then, as I stood transfixed, unable to move, she let out that Indian yell. "Whoo-oo-oo black, black, black." I guessed she did not like black, which was funny since Grandfather, her husband, was blacker than I was. I figured out all by myself that she was just angry because I had snooped and caught them smoking.

This remarkable woman had a small volume of her poems published in Philadelphia sometime around 1879-81. She composed both the words and the music. She taught classes of Whites and Indians and still had the time and energy to bear 11 children – seven boys and four girls. My mother was the baby. Pert and pretty Jane married Rex Stewart from out Kansas way. I am told that they met while Mother was at Bryn Mawr and father was singing with a quartet from Lincoln University. Aside from singing, Pop also played violin, piano and mandolin.

As a boy, I used to feel flattered when people would comment on how much I resembled Mother. To my eyes, she was the prettiest woman in the world with her waist-length, jet-black hair, well-turned ankles and cherry-brown face. She was about 5 feet 2 with a slim figure. I don't think I had more than the usual Oedipal complex about Mother – but I certainly approved of her looks. When she married at 16, she had only one more year of college to complete her course. Even though she continued her studies at home, she never graduated. My parents were divorced when I was quite young so my father was not in my life at all, and from childhood I did not see him again until I was a youth of 16. I have only a few very dim childhood memories of him. I remember being on a boat and then the spanking some big man gave me when I tossed my ball overboard. The big man was Dad and I was only two years old when this happened, according to Mom. Then I remember my short introduction to the violin. Pop proudly started me on the instrument and I did catch on quickly to the principles of fingering, the notes of the scale, etc. But I was too small to relate what he was trying to teach me to his beautiful tone and technique. I also remember being so overawed that I said to myself, "I don't want any old violin." And I never touched the instrument again, especially after that spanking in the woodshed just for taking the bridge off the fiddle to see if it would sound like a mandolin, which Pop also played. Outside of those few memories, I forgot Rex Sr as a person for many years. When we met after that long separation I recognized him immediately, but it took many years for us to become acquainted and for our mutual love and respect to develop.

As I grew older, I regretted that Mother did not remarry, as I was lonesome for a brother or sister. We used to kid about that. However, in spite of being attractive and still very young when she and Dad separated, Mother was not too popular. Most people in the neighborhood considered her an oddball. She had been a gifted child and had attended Bryn Mawr on a scholarship. Her major there was French, an unheard-of undertaking for a negro girl at the turn of the century. Then, too, the combination of her frankness in discussing subjects such as politics, segregation and woman's role in life, plus speaking and reading French, frightened away most of Mother's male friends.

Mother and I were a part of Grandma and Grandpa's menage, which included my cousins Georgetta and Angelina part of the time. Our family atmosphere was always literary and musical, more Christian than worldly. We were considered a weird family because of Mother, Uncle Fred's devotion to positivism and Aunt Dora's speeches for the suffragettes. But since most of the people who came to our house were either musical or intellectual, the family had few contacts with the regular outside world. It was a strict household. As a little tyke, I had to be in the house by sundown. Angie and Georgie, being girls, had even less freedom. None of us kids went to a public school until we were at least nine years old. We attended private school. Later, I went to a Quaker school when our family moved next door to it. I was an unofficial student there – the other kids were from some of the best homes in Washington. I can still see myself pushing back the board fence, slipping into the classroom and, on being noticed, immediately trying to captivate the teacher. She would then invite me to return, which I did for a long time, perhaps six months, until one of the kids mentioned me to his parents. Then the teacher told me that I had finished school there. About that time, we moved back to Georgetown again.

During the long winters in Georgetown, I used to sprawl in front of the kitchen stove, entranced by the family Bible. In those days, the Lord's book was the main repository for almost everything of value – birth dates, weddings and death dates were recorded in the Bible. From looking at the pictures to the words about them was a short step, and my mother told me I started reading when I was four years old. Later on, I began asking questions about the other writing in the book. The hand-written entries were in various scripts but the ones I found most interesting looked like hen scratchings. These I was told referred to the purchase of a cow and some tax entries. In addition, there were all the names of Grandfather's brothers and sisters with the dates of their births and, in most cases, their deaths. There was also a little hand-drawn map showing the boundaries of a farm belonging to Grandpa. In later years I wondered whether these entries really were the writings of Seth (Grandpa's father) or his great-grandfather. In either case, it was extraordinary in those times for the family to have owned a farm, even though they were then free men. I would give a lot to know whatever became of the Johnson family Bible.

From early childhood I've been blessed with a combination of curiosity about everything and the ability to retain impressions about most of what I'd seen, heard or read. This has made me the sort of unconventional person that intrigued folks throughout my life. In those days I pored over anything I could get my hands on, from Grandpop's *National Geographic* magazines to Mama's so-called novels. I say so-called because these French novels were mostly translated into English but some were in the original language. Even though I was precocious, I couldn't get anywhere with the French!

Outside of the family singing around the old organ and listening to Uncle Fred and mother playing duets, music did not mean anything in particular to me at that point. However, soon thereafter, when Mother began working at the Blue Mouse Theater accompanying the movies, we were exposed to all kinds of music. That was about the time the moving picture companies started giving the theaters music scores to their more important pictures. I soon found out that when Mother went into the parlor with her piano score she wanted privacy. Most of the time she would emerge, beaming, and say, "Papa, you should come to work with me tonight. It's a wonderful picture and the score is so beautiful." Grandpa would always shake his head and beg off because of a prayer meeting or some other excuse. As far as I know, Grandpa never went to a movie. As soon as Grandpa had refused, I used to pipe up that I would like to go. Sometimes she took me. Later, as I grew older, I would just walk into the theater without paying. This made me the envy of all the kids in the neighborhood.

Aside from my exposure to the cinema, I was taught another kind of acting by Grandma. We three cousins were all instructed to conceal our true feelings. I'll never forget how strongly Grandmother tried to influence us to act like the Indians, to be stoic, impervious to pain, etc. As a result of Grandmother's firm influence on the family, I don't recall seeing or hearing anyone in the family crying except at funerals. They did laugh in private but never in public. Later on my mother, who had no doubt been reared to show no emotion, continued the lessons. Sometimes, when we were riding the street car, she would say to me without moving her head, "There's a man to your left who is certainly tipsy. Look but don't stare. And don't laugh! No, no. Don't turn your head and look. Just use your eyes."

I guess that was part of the Indian heritage? But there was one time when Mother's mask slipped. We went downtown in Washington to see President Wilson inaugurated. It was a bitter cold day, with snow and sleet. We both grew colder and I noticed that mother kept glancing at a coffee stand down the street from us. Finally, she said, "Come on, son. We'll get some hot coffee." I was all for it, as we children were never allowed coffee at home. When we reached the stand the vendor just looked at us and looked away, looked at us and looked away, as if we were not there. At last Mother said, "I want two cups of coffee," in a loud voice which seemed to shock the attendant into answering, "How's that, auntie?" It was the first time I had ever seen my mother angry. She seemed to start swelling up like a giant, as she replied, "I'm not your auntie and I am not here to be insulted. This is a very cold day and I demand a hot beverage for my son and myself, in the name of common decency." The fellow turned beet red and said, "This ain't no nigger coffee and, if it was, I wouldn't be sellin' you none. I just don' lak smaht niggers."

Before Mom could reply, a big white fellow stepped up close to the stand and said very quietly, "You don't know me and I don't know you. But if you don't get some coffee in two cups – and damn quick, you and me will go to hell together." I can still visualize those two men glaring at each other. Then the coffee man slowly drew two cups of java, and as he slammed them on the counter he snarled, "Gimme a dollar." At that time, coffee was a nickel or less, but Mother smiled sweetly as she laid a dollar down. When we had finished drinking, the coffee man snatched the cups and smashed them on the ground. And I wondered why.

Mother was so upset that I waited until we were back home before I dared to ask her what a "nigger" was and why the coffee man was so angry. She explained all, including the smashing of the cups. I'll never forget that first time I heard the word "nigger." It was a very traumatic experience for me, probably because I was raised in such a sheltered environment.

I loved Mother even when I made her angry enough to throw something at me, which happened quite often. The fact that we had a relationship of mutual respect did not deter her in the least if I got out of line. I remember making a smart-aleck crack in front of some guest, and right there and then Mom gave me a back-hand slap that I'll never forget. How could a little woman hit so hard, I wondered? On the rare occasions when she would apply the hairbrush to my bottom, she'd pause between strokes and sigh, "Why, oh why, can't you be a good boy? Don't you know this hurts your mother more than it hurts you?" Then I begged her not to hurt herself, which always changed her mood from crying to laughter.

Then there was the time I bummed a cigarette from an older boy and was walking home enjoying it so much, when all of a sudden the ground reared up from the dark of night. As I found myself getting up, I heard Mom, whom I hadn't known was anywhere around, say gently, "Son, you are too young to smoke." This scene came back to my mind years later when I came home for a visit. Mother drove up to meet me in a little car – a Maxwell – with a cigarette dangling from her lips. We both giggled like idiots when I told her, "Mother, look at you driving an auto! And you are too *old* to start smoking cigarettes."

Mother was the youngest of my Grandpa George Johnson's 11 children. And he was the youngest of 17 children born to Seth. According to family lore, Seth was descended from

Barbee, who was an African, a fisherman and a celebrated drummer. Barbee was brought to America as a young boy. We were told that he grew up in Virginia and the name Johnson was undoubtedly acquired from his slave-owner. If legend is true, then it was Barbee's musical gifts which were strong enough to become a part of the family heritage for generations.

Of Grandpa's 11 children, the ones I remember best are Uncle Fred, who played piano, violin and sang, Uncle Harry, who played mandolin and the long-necked guitar, and Aunt Dora, who played piano. Uncle Fred was the colorful member of the family. He was the cut-up, always full of life and mischief. His story of escape from the mob during a race riot in New York was one of his best. As he told it, he hid on the roof under some rugs. Then he hopped from roof to roof until he found himself in a cemetery, and when it grew dark he stole a sheet from a clothes line and moaned like a ghost, frightening people until he was way north of the city. From there, he got a ride in a wagon to Bridgeport, stowed away on the Baltimore Packet and then walked home to Washington. And never left home again.

Uncle Jacob was Grandma's favorite son and perhaps the most gifted musically, playing banjo, trombone, violin, guitar and piano. He was one of the older uncles who left home before I was born, but the stories the family told about Jake made me yearn to have known him. It seems that he left home because Grandma objected to his playing "rags" on the piano and also because Grandma knew he drank. Uncle Jake left Philadelphia with a minstrel show of some kind and was never heard of again. Poor Grandma! There were rumors that he had settled in Texas but I was never able to track them down. We never knew what became of him. You can well imagine that, from that time on, leaving home with a show was not a topic for discussion in our family.

My grandfather, George Johnson, was the benign patriarch of our menage. His musical activities were sandwiched among his many trades and skills. He played organ and trained the church choir, acted as sexton and was also caretaker of the old ladies home as well as a house painter. As a kid, I admired these many talents and thought he was wonderful. As an adult, and writing about him now, I am amazed at what a fantastic human being he really was. By the time I was seven, the many family members had dwindled away to just my grandparents and my mother. Grandpa was a tower of strength and a pillar of integrity. His philosophy embraced and embodied, without any reservations, the Christian way of life. Even as I write, I have to stop and wonder – was this really my mother's father? Was he actually as I remember? Or has the passage of time glorified Grandpa in my recollections? Then I answer myself: this man was even greater than I shall ever know, as I saw him through the eyes of a child and as a very young boy. Among my memories, one of the strongest was the time late one Sunday night when he took me to help him clean the church. Now I had nothing against churches, but I had been there all day from Sunday school to Christian Endeavor to evening services. So I was chock full of church. Besides, I never knew Grandpa cleaned the church until that night. We were hard at work sweeping when Sister Fullbosom knocked and peered in. "My land, Brother George," she exclaimed, "what on earth are ye doing?" "Cleaning, Sister, cleaning God's house." "But, Brother George, we hired Brother So-and-So to do that! You are the sexton and organist. You are the choir leader. You are not supposed to work like this! Where is your dignity?" "Brother So-and-So happens to be ill," Grandfather retorted, "and the good Lord dignified all men by dying on the cross, did he not? Let us not forget that cleanliness is next to Godliness." Sister Fullbosom said no more.

By any measure of mankind, this gentleman was just that – a gentle man. I remember that he was a plasterer, bricklayer, carpenter and gardener. Among his other skills, which he no longer utilized when I was a child, were those of a surveyor, a coachman and a woodsman. He knew and recognized an incredible assortment of medicine, roots and herbs, food such as the edible grasses, etc. One never knew hunger when a man was as resourceful as Grandpa. During the height of the so-called Spanish influenza epidemic, the merchants of the community were virtually closed for business. I say "virtually" because all of the neighborhood markets were closed and you could not buy any bread, milk or anything else to eat. In our house we were all sick, too, and hungry. I recall my mother's saying, "Daddy, what shall I cook today? There's no flour or cornmeal, no eggs or beans. I can't find anything to cook outside of that old Virginia ham down in the cellar." Grandpa said, "Don't worry, Janie. Boil up some of that starch that you use to starch clothes with. Dry it out, real dry. Then fry it in the grease from the ham. Everybody will go to sleep on a full stomach, and in the morning I will go up to Sandy Springs to my brother's and bring back enough food to last us until this time passes." On looking back, I suppose I owe a vote of thanks to starch for keeping us alive, and certainly another vote for Grandpa's originality with foods. In later years I was to make an attempt to try my own hand and imagination with food.

Grandfather was a very striking man. He stood about 6 feet tall, and, until he grew quite old, was as straight as an arrow. He wore the fashionable sideburns and his linen was always immaculate, even in his work clothes. Grandpa washed and starched his clothing himself. I often used to wonder how he could get so much done in a day. A typical day started at 5 a.m., when he would arise, shake down the kitchen stove, bring up coal, then wake me up. I was called to help him in our flower garden with the weeding – ugh. Then, if it was the summer season, off we would go to pick up some chairs to cane or upholster. Lunch time would find us pruning hedges or white-washing someone's fence. In the winter we would clean off the steps and pavement in front of our house, then go to everyone who was ill carrying broth that he had made. Grandpa could fix clocks, sharpen knives and scythes, and he laid bricks. Even when he was elderly, people would send for him out in the country to treat and gentle their horses for them. But Grandma made him stop gentling horses.

Grandpa was not prejudiced like Grandma. I never saw him lose his temper or heard him use an angry word, despite the crosses he had to bear. I recall one incident that reflects these qualities. Across the street from us lived an Irish family that we were fairly friendly toward, always speaking to each other on the street, which was rare for the neighborhood in those days. When my family would get together for a Songfest or musical evening, these people would gather out on their stoop to listen. And we would do the same on Saturday night when they would have a family dance. I particularly liked the music because it was so lively.

Their music was from the homeland, Irish jigs and such. At any rate, one Saturday night the father of the family asked to borrow a fiddle so they could have their dance. I watched Grandpa's face when the man asked, because I knew he wished the Irish neighbor had not asked and I also knew that my grandfather did not approve of drinking, lending or borrowing. It was obviously against his better judgement that Grandfather told me to bring Uncle Jacob's violin for the fellow. As the Irishman walked across the street with it, Grandpa remarked that we would probably not see the fiddle again, so I popped up with questions. "Grandpop, if you think that, why did you lend it to him?" With a smile, George Johnson replied, "I gave it to him because he asked, and I know it will probably not be returned because when they dance, they drink. When they drink, they fight. And in the fight, most likely the fiddle will get damaged." And that is exactly what happened! Sunday morning, when the Irishman told Grandpa how sorry he was that the violin had been broken and how he hoped to pay us back at so much a week until it was paid for, Grandpa said, "It was the will of God. I am happy to have been of service to you."

I suppose Saturday night functions have been the rule for a long time. Going back in time a little, for many colored folk Saturday night was enjoyable because of what some people called the "walk around." These get-togethers were very important as a social outlet. It was really a sort of dance contest and the prize usually was a cake. The "cakewalk" and its rhythm was a forerunner of ragtime, combining the European melodies and harmonies with African rhythms. This ragtime of the plantations traveled north as these people migrated. It collided head on with the northern ideas of culture which existed in the form of square dances, the more staid and stately waltzes, folk dances, etc. Ragtime hung around, not really accepted until it grew – probably from being played at the Saturday night functions. It was somewhat later that I became exposed to this music.

One of my greatest pleasures was going with Grandpa to the market once a week. Off we'd go, he with a gunny sack and me with a smaller sack. Everybody knew George Johnson and they would say, "Hello, George," or "How are you, Uncle George – and this is the boy?" meaning me. I guess he had been talking about me. Anyway, people would give me candy, fried oysters or whatever they sold that a kid would like.

Next to market, I liked going into the woods with my grandfather, because he knew every bush, every flower. I remember once I was frightened by a snake and picked up a stick to kill it. But Gramps stopped me, saying, "No, son, you shall not kill the reptile. It, too, is a child of God, like you. You may kill only what you need to live or to protect your own life or that of another human. I don't want you to ever hunt animals for sport or fish just for the fun of it. It is no fun to destroy what God put here on earth." I have remembered these words and tried to live by them, but I don't think it is possible for me or most other human beings to be the man my grandfather was.

My introduction to opulence was through Aunt Lucretia, Uncle Fred's wife, who was housekeeper at the office of J. R. McClain. He was owner of the *Washington Star* newspaper on H Street, NW. Auntie had complete charge of the place, doing all of the ordering from Delmonico's and other swank purveyors of the best viands and liquors. She was responsible for the cook, two cleaning maids, the houseman and McClain's personal valet. This establishment was in a three-story building – or, rather, four – counting the kitchen and Auntie's office in the basement. The street floor contained Mr McClain's private offices. The next floor had two huge rooms, like banquet halls. Above that there were sleeping quarters, I believe, but I never went up there. I only visited Auntie in her own domain.

One day, while I was visiting, McClain came into Auntie's office. For some reason he took an interest in me. He and I had a long chat and I must have amused him because this encounter resulted in my being invited to spend the day at Friendship, as his country house was called. I met his children and we got along fine after I stopped being overawed by my surroundings. I had read about kings' palaces. Friendship was the modern equivalent and McClain was a "king" of industry. I never realized that houses were built that colossal, that majestic. Even the children's quarters in a separate wing dwarfed anything I had ever seen. Not only did those kids have just about all of the toys in the world but they also had ponies. I was completely flabbergasted. Ponies!

After that I was often taken to play with the McClain children. For a while there was even talk of his adopting me. I've sometimes wondered what my life would have been had I been raised in that setting with all its advantages. But Mother vetoed the idea. On reflection I still don't quite understand why Mother Jane would not permit my adoption by them. The Johnsons had a family conclave to talk about my being a companion to the youngsters and I was really surprised when Mother said no. Later I found out that my father was all for it. He had the idea that I would make a swell jockey because I really loved horses. And I would have loved working with them. But perhaps "Mother knew best," as she was always quick to say. I've often wondered how differently I would have turned out. Probably not as a musician. Perhaps blasé from a surfeit of all the good things? And doubtless my days as a jockey would have been limited. When there was plenty to eat, I did, and grew totally out of jockey size by the time I was into my teens. So just maybe what happened was even better?

3

Pop Johnson

My first adventure in music began when a policeman by the name of Johnson, a friend of the family but no relative, formed a kid's military band of about 25 pieces. I was nearly ten years old and, as Mr Johnson went to AME Zion and sang in Grandfather's choir, it was natural for him to tell my mother he wanted me to be in his band. I started off playing fourth alto horn, which is just about the lowest man on the totem pole of band instruments, or so it seemed to me. But it was not long before I was told I was ready for the cornet. I will never forget the night Pop Johnson came by my house and said, "Mrs Stewart, your boy is ready for the cornet. Will you buy him one?" I couldn't believe my ears, but that's what he said and, sure enough, Mother bought me my first cornet, a second-hand J. W. Pepper silver beauty. Oh, cornet! I was in seventh heaven the day I received that cornet. By the way, has anybody besides me ever heard of a J. W. Pepper?

I didn't want to be separated from that horn for even a minute. I took it to school. I slept with it. I no longer had time for the gang. I would sit in the cellar or go out to the woodshed and blow, just blow until I drove everyone out of his mind, including Grandpa. How the neighbors hated both the horn and Stewardie, because before school and after school I was blowing into that cornet! I would sit in my school class and imagine playing those sweet notes in my mind, but everybody within a radius of three city blocks agreed that the notes were a long way from being sweet.

However, Police Johnson was pleased with my progress. He was so pleased that he moved me from fourth chair to third chair to second chair, and only clumped me on the head every once in a while when I goofed a note (which was often enough). He had a unique method of imparting musical knowledge. First, each kid had individual instruction, then sections would play together, and twice a week the entire band would rehearse while Pop would supervise, playing bass drum.

We kids thought that Police Johnson was a ringer in physical appearance for Jack Johnson, the celebrated prizefighter of that era. He directed and tutored the group, and here's the picture. Imagine a wheel of kids. At the hub sat a 6 foot plus giant perched on a high stool, and his tremendous reach was further enhanced by a bass drumstick. None of us will ever forget that man or his drumstick as, inevitably, with uncanny aim and intuitive precision, a wrong note was rewarded by a clump on the noggin. This skill soon made us more careful about playing the right notes. We weren't too safe even in public appearances, as he carried three spare sticks and could throw them with deadly aim. It certainly was humiliating to be conked in a parade, then have to pick up the stick and pass it back to him while everybody laughed.

I remember one time that we were working very hard on a Sousa march which happened to have a difficult trombone part. The solo trombone player was one of the instructors, but he just couldn't play the part correctly. Every time we reached a certain place that was supposed to go toot-toot-ta-toot, this man would miss again. Well, Pop obviously tried not to say anything that would embarrass Mr Jones (not his real name), because he was one of the adults who had volunteered to help form this band. He was also a deacon at the church, had a responsible government position and was a pillar of the community. Pop said gently, "Jones, seems like you are having a bit of trouble." To which Jones replied, "No, no, Brother Johnson, I'm all right." So we went over the music again and the same thing occurred. Pop stopped the band and said to him, "Wait a minute, Brother Jones, lend me your trombone. Here's the way it goes." After playing the passage he handed the horn back and said, with a big grin, "There you are, Brother Jones. That's the way it's writ." So off we went again, but when we got to the spot, while everybody waited on pins and needles, here sounded toot-toot-ta-toot-tweet. There was a split second of stunned silence because Pop had forgotten himself and bopped Mr Jones with the mallet! And that finished band practice for that evening.

Fortunately, the parents did not have to find money for the uniforms and very little either for the horns. Pop Johnson spent most of his off-duty time scrounging horns and repairing them. He was determined that his band would have instruments. For example, this is how he obtained a tuba. Many a night we skated past a particular apartment house where one of the President's bodyguards lived. This fellow loved to toot on a bass horn. We would hear a sound like a bellowing bull and, looking up to the second floor, there was a man sitting by the window in his undershirt with a great big can of beer and a huge helicon bass. Every time he drank a slug of beer, he belched, and every time he belched, he blew his horn. It was a fascinating sight to us youngsters.

One of my buddies, Otis Boyd, lived in this apartment house since his folks were the caretakers. As Otis told it, one night Police Johnson rang the man's bell and very politely told him that he was disturbing the peace with his horn. The man stopped playing that evening. Later on in the week the man played again and Pop returned to tell him it would be better if he played only in the daytime, knowing full well that the man was on duty during the day. Again, the bodyguard regretfully stopped. When Johnson returned for a third time that week, he was greeted with a large-sized fist and a fight ensued. But Pop was more than a match for the fellow, so they shook hands and everything seemed to be all right. However, the next day, when Pop reported for duty, the Captain chewed him out because the tuba player had complained. Johnson explained that he didn't have anything personal against the other officer, it was just that he needed the horn so badly for his band and was trying to figure out a way to borrow it or something. This so amused Pop's brother officers that they chipped in and bought a beat-up tuba for us. When the President's bodyguard heard the whole story, he bought us one, too!

We really were proud of our band with two great big basses and even prouder when we were allowed to discard our customary knickers in favor of long, white duck trousers, red ties and a real band cap. It also made us aware that we were growing up. I clearly remember thinking at this point that playing music was a wonderful life – you could wear long pants, travel and get lots of free eats. I decided right there and then that this was for me!

Gradually, the band got better and better. Soon we were playing well enough to play for the public – or so we thought. However, on those first appearances we all froze with fright so badly that there was many a sore head from Mr Johnson's drumsticks. But finally we were in demand for picnics and church concerts. I'll never forget how thrilled I was when, as a member of Pop Johnson's band, I played for a wedding. It was my first real exposure to elegant sophistication. The bride was the daughter of some government big-shot. Now, somewhere in the back of my mind, I had always thought people had to get married in a church. When we were taken to the beautiful garden, I was sure there had been a mistake. But how could that be, when they had us dressed up like little angels? We were wearing some type of long white dresses! Pop Johnson had to hit one of the fellows who rebelled at wearing the dress. I was too curious to do anything but goggle at the vast amount of food – dozens of turkeys, hams, barbecue. They even had a whole pig with an apple in its mouth. It looked as if somebody had bought out the grocery store, the meat market and everything else. And that wasn't all – they had little statues carved out of ice. It was a beautiful sight, with all those flowers and candles.

I strolled down a path looking for a place to you-know-what, before we were called to play. And right there in broad daylight I saw the most amazing sight of all. I couldn't believe my eyes – a statue of two naked women! At first I only peeped at it until I realized that it had to be all right to look at it or they wouldn't have it right out in the open, would they? The other fellows wouldn't believe me when I told them. First I took my buddy, Jack Rags, and showed him the statue. Then, one by one, everybody saw it. There was certainly a lot of talk at school the next day as we described to the other youngsters what we had eaten, about the champagne fountain and especially about that statue.

Pop was not in favor of parades, which he used to say were "only fit for monkeys and mules," and he was too old to be a monkey and too stubborn to be a mule. But he did make one exception, though, and that was for the competitive drill, an annual and outstanding event. The reason was that we would not have to march and could play sitting down. Also, our star trombone player and assistant bandleader, Danny Doy, had pleaded with Pop to let us play this event. Danny was quite a fellow. He played piano and trombone better than anybody we had ever heard. Not only that, he was invaluable to Mr Johnson because, after fooling with the baton for only a few weeks, he was a capable drum major. He led our band with such grace and elegance that every move was a picture. His rare type of coordination had been taught him in the Dunbar High School Cadet Corps and, among Danny's many talents, he had been captain of the winning team the year before he joined us.

I have no idea when or by whom the Corps was originated, but it was the prettiest sight you might want to see. Imagine a June day, thousands of people, beautiful girls and well-dressed men; almost everybody and his brother turned out for the annual competitive drill, making this a gala holiday for the hundreds of students from the various high schools. These youngsters had been training, praying and planning that their school would win that coveted flag along with the glory of being the winning company in the annual competitive drill. Usually there were about 15 to 20 companies trained to the finest possible point of perfection, each youngster in it proud of the splendid appearance his group made and hopeful of winning this event of a lifetime. The drills were executed in a manner that would have been a credit to West Point cadets and was a breath-taking demonstration of what was possible in coordinated movements. All of the pretty girls from miles around were there; Foggy Bottom misses sat with Anacostia elite, Southwest bootleggers shared benches with Northwest lawyers and doctors. There was even a goodly sprinkling of white society people enjoying the brilliant spectacle. On that day, Jim Crow disappeared.

Whether or not they still have this drill, I don't know. But if it still exists as a part of the pageantry of Washington, it is not to be missed. And if it is no more, then that's a pity. The only time since the old days that I have seen a spectacle to compare with it was in Berlin when I had the pleasure of watching General Clay's honor guard perform the magnificent silent rifle drill. That was a stirring, never to be forgotten sight.

But, getting back to our music, we didn't play for that drill after all. Our mighty leader, Policeman Johnson, got caught in a spring rain storm. He came down with a severe cold which turned into Spanish influenza during that terrible epidemic, and he was gone in a week! I sincerely believe that the day I was told that Pop had passed away was the saddest day in my life. I wouldn't go to school. I couldn't eat or sleep. It was the end of the world for me. I must have been about 11 years old at that time, but, if I live to be 111, I'll never forget that funeral. We 35 or so kids in his group were supposed to play *Rock of Ages* and *Onward Christian Soldiers*. There we stood with our eyes so full of tears that we couldn't see the casket. And when Daniel Johnson, Pop's stepson, cracked on the melody and let out a sob, that finished our part of the ceremony.

Danny Doy took over and he was really a ball of fire. Although he was a fine musician, he was too young and inexperienced to hold the big band together. Instead, he opted for a seven-man group which played the new music called ragtime. The grapevine spread the news that Danny's group was going to play – shoosh, whisper – *ragtime*, and the old folks shook their heads. In those days, polite people only knew about orchestras or brass bands. Ragtime had an unspeakable connotation. But Danny had a vision, and chose me as one of his new group. At the time I was floored, as I had the impression that he didn't think much of me or my playing. I could only figure one reason for this unexpected decision – a guilty conscience. Let me explain.

There had been an unpleasant incident not too long before.

Doy, along with his various skills, aspired to be a drill master with Pop Johnson. This was probably a hold-over from his cadet days. In any case, he had worked very hard helping us to learn to play and march simultaneously. This looks easy, but just try it sometime! As soon as we had this down pat, he started us on several drill formations. For us, this was too much. Between band practices, school and Doy, we never had time to swim, play ball, lollygag on the corner or play our many games anymore.

I can see it all so clearly! It all seems like only yesterday. We wore those long johns which itched like mad in the spring, the corduroy pants, and those heavy black stockings that you couldn't keep from slipping down. There were those old-maid schoolteachers who seemed to single me out to recite poetry for an occasion, and this I really hated. And the fun of playing with the gang after school. We kids had some great games, such as the one we called "Shot Gun," which necessitated gathering a supply of cockroaches. These were placed on top of bread squares which were formed into water lanes. The first roach to reach the other end of a 6-inch course was the winner. The game was called Shot Gun because it would practically take a shot gun to get the roaches off the squares and into the water. Other games we played were Red Dog, Georgia, Coon Can and Angel Tits. This last one had to do with flies being released into a bowl or similar glass-covered receptacle.

Anyway, the fellows all began to grumble, and before I knew it I had been elected spokesman to tell Cap Doy that the guys wanted more time off. Maybe I didn't tell him in the most tactful way, because before I knew what was happening I had been rewarded with a swift kick in the pants! I'll never forget that kick. Danny happened to be wearing the newest style in pointed shoes. Perhaps later he regretted the top sergeant-type response. He didn't say anything and I didn't complain at the time. But he must have known how angry I was about the unjustified kick, and I guess he picked me for his group as a way of apologizing. Actually, I was probably a bit too cocky for my own good, anyway. After that memorable football game and being given the nickname Devil, I'm afraid I strutted about and was hard to live with for a long time. So when Danny Doy came by my house to ask me to try out for his band, I was really astounded. There were three or four other cornet players right in the neighborhood about as good or better than I was, such as my friend Henry Goodwin.

Henry lived two blocks from me on Dunbaston Avenue in Georgetown. I first knew him when he and two other guys chased me all the way home from 11th and P streets to the Georgetown Bridge. The next time I saw him he was sitting on his stoop fooling with a cornet. I later heard talk about a fellow who could "buzz" on a horn like Johnny Dunn, which made me feel very low because, try as I might, I could not make that damn buzz. Henry could sort of do it but he wouldn't show me how.

However, it was not these others fellows who were the ones being auditioned. It was me! Danny had me play a piece called *Cuban Moon* from the music. This scared me because I was a poor reader. Luckily, as it was written in all whole notes, I managed to struggle through and so I became a member of Danny Doy's Melody Mixers.

We went south to Norfolk and as far north as Wilmington, Delaware. But we had the most fun on the eastern shore of Maryland, playing places like Indian Head, La Plata, Aberdeen and a lot of other hamlets on both sides of the Potomac River. Half of the fun would be the trip down the river, and this is how we did it. We would meet at the navy yard and play our way down on a government boat. The sailors were glad to have any diversion and would accomodate us by letting us off on either side of the river. We would generally play the dance, stay over at someone's house that night, get up in the morning and take the up-boat home. These boats were apparently operated by the navy department as a courtesy for the folks who lived on the river, as I never saw anyone pay. I know we were well liked by someone at the navy yard because one time, when we missed the big launch which carried about 100 people, we were sent down river in some kind of speed boat instead, which only held ten people!

Yep, the navy was kind to us. Only once did we run into a

captain who refused to let us off where we had to play. He said, "I don't give a damn where you've got to go. This here tub is going to the Virginia side and you can swim across for all I care." We were sad when he let us off at the thought of missing our dance that night. But Bunky Addison, our banjo man, said, "Shucks, I bet we can pay one of these guys at the dock to ferry us across the river." So a deal was made and we took off again, all grins, as we knew we would make our date in plenty of time after all.

Just as we reached the half-way point, someone noticed a speedboat racing parallel to our course about 200 yards starboard. This was a big speed-boat and it bore a flag which we had never seen before, white with a big red ball in the center. We asked the skipper of our craft what that boat was and what kind of flag, but he just grunted. Then everyone spied another boat, farther down river, also paralleling our position. This one not only had the same flag but also had a siren which was wailing. Suddenly from out of nowhere it seemed like judgement day. We heard a salvo of sound, the likes of which must have come from hell, and all hell broke loose as even the sun seemed to dive on our boat! The only way I can describe my reaction is to say that I was so busy being scared to death that I couldn't see for crying and I have no idea what the others did.

After about ten minutes of our little skiff's being tossed about like a leaf in a hurricane, both of the coast-guard cutters came alongside. A man who I guess was the senior officer boarded us, cussing. He cussed us collectively and individually. I began to wonder if he was going to run out of words or out of breath first. Then he knocked down the fellow who owned the boat and told a sailor to handcuff him, he was jail bound. Another crewman was assigned to take us ashore, and then we had a chance to find out what it was all about. This sailor told us that the peckerwood knew better than to come out on the river when they were testing at the proving grounds and how lucky we were not to be in little pieces at the bottom of the river.

Later at Aunt Jennie's the guys started kidding me, watching me eat everything in sight. It was a good dinner of roast pork and sweet potatoes, fried porgies and mixed greens (mustard and collards), those famed Maryland beaten biscuits, plus apple pie topped with home-made fresh strawberry ice cream. I was glad to be alive and happy to eat like that to prove it!

Gradually, the gang began to change. No more walking home from school the tow-path route. In those days, canals ran through Georgetown and Foggy Bottom and they fascinated us. We used to walk home from school via the tow path, all slippery mud when it rained, and every rainy day some kid fell into the canal. But now we were all growing up and there were new avenues to explore.

Going back a little, the year that Danny Doy won the competitive drill for Dunbar High's "War Babies of Company B," his company became famous by defeating Armstrong High School's crack drill unit, "Company D," which was captained by Oliver Blackwell. Ollie's group was runner up. There was intense rivalry between the schools fueled by the color discrimination at that time. This attitude was even evident in the high schools. Dunbar is where the light-colored kids went and Armstrong was for the others of various darker shades.

In spite of these rivalries, Ollie and Danny became buddies after that, probably because they both played piano and liked ragtime. Danny, who could read music well, would teach Ollie Blackwell all of the new tunes as fast as they came out because Ollie couldn't read. In turn, when Ollie would get a job, he would hire Danny to play trombone. And that's how I came to meet Ollie. In Danny's own band he also played trombone. We didn't, in fact, have a piano player. Our instrumentation was Ernest Hall on clarinet, Jack "Rags" Richardson on drums, Ralph Dorsey on bass, Reggie Martin on banjo, Danny on trombone and me on cornet. We really had a dixieland band without any of us ever having been to New Orleans or ever having heard any New Orleans music! Among the tunes we played were *All by Myself in the Morning*, *Walking the Dog*, *Balling the Jack*, my try-out tune *Cuban Moon* and also a lot of blues, the same kind of blues that I heard and liked at the function at King's house.

Doy's group played one special party which was a fox hunt. To this day I can't figure out why they needed music so early in the morning. They had what Doy told us was a "hunt club" breakfast, and we stuffed ourselves too. One of the help even slipped us some whiskey – my first taste! I liked it, but it made me sleepy, so I was glad when we finished playing.

Around that time, Danny Doy opened an important avenue for me when he told us fellows that he expected us to be at Lincoln Colonnades to learn how ragtime should really be played. I was overjoyed. I had never heard a jazz band play up until that time.

If one of the axioms of this business is to be the right guy in the right place at the right time, then Washington, DC, in 1921 was the right time and place for me to hear music. I don't think there were many towns with more dance halls than Washington, excluding only maybe that fabled New Orleans scene. Starting with the then spanking new Lincoln Colonnades, there was Murray's Casino, True Reformer's Hall, Eye Street Hall, Stack O'Lee's in Foggy Bottom, Odd Fellows Hall in Georgetown, the Woodman"s Hall in Anacostia, Eagle's Hall in the Northeast section, the Masonic Hall in midtown, and Convention Hall, plus at least ten or so smaller halls.

There was a dance somewhere every night. Of course, you had to know what the social climate might be before venturing into a hall where you were not known, as the natives were mighty clannish in those days. Sometimes you might have to leave a dance without your overcoat, your hat or even your head! Ambulances were rarely seen in a colored neighborhood in those days, and the victim generally bled to death. One of the features at these halls was a battle of the bands. No doubt the idea of bands trying to outplay each other is as old as mankind, and it doesn't require too much imagination to visualize one small band of itinerant players trying to outplay another group of musicians. At any rate, my first awareness of this delightful phenomenon was at the Lincoln Colonnades. There were three bands, but the main battle was between Doc Perry and Sam Taylor. The third outfit was only a pick-up group with Duke Ellington on piano, a fellow named Tobin on C-melody sax, Otto Hardwicke on bass violin and Stick-A-Makum on drums. There were others in the band, too, but I don't recall their names or faces.

The formula for band battles has remained the same over the years, it seems to me. First one orchestra plays, then the other takes over, and they alternate until the crucial magic moment when complete empathy with the audience is reached and the battle is over. The jazz band battle was not only fun, it was also an education, a proving ground and a moment of truth for many a musician. These battles in Washington had various ramifications because it was a border town with both clear distinctions between colored versus white people and, more important to me, the indisputable differentiation between negro people of various hues. There was very little mixing in the homes, in the churches or in the dance halls. Therefore, when the news that Doc Perry, the pride of the elite, was to play against Sam Taylor, the favorite of the masses, the whole town was agog.

Doc represented the group who mostly lived in the northwest section of the city. These were the lighter complexioned people with better-type jobs, such as schoolteachers, postmen, clerks or in government service. Sam Taylor was the idol of the southwest area. His followers were the working class, the coal men, the fishmongers, the gamblers, pimps and sporting females. This dance was more like a championship bowling match than like a special event.

Strange as it seems when I look back, up until then I had never heard any orchestra in person except when I stood outside of Odd Fellows Hall in Georgetown. We kids had all heard about and wanted to go to the Colonnades for this battle of the bands. But stern dictates were issued by parents telling their youngsters that they could not attend the dance. However, when Doy instructed us to be there, that was different. I was ecstatic until I realized I couldn't get in wearing short pants. Bernard Addison came to my rescue by lending me a pair of his trousers.

I can see the scene as if it were yesterday. It looked like the entire police force was on hand to keep order, whiskey was flowing like water and guys were betting on who had the best band. Artie Whetsol, John Adams from Annapolis, and I suppose every musician within 40 miles was there. I remember Big Jim

Blair from the eastern shore of Maryland with his violin, Da Da from Falls Church with his guitar, and Pike Davis from Baltimore, who was pointed out as the only trumpet that Johnny Dunn of New York fame wouldn't tangle with. Yes, this was the night, my first exposure to Big Time, the battle of the bands. That hall was so packed that I'm sure you couldn't get a sardine in after nine o'clock. We were there at 7:30 and got right on the bandstand out of the crowd. Doc, as I remember, had Artie Whetsol on trumpet, and rarely have I heard a sweeter tone. My arch rival Henry Goodwin was the trumpet with Sam. Henry, Hank, or Cuz, as we called each other, was the one who learned the flutter tongue and didn't want to teach me. Anyway, that was the night of nights for me. The music was prettier than I had ever dreamed. Doc Perry had perhaps the best musicians, but old Sam Taylor had that beat – and above all he had something. The only word that would describe it actually is funk, which by the way was never mentioned in polite society in those days. But now it is "in" and not a naughty word anymore.

It seemed like the end of the world to me when, shortly after that, Danny Doy called us together and announced his departure to Europe. He took off along with Claude Hopkins and some other Washington musicians. We wished him well, but each of us slunk home with heavy heart because we knew that was the end of the band. The next afternoon I sat on my back porch fingering my horn, feeling too low to even blow a few notes. I heard the door bell ring and Grandpa saying to someone, "Reggie, oh yes, he's out back." I must pause to explain why the family called me Reggie. It's because the name on my christening papers was Reginald. But as soon as I found out that names like Percival and Reginald were considered sissy, I became Rex, like my dad. However, strangely enough, years later when I asked Pop if his name was Reginald or Rex, he got angry! Anyway, I became Rex early and stayed that way from then on.

To my surprise, the person at the door was Ollie Blackwell, and I was even more surprised when he asked, "Stewardie, how about you working with me now that Danny has gone abroad?" It hadn't occurred to me before, but actually it was quite logical that Doy had turned the band over to Ollie. I answered that I'd like to join him but wondered what would happened to Henry Goodwin, the horn player who had been working with him. Ollie smiled and said, "He was with me, but Sam Taylor hired him away from me last night, so you can have the job. I sure hope you can growl, though." That threw me because I couldn't even flutter-tongue. But I promised Ollie that I would try to learn how to growl and flutter.

Although Ollie was a real smart dresser and a favorite with the girls, he was on the homely side, bow-legged and with a beak for a nose. But his assets were his 6-foot height, his erect carriage, his beautiful Indian complexion, his quick wit and his good ear for music. Ollie was a regular go-getter. Up until this time he had played only parlor socials. In those days there were two types. There were the social receptions where people got together in someone's parlor and danced sedately until about 11 p.m., drank punch and ate cookies. There would be no charge, but you had to be known by the family to enter. The other type was the "bow wow" and was as different as day and night. This kind, anybody who had a quarter was welcome to attend. They served fried chicken, fried fish, chitterlins and hog maws along with plenty of corn liquor. These events went on until everybody passed out or the cops broke it up. Ollie got us both types of parties, and engagements began to come to us right and left. We roamed farther and farther afield: Virgina Beach, Castle Point, Baltimore. I remember well a dance I played with Ollie. By then I had become exposed to various aspects of life. On my way to rehearsal, for instance, I used to pass a certain block of houses, and each one had a female beckoning to the passers-by. I was amazed when I saw one slip off a house-dress and try to entice a man into her parlor, because she wore nothing underneath that house-dress. This was something very new and strange to me.

By this time I was on the threshold of puberty. At the Saturday night dance I mentioned, the smell of cheap perfume plus the odor of musk from the dancers' bodies wafting up to the bandstand made me yearn to prove my maleness. Ollie, sensing my state of mind, leaned over to me, grinning and saying, "I bet this is the first time you ever saw anything like this, eh Stewardie? Say, do you know that most of those babes don't wear any drawers. No, sir, there's nothing under those dresses, so they can get into action quick!" Wow! Like the woman I had seen in that block of houses! Going home on the street car I fought sleep on the way back to Georgetown and, thinking about the dance, I decided not to tell mother all, figuring that she wouldn't know about such things.

All our hearts took a leap when we were chosen to play for a real up-to-date musical comedy with girls, dancing and bright lights. Here we come! *Go-Get-It* was my introduction into the big time, deciding to make music my career and leaving home.

As I think it all over, perhaps it was inevitable that I should have wound up in music, even though I had shied away from it like the plague earlier. This was because my father, mother and, in fact, the entire Johnson family had tried too hard to interest me in the art. My dad especially had made music distasteful. He wanted so much for me to play the violin, but my fingers were too short, so it became a tug of war between us. Then the competition was between violin and piano. I hated piano practice, because I could see the other kids through the window outside having fun while I sat there perched on pillows, pounding my stubby fingers to a nub under the alert supervision of Uncle Fred or Grandma or sometimes Mother. I'll bet no kid had more teachers at the same time than I did. The whole family labored in vain because I never got out of the second book. It took being inspired by Policeman Johnson, the boys' band and the cornet to turn me into a musician. Looking back, at every stage of my life there have been teachers, and as we proceed I'll tell you about some more of them and the lessons they taught me.

4

With the Spillers

Let's return to *Go-Get-It*. The show played Baltimore after opening in Washington. Then we traveled on to Norfolk, Virginia. Finally we reached Philadelphia where, after three weeks at John Gibson's Theatre on South Street, we realized we had had it. *Go-Get-It* was no more. But by now I was convinced that the music business was what I wanted, and decided to explore the world more fully. I had not cared much for school in the last few years, anyway. The other guys in the band were not dismayed and wanted to stick together, all except Hallie, the clarinet man. He had a gal back home and cut out for Washington to get married.

One night after I had finished a big bowl of chili up at Mose McQuiddy's combination rooming and boarding house (which catered to TOBA members only), Bernard Addison took me to a honky-tonk. That's what a nightclub was called in those days. We played some ragtime music and, while I don't remember where this place was, I do remember meeting Willie Lewis. He introduced himself as "the world's greatest clarinetist starring the world's greatest ragtime orchestra, the Musical Spillers." This kind of bragging was the usual spiel between musicians and performers during that period.

Willie told me to bring my horn to the burlesque theater the next day and maybe Mr Spiller would hire me. I really didn't want to leave Ollie and the guys, but winter was right at hand and I figured we'd wind up together in New York. This is where the Spillers were bound, and it seemed inevitable that the fellows would make it to the big city, too. Arriving on the scene, I found it was indeed already arranged with Mr Spiller (for the life of me, I still can only think of him as *Mister* Spiller). He sent me at once to a tailor to have a costume altered to fit. And as soon as that was done I was to report to Fred Pinder, the first trumpet man, to be taught the second trumpet parts. I thought to myself that they sure did things in a hurry, but, after I finish with this, I'll eat. I seemed to have constant hunger pangs during that period. But that day there was to be no lunch for me, because Isabelle came into the picture. She was the boss's wife, a great big woman about 5 foot 7 tall with a manner like a top sergeant. Nobody introduced me to Mrs Spiller, so I was flabbergasted when she strode up to me. Her first words were, "I guess you can't read music, but we'll soon fix *that*. And of course you are breathing wrong and blowing the instrument quite incorrectly. We'll fix *that*. Let's see your teeth, boy . . . hmm. I guess you shall double on tenor sax and I'll fix that *personally*."

Even now, as I look back, I remember how much Mrs Isabelle Spiller frightened me that first time we met. And, at the same time, I thank my lucky stars for all of the time and effort that most gracious lady spent on me. Isabelle undoubtedly was the greatest music teacher I've ever known, and the way she alternately cajoled me one moment and drove me the next was exactly what I needed. Then, along with the sugar and vinegar, this unusual person came up with real thought-provoking exercises that we had never known existed and which extracted results from all of us. For instance, she had the bass sax man carry weights for half an hour so that he became accustomed to doing the steps with that giant horn (this happened after the original bass sax man returned to his home in Baltimore). The basis of her method of teaching intonation on the trumpet was solfeggio. Isabelle would strike a note on the piano and I would blow the note on just the mouthpiece. She also had me twirling a broomstick around my fingers to promote dexterity. Over and over she told us that there was no angle of training in music that could be overlooked.

That first day we went from trumpet parts to the tenor saxophone, and I tried with all my might to produce a tone on that devilish instrument. The longer I tried, the hungrier I became and the worse I sounded. Just when I was about to faint Isabelle said, "That's enough for today." I sighed with short-lived relief as she continued, "Now we'll go get Dinah so he can start you on the dance steps." Dinah, whose real name was George Taylor, was both drummer and featured tap-dancer in the group. Well, that remark made the pot boil over because, as much as I was intimidated by this amazon of a woman, I was too hungry to care what happened. So I said, "Excuse me, but I'm very hungry. Could we get a sandwich first?" The smile was gentle but the answer wasn't. "Just tell me what you want and I'll send someone for it. You may eat while you are being shown the steps." My heart sank as I wondered what I had let myself in for.

But that's the way it was with the Musical Spillers, a really thorough organization. The Seven Spillers were among the first big-time colored acts in show business. They only played the best show houses in the country and burlesque theaters. Playing with the Spillers was quite an experience for me. Having never been on the stage, I had to be taught to bow, smile, say cheese, enter and exit. Then I had to learn where and how to keep my clothes ready for the changes of costume. When I joined them they were featured in a burlesque show, the exact name of which I've forgotten. But I do remember well the ever-present crap games in the dressing room with Al Jolson, Eddie Cantor, Bojangles and a lot of other celebrities.

The first engagement I played in New York was with the Spillers at Hurtig and Seamon's Apollo Theatre, which was located on 125th Street in Harlem. The burlesque house at that time was catering to white audiences only – unless you could count that small section of the peanut gallery where approximately one-third of this section or about 50 seats were allotted to colored patrons. This remains firmly in my mind, not because it was my first exposure to New York, but, for the first time in my life, I saw at least $5000 in cold cash! After our last performance some big-time show people came up from downtown to shoot craps with my boss, Mr William Hezekiah Spiller. I was 14 years old at the time and completely overwhelmed by the glamor. Jimmy Durante was playing piano next door and later Evelyn Nesbitt Thaw was featured there.

In the Spiller group I played second tenor in the saxophone section. The others were Spiller on bass, Willie Lewis on first alto, Seymour Todd on C-melody saxophone, Isabelle Spiller on first tenor and Fred Pinder on baritone and also bass sax. The dance was done while playing the saxophone and, although it was not much, in retrospect it certainly took a lot of concentration for me to play the right notes and do the correct steps at the same time. It was even worse than the marching and playing that Danny Doy had made us do.

We opened playing march music in a military-type uniform. When the setting segued into various specialty turns, we all changed clothes. For the ensemble spiritual singing we wore varicolored silk overalls. After that there were more solos, which led us into the finale. The finale was ragtime music and we wore tuxedos. I was on my own and could blow any kind of notes I wanted on my cornet. How I loved it! Spiller would milk the crowd for encores, yelling "Wait! Wait a minute! You ain't heard nothing yet!" Many acts copied this exhortation and in later years this spiel became identified with Al Jolson.

The Spillers taught me so many skills and actually expanded my youthful horizons to such an extent that I could hardly bear the pressures. As a matter of fact, I was crammed daily with harmony and theory lessons along with trumpet and tenor sax, and even now I recoil at the thought of the marimba lessons. However, at the same time I regret not having assimilated everything they taught me. But, alas, most of this went down the drain.

Altogether, I remained with the Spillers about two years, and perhaps would have gone on and on with them except it got so rough on me to get up at 7 a.m., what with the late hours and booze the night before. Every morning, rain or shine, Isabelle would knock at my door. This was the routine. I had to get up, whether we were on the road or at home. No breakfast now, no matter how hungry I was. First there was a brisk walk of at least six blocks. And Isabelle accompanied me so I couldn't get away with less. Then back to the hotel or house for hot drinks. Mine was always milk and hot water. This was followed by setting up exercises for ten minutes, and mine included twirling a broomstick to make my fingers nimble. To rest up, we stood on the front porch for about ten minutes doing breathing exercises. Inhale – hold it. Exhale – hold it. Hop ten beats on one foot – breathe. Now the next foot – breathe. Then, at last, I was allowed to have breakfast. This was followed by the saxophone lessons for about an hour, and, after a small rest, get out the mallets and on to the marimba. What a despot Isabelle Spiller was! But what a devoted, intelligent teacher! At the time I thought, "What a hell of a life this is." Of course, now I realize what she was doing, and I'll never stop thanking her.

To be factual, credit, or discredit, must be given Willie Lewis for both my entrance into and my departure from the musical Spillers. Willie used to take me to the cabarets. In Harlem at that time, the glamorous place was the Garden of Joy, which sat high on a hill at the corner of 137th and Seventh Avenue. I only recall two men in there, but these were two tremendous musicians – Coleman Hawkins and Sidney Bechet. Hawk I had always remembered since hearing him play with Mamie Smith at the Gaiety Theatre in Washington, DC. This was an unforgettable experience for a 12-year-old, which I was at the time. Anyway, Willie took me to all the hot spots – the Capitol Palace, Gold Grabbens, Leroy's and Smalls' on Fifth Avenue, the 101 Ranch, the Bucket of Blood and many others. One night at the dinner table (at Spillers, we all ate together family style) Willie gave me the signal. This usually meant for me to sneak out, meet him on the corner and we would go hear some music. When I got to the corner this evening, he told me to take the horn back to the house because we were going out with some girls.

"Not me," I said. "You go ahead. I'm going down to Smalls'." Willie was agreeable and told me what time to meet him later so that I could get into the house without the Spillers knowing that I had been out. I was not allowed to go out by myself at night and had no key. Isabelle was very strict about this rule. The penalty for disobeying was the threat of being fired, and to get bumped for sure.

Let me explain about getting bumped. Mrs Spiller weighed about 140 to150 pounds, and I think she must have been all muscle. She often times cornered one of the fellows and bounced him against the wall like a rubber ball. Even now, I can't figure out just how she did it, but she did. The first few times I got caught sneaking in I was let off with a reprimand, but this evening was the pay-off. I was not able to sneak in and, instead, was greeted on my return by both the Spillers. I didn't get the usual bumping. This time I was really through – fired! I packed my very few belongings and was really on my own.

5

On my Own

I didn't mind getting fired too much, as the transition to playing clubs in New York proved to be easy for me. I got my first cabaret job at Smalls' Sugar Cane and started living at Mr Smalls's house. Bernard Addison, my old buddy, had turned up in New York and engineered everything.

At that time, the team of June Clark and Jimmy Harrison were just closing at Smalls'. I caught them at the Lincoln Theater, where I heard this trombone playing real high like a cornet and not like any trombone I had listened to before. His style was long smears, just like the dixieland boys play now. I can picture him now with his long legs crossed, lolling in an inadequate chair, big head leaning on one side while he held a Coca-Cola bottle in the bell of his trombone, and he was just swinging like mad. It was new to me and the rest of the cats, because Jim Harrison had recently come off the road where he had picked up Louis Armstrong's stuff, and we could hardly wait until the show was over to meet this genial giant. Jimmy and June had played around Chicago a lot and absorbed the feeling of what we later discovered was the greatest team of them all. They played what they called "Western style" and started the New Yorkers thinking when they told us that King Oliver and Louis were the greatest in the world. These statements were greeted by derision and questions like "How about Johnny Dunn and Bubber Miley and Jack Hatton?," who were considered the blowingest cats in those parts at that time. That made Jimmy roar, and he had a mighty laugh, telling us that Louis would get to New York one of these days and he'd show us how to blow. Jimmy was born or grew up in Louisville,

Kentucky, but the family soon moved to Detroit where his father ran a restaurant. His two sisters and his mother baked wonderful pies which were famous in that neighborhood. Jim, who was the night cook, ate a lot of them, too. Jimmy was some eater. Finally his father had to tell him that business was not good enough for him to eat all those pies and he had to hire a different man. Lucky for us that he gave up cooking to be a trombone player!

So here I was hired by Smalls to replace June Clark, and a real swinging trombone player from Newark, New Jersey, Herb Gregory, replaced Jimmy Harrison. Herb and I tried our best to copy Jimmy and June but we didn't get anywhere with that. However, we did swing pretty well together until the drinks got too potent too often and we were fired. We really couldn't have cared less. In those days there were plenty of jobs and a guy could get fired at 9 o'clock and be on another gig at 10 o'clock. Really!

Later, after I was fired by Smalls, I did what we all used to do when we were out of a job. We called it "going hunting." This meant standing in a bar quaffing Top 'n' Bottom, our favorite mixture of port wine and gin. Then Herb or one of the others would say, "Tomorrow night, let's go blow So-and-So off the stand." We had our own code of ethics; everyone played against everyone else. Fair was fair. The best man won and got the job. I've seen this happen many times. A bunch would be playing great until a hotter gang would walk in and, on sight, the band would finish the tune and start packing because they knew there was no competition. This reads like make-believe but it is a fact. Jobs were plentiful and there was no union for us in New York during the early 20s.

I bummed around New York playing in various cabarets in Harlem. After playing at the Sugar Cane on Fifth Avenue sometime later I worked at the Green Parrot on 135th Street. When I took that job I didn't know anything about a curfew for nightspots, nor that the Green Parrot intentionally stayed open to cash in on the action when the other joints obeyed the law. The arrangement was for them to operate as long as possible. Then the police would raid the place and take the band and entertainers down to the police station, where we would have to cool our heels until a magistrate held court and dismissed the case for insufficient evidence. This sort of hanky-panky was a lark the first two times because I had never been in jail before, but after that I began to dread Saturday night, so I quit and started playing way up in the Bronx at a club called Dashy's Inn.

The boss there was Dashy Grant and he had a swinging hangout for the race-track crowd. The salary was good and the tips were even better. Every night the kitty was at least 100 dollars and would be divided up between just three of us – piano, drums and me. Sometimes there was even more, and it was here I acquired the champagne habit, thanks to the Jewish and Irish race-track plungers who scorned any other beverage. But one night we arrived for work and there was a big padlock on the door: "Closed by Government Order!" I never did find out whether it was a liquor violation or taxes, but Bobbie Johnson, our drummer, had to get a court order to extricate his drums from the place.

After that I fell into one of the most pleasant associations I can recall in a band. I joined Johnny Montague, a piano man whose group was playing at a dance hall downtown on Columbus Circle. In his band there was my trombone partner Herb Gregory, George Taylor on drums and Cecil Benjamin on clarinet. On looking back I can see why this combo made such a deep impression on me. First of all, there was so much togetherness. If one guy had a problem, he could count on its being shared by the other fellows. We were closer than most brothers, roomed in the same house, ate together and boozed together. We wore each others' clothes and, on several occasions, fought together. From a musical standpoint, we were closer than peas in a pod and could anticipate each others' breaks and so on, almost as if we were playing written scores. We had rehearsals every day, but usually these were a joke with lots of arguing about chords intermixed with one of us running downstairs to get another bottle from our friendly bootlegger. Strangely, since this was the Prohibition era, or perhaps not so strangely, we all drank like fishes! Liquor was not hard to come by. In the building where Leaky Pease, a drummer, lived, there was a giant still. The cooker was his pal and we would watch as he mixed the stuff in the bathtub, making scotch flavor, bourbon flavor and gin flavor for the trade. And some for us.

Now let me tell you a little more about the New York scene when I arrived, which must have been about 1922. Everybody who was anybody hung out at 135th and Lenox Avenue, as that area was the Broadway of Harlem, and the Lincoln Theater drew all kinds of performers and musicians like a magnet. Johnny Dunn was a big man in that New York milieu and this is where he chose to hold court. The crowd would congregate, and I must say that he was always the picture of elegance with his big cigarette holder and his glistening patent-leather shoes which were discreetly muted with natty gray spats. There was no question that he was the idol of the vaudeville set. Dunn was a transplanted Southerner and East Coaster, born in Memphis, Tennessee, but he really started his claim to fame when he toured with W. C. Handy's orchestra.

I had first heard Johnny Dunn play back home in Washington when I was a boy. I thrilled to his artistry when he appeared at our local theater. He was the first fellow I ever saw and heard playing the ragtime music, and you can bet that I was impressed. I gaped open-mouthed when I heard the sounds emanating from a long slender contraption played by a tall slender brownskin fellow on the stage. The contraption was a trumpet, a special type which I later found out was called an English coach horn (but to this day I don't know why or who manufactured this horn). It was all of four feet long and had a very piercing tone. My uncle, with a smirk, told me that the player was Johnny Dunn, the "Ragtime King of the Trumpet." The smirk indicated that ragtime was something naughty, along with bootleg whiskey and the *Police Gazette* magazine. I was just flabbergasted when, later in the program, Dunn picked up another much shorter trumpet and made sounds like a horse whinnying and a rooster crowing! This was in a ragtime piece they called the *Livery Stable Blues*. On that same bill was the sensational Mamie Smith. Everybody in that crowded playhouse called for more of Mamie's songs, but I remember wishing that they would be quiet and let this tall, lanky brownskinned musician weave his own spell with that shiny gold trumpet.

That was my introduction to ragtime trumpet which, over the years, has had names like "get-off horn," "swing," "hot," "bop," etc. Johnny Dunn was my first influence and, for his times, he was king with those tricks he did on his horn as well as for possessing a clarity and power that was virtually unmatched.

I am sure that that show was the first time I had laid eyes on a real trumpet, and being told that that shiny gold instrument was the same thing as my little silver cornet didn't cut any ice with me. Further, Johnny made sounds on that horn such as I had never imagined. He made that horn moan, he made it chitter and wa-wa like a baby's crying. But the greatest effect of all was when he did the flutter tongue. This gimmick broke up the house. Dunn reserved it for special moments like when the band would be playing soft and sweet, with the lights way down low. He'd start on about the twelfth bar of a 16-bar strain and go from a whisper to a roar, flutter tonguing, and the crowd in the dance hall would answer with yells of approval.

However, New York's own local favorite was not Dunn but Jack Hatton. He had already been around New York for several years, but I understood that he came from South Carolina, where he had matriculated from that bastion of brass, Jenkins' Orphanage Band. This amazing place turned out many an outstanding trumpet man – to name another famed alumnus, many years later of course, high-note man Cat Anderson. Jack Hatton represented the other side of the coin from a trumpet player's viewpoint. First of all, he had tremendous power, blowing that horn such as I had never heard before – nor since, for that matter. He played with such force that he was not welcome in the cabarets. Most of the time, the boss of the place would catch him coming in and say, "No playing, Jack. Keep that bugle in the box. I won't have you running my customers out of here." So Hatton had to do his playing in big dance halls like the New Star Casino and at outdoor picnics, where he was much in demand. I can still hear Jack saying, "Hell, what's the use of playing if everybody can't hear you?" Later he toned down and started employing all sorts of gadgets to make his sound more subdued and not so ear-blasting. Part of this paraphanalia consisted of four kazoos held together with rubber bands, a metal chamber pot and a wooden flower pot.

Bubber Miley was the other famous trumpet player of the time. I wonder how many music writers today know about Bubber's playing behind a screen with society's favorite band, Leo Reisman? The elite audience wondered mightily at the hot jazz coming from nowhere! It attracted so much attention that Reisman was forced to have a white trumpet player go though the motions as if he were playing.

In late 1921, when I arrived with the Spillers in New York, I was starry eyed, full of beans and ready to grab the tiger by the tail. Playing the top vaudeville circuit, I thought show business was all about perfectionism and doing the best you could. I was that surprised to notice that most white orchestras could not even hold a tempo, much less a beat! They would start out playing a foxtrot and end up playing a one-step. That was the rule, and the exception were groups like the Dixieland Band, the Memphis Five and a few others. I remember the fellows around the Clef Club laughing about the efforts of white musicians of that era. The Original Dixieland Band had soaked everything that they knew musically from the Negroes in New Orleans, and still it was amusing to us when they soloed in comparison with their colored counterparts.

Those were great days. Life was a ball for us youngsters. We would play on a job all night, and we played hard, seldom taking an intermission. Then, after work, most of the time we would go to a bar – not particularly for the booze (we always got plenty of that on our jobs), but to compare notes and get the scuttlebutt on who outblew who and where the cutting session was this morning.

We were a motley crew, consisting of almost every race and color. I well remember Seminole, an Indian banjo and piano player, who was left-handed and could play as much bass on the piano as Art Tatum developed years later. There was Spivvy, a Portuguese, who was a great banjo player. Another great musican was Carmelo Jejo, a Puerto Rican clarinetist. There was a Chinese sax man who doubled on oboe. His first name was George and he was not only the first oboe player I had ever known, he played jazz on the instrument. I've forgotten his last name, maybe because everyone called him Confucius.

6

The New York Scene

Lots of West Indian musicians were in New York. We used to kid them by imitating their accent and also by playing a popular song of the times when they walked in. It was called *The West Indian Blues*, which went like this:

> Gwine home, sure's ya born
> Gwine home, t'won't be long
> Cause I got those West Indian Blues.

It was all in fun, and I guess it was a real indication of the *esprit de corps* that existed among us guys that we all hung out together. Those of us who were not in Big John's, or one of the 30 or so bars which lined Seventh Avenue starting at 110th Street all the way up to 145th Street, would be playing pool at the Rhythm Club, or standing on the corner listening to Jelly Roll Morton or Chick Webb talk about music. We used to go roller skating at 6 o'clock in the morning, starting out at the club 200 strong, until the law made us quit congregating. Then we would all meet in Central Park and scare hell out of the squirrels and pigeons, or whatever wildlife lived in the park. The next year we young fellows changed to bicycles and bought all sorts of fancy rigs. But that phase didn't last too long – we found out that Top 'n' Bottom drinking almost always led to a cracked crown, and lots of unlucky fellows wound up on the bottom of the bicycle. Then we returned to roller skating, but in smaller groups because some of the guys graduated into autos.

We did a lot of swimming the whole year round. I had always been fascinated by water, and when we moved to

Georgetown when I was a kid I was ready at the drop of a hat
to go down to the "crick," as Rock Creek was called. The larger
boys would chase us away and sometimes kick us in the tail to
emphasize that they didn't want the small kids tagging along.
However, I kept trying, so one day they let me undress on the
bank. As I watched them cavort, they didn't stop me from
paddling in the shallow water. All of a sudden, one of the
bigger boys had me by the waist. He carried me to the middle
where it was about nine feet deep and said, "Now swim, damn
you, swim!" Well, I went under. I went under twice and then I
swam out. But that was just the beginning. As soon as I got my
breath, they repeated the treatment ten times. Then Alf Johnson
said, "Now you are a member of our gang. We won't chase you
any more and you can hang out with us." How proud I was,
and I've loved to swim ever since.

In the summer we would go to Coney Island. Or, if the
hangover was too unbearable, we would swim in the nearby
Hudson River. As time marched on we became more selective
and hung out at the Lido Pool on Lenox Avenue. On a nice clear
day you could see the giants of jazz there: Don Redman, Buster
Bailey, J. C. Higginbotham, Bud Freeman, Sid Catlett, Fats
Waller, Tommy Dorsey, Ben Webster, Davy Tough – almost
anybody you can think of.

We had a lot of fun, which is why I look back on those days
with such nostalgia and affection. It seems to me that the entire
attitude toward life and the pursuit of happiness has undergone
such a drastic change from the times I speak of that I wonder
what happened to fun? You don't see a bunch of young fellows
biking, skating and swimming any more. These days, it seems
to me that gangs of teenagers are more likely to be involved
with stealing hub caps and similar shady activities, a far cry
from the diversions of my era.

It has been my experience that musicians usually hang out
with other musicians and, as a rule, they tend to live for music.
Seldom does any brother employ the art as a cover for another
activity. But here's a strange one, an exception to the rule.
Hawkshaw Harris was his real name and he hailed from
somewhere in Ohio. Now, while he was no Django Reinhardt

on his guitar, he was a better than average player. Unfortunately, that didn't mean much during the Depression, as a lot of the best musicians were not doing too much. At 6 p.m. every night you could see Hawkshaw standing in front of the Rhythm Club, immaculate in his tux, *en route* to his gig. But what we could never understand was his secrecy about where he was working. Whenever anybody would ask him, he'd change the subject by saying something like, "C'mon, let's get a taste," or "I'm working over in Jersey," which covered a lot of territory. This went on for a few years until a hometown buddy of his, who also happened to be a pal of mine, remarked to me, "I don't get it. Hawk left his guitar case standing at the bar last night, and when I picked it up to keep it for him it was so light that I looked inside. There was no guitar in it. Do you suppose somebody clipped him before I saw him or maybe he left the box on the job?" It suddenly occurred to me then that maybe he really didn't have a gig at all! Could he have been a head waiter someplace? We never did find out.

During this period I was a sideman in so many bands that there were some whose leaders' names I've even forgotten. Somehow a picture was taken of me with Willie Gant's band playing at Smalls' Paradise. However, I never played with this group, but the photo was one of my favorites because I fancied that I looked like a young Louis Armstrong. He was my hero – and idolized by all of us in the gang. But look alike or not, that's as far as it went, because nobody ever did fill King Satchmo's shoes and I doubt if anyone ever will.

Later the Comedy Club and the Rhythm Club opened up, becoming schools for dancers, for musicians, for everyone. You name them and you can bet, if they became great, they went to "school" at Seventh Avenue at 132nd Street. Where can a youngster go these days, and who is there now to help a budding musician like so many did me? Looking back, I owe a debt of gratitude to many people who helped me in my formative years, and now is a good time to give a very special thank you to that great gentleman Willie "the Lion" Smith. Yes, the Lion was another person who had much to do with my formative years. He was a scholar, a piano master and an unsung hero to the profession, particularly to the young. When I first met the Lion he scared me to death, because I had never heard a piano played with such force. This was at the Capitol Palace, where I had been taken by Willie Lewis. The joint was jumpin', presided over by a majestic figure of a cigar-chomping fellow, Mr Willie "the Lion" Smith. As Lewis unpacked his clarinet, the Lion roared, "Who's this tomato?" meaning me. I left my horn in the case.

Months later, after hanging around, I ventured, "Mr Smith, I know this tune. Would it be okay for me to play it with you?" The Lion growled, "Yeah, kid, if you know your tonics." For all the musical education I had had by then, I didn't have a clue what he meant by "tonics." Nevertheless, I hopped on the stand. Then I found out as Willie played on, each chorus in another key: A sharp to A flat, B flat to B natural, and so on. But I struggled on. So we got to be friends, kind of like a cat looking up to a king. And I'll never stop thanking Willie "the Lion" Smith for his important part in my musical education.

Those days, I didn't need to grow too much musically. Most groups played a semi-dixieland style, and we woodshedded our way from gig to gig. As I said, jobs were usually easy to find and I worked with whoever asked me. Some of the bands with whom I played, for varying periods from a few weeks to several months, were Alex Jackson's, Billy Paige's Broadway Syncopators and Billy Fowler's.

Here's one I remember that was over pretty quickly. I was playing with a burlesque show which took us on the road, the first stop being Montreal, Canada. We opened with a bang, stopping the show and no wonder, seeing that we were loaded to the gills with shake-'em-up booze which we had thoughtfully brought up from New York, just in case we got stage fright. The first part of the week went great, then some things happened which led to our being back on the corner of 135th and Lenox Avenue, looking for another job after only being away for three weeks.

The first thing was that the house manager objected to our milk bottles, which we used in our act. I'll explain the act. Our scene opened with us dressed like the ship's crew. We lounged at the bow of the vessel until an officer arrived leading a beautiful blond (the star of the show) and saying, "Tut, tut, my dear, you are not seasick. What you need is a little music to get your mind off the ship's motion." Turning to us, he'd continue, "C'mon, boys, let's have some music to cheer the little lady up." That was our cue to start beating out a slow bump and grind-type number, *No, No, Nora*, which was a popular tune of the times. Then, as the couple left the stage, we'd go into our act of several musical pieces climaxed by the then show-stopping *Tiger Rag*.

After returning to New York, I joined Billy Paige's Syncopators, a Pittsburgh band that was playing on Lenox Avenue at Johnny Powell's Capitol Palace Club. Don Redman came to New York with this group and this is the club where I first met Lizzie Miles. However, I didn't remain with Paige's orchestra very long. This time I quit because I fell in love with one of the cutest entertainers I'd ever seen and, after I discovered that she was taking my money and giving it to a dancer in the floorshow, I was so angry I couldn't stay. I had enjoyed playing those symphonic arrangements of the light classics such as *By the Waters of the Minnetonka*, *After the Storm*, etc. But this little lady taught me one of the many important lessons I learned.

The following spring found me on the road with the Alex Jackson orchestra, which took us as far west as Cincinnati. But I grew homesick for the Apple, where once again I nearly got myself on the wrong track. By this time I had been away from home more than three years. I was nearly 18 and had seen a lot and done a lot, so I figured that no one could tell me anything I had not heard before. But the fact is that I still had some important lessons to learn.

It was about this time that I met three characters, Country, Philadelphia Jimmy and Sweet Singer, who played an important part in my unorthodox schooling. Country was perhaps the most colorful. The best description I can give of him would be a ginger colored, skinny version of Peter Lorre. Country ran a joint on 133rd Street which he called Seventh Heaven. He considered himself one of the elite among the hierarchy of hoodlums, based on his boyhood friendship with the police commissioner. His Seventh Heaven was just that for all of the pimps, whores, boosters and other assorted gentry of that dim half-world, especially the opium smokers who really looked down upon anybody who couldn't support a 50-dollar a day habit.

As I recall, there were about eight or nine of these fellows, and Country provided special facilities for those chosen few. You might call it a bank. Behind the bar there was an arrangement of compartments like vault boxes, each locked, and the bartender had a key. He used to gauge which pimp had the most industrious stable of whores by the number of times a box had something deposited in it. One would think that the common knowledge of all that money there would prove to be too great a temptation in this thieves' den, but Seventh Heaven had only one way in and one way out. Old Whistling Sefus was the inside doorman, perched on a high stool, sawed-off shotgun across his knees. He didn't drink or smoke and he saw everything. If a real rumble started, Sefus would merely bar the door and push the buzzer, which let Philadelphia Jimmy know about the trouble. Nobody could get in, not even the police! What began in Seventh Heaven ended right there. I started at a salary of 25 dollars per week, but I never knew what I would really be paid. Country would usually give me a 50-dollar bill and, before the week was up, hand me another 20 or, once in a while, 100. Tips were great and whiskey was free to the band. We never dared ask Mr Country for wages for fear he just might jump salty on us. So we let well enough alone.

One morning around seven or eight we quit playing and Country, who was tending bar at the time, yelled, "Hey, you little sad-assed horn-tooter, come on and have a drink with me." I was flattered. Country never drank with his help. He put a pint of good rye on the bar, not the shake-up he generally served but real Canadian rye. Pouring some high-class sherry for himself, he started telling me about how he started as a runner for the Old Hudson Dusters band and then worked his way up to being part of Monk Eastman's mob. Finally he got his own organization up on San Juan Hill, where most of his people lived at that time, saying he no longer had anything to do with sporting women or dope except smoking the poppy. He would like to make one more good haul at his specialty, which he said was safe-cracking, and retire to a farm away from everything illegal. Looking back, I'll never know if Country was conning me or setting me up for the pitch that came next.

"Boy, you look like a good kid. I like you. I think I'll take you under my wing. Now you listen and listen good, 'cause I ain't gonna say this but once. Do as I tell you and you'll never be sorry. Smarten up! Be somebody! First of all, ya gotta cut way down on the whiskey. Drinkin' is okay, but gettin' drunk all the time is out – get me? Out! Next is women. Ya gotta learn how to live with 'em and how to handle 'em. If ya don't, they'll handle you. When that happens, ya ain't a man – and if ya ain't a man ya might as well be daid – ya get me?" He poured us another drink and continued. "So the way you handle 'em is never get one that you love. Get you one that loves you, but don't you fall in love with her. If in case you do fall in love, quit her. Quit the bitch! Get the hell out while you're still a man. 'Cause the breed can't help but devour a man, 'specially if she knows he loves her. Hold on to these truths as long as you live and you'll find them to be true. Now dough is important but it ain't everythin'. The thing to do if you get a chance is to grab a bundle, run like hell, clam up and go straight from then on. I'm gonna give you that chance because you're young and I wanna do somebody good. Besides, I got a hunch I can trust you."

Then he opened a big compartment behind the bar and started piling money up in front of me. You can believe my eyes popped wider and wider and I started sobering up. I had never seen that much money in my whole life. All kinds of thoughts tumbled through my head. I was completely at a loss about what Country had in mind when he displayed all of this geetus. It suddenly occurred to me that I was still a green kid, as naive as they come. I guess he got quite a kick from the expression on my face because, laughing, he said, "Don't get so excited, kid! Ain't ya never seen no queer dough before?" Then I became absolutely sober as he continued, "Here's the deal. Every day I will give you 100 or so. I want you to go to Philly, Stamford, any close in town. Buy suits, shirts or anything with this scratch and I'll give you 20 per cent of the good money you bring back. If you get caught, telephone this number. I'll have a lawman spring ya. Just don't let anybody know my name. If you have to take a beatin', take it. I'll pay you for takin' it. Just stick to your story – ya found this in the street and didn't know it was queer."

Every syllable registered like the blow of a hammer, while something inside of me said, "No! No! This is not for me." The problem was how to get out of this without making an enemy of Mr Country or, at the very least, hurting his feelings. I think I said, in a quavering voice, "Mr Country, I appreciate all the things you've told me and thank you for the chance to get into the big dough. But I'll need a little time to think it over." I thought and thought all day and up until time to go to work. Then I went out jamming my way downtown. I just couldn't go Country's route. The next night I was working in a little joint in Hackensack, New Jersey, with no intention of even passing by 133rd Street or the Seventh Heaven. In fact I was so scared I stayed away from New York for about two months and only mention this now because I know Country has been dead a long time.

The above reminds me of how much at home I felt reading Damon Runyon in later years. The names were different but I knew all kinds of very similar characters who hung around Broadway or the Harlem spots. Here are a few more that I recall. The Black Eagle was Hubert Julian. There was Tony the Wop, who knew every song, and Tack Annie, who put tacks on subway seats! Chippy Mayme had five whores working for her. The head of White's Lindy Hoppers was Herbert White. Memphis Slim was a pool shark and played with James Evans, doing a Stepin Fetchit with Broadway's best. Charlie Piano outwitted the government for years and never was drafted. There was Casper the Coot, and people said he was crazy as a cootie beause he pulled all kinds of confidence games just so he could support anybody that told him a hard-luck story. Fearless Johnny Blue Eyes was a coon-can dealer, a bouncer and one of the few guys that knife-men and gunmen respected. But his 98-pound wife whipped him whenever she was in the mood until she brought another man into their home. Yes, there were many bizarre characters around in those days and I was somewhat acquainted with many of them.

Philadelphia Jimmy I knew well, and he was another fellow who taught me a long-remembered lesson. I had seen Jimmy lots of times in the Touraine Restaurant, usually in the company of Wintergarden Eddie, Broadway Al, Chippy Charlie and people like that. These were the hard hustlers – the top dogs of the underworld. No nickel and dime stuff for them. They didn't bother with street women. When they congregated to talk shop or while away the time, if a female was along she was a stunning dreamboat. She would be stashed at a corner table looking like an angel swathed in mink and ermine, dripping with diamonds.

Anyway, Jimmy was never seen with a woman until he started dropping by the Bucket of Blood. This is where I was working after I figured the heat had died down at Country's. Jimmy would arrive in the late morning, about 4 or 5 a.m., and always asked me to play the Irving Berlin tune *All Alone*. He wanted it played sweet and as a waltz – which is the way it was written. Although the other people in the place didn't like that kind of music, no one dared say so until Jim left. Generally, after hearing the tune, he would give me five or ten dollars and that would be that.

Then he started bringing two girls with him. One was a red-haired Junoesque type of beauty; the other, a lovely molded little goddess, a coffee with heavy cream color. Many years later I saw quite a few women in Paris, originally from Martinique, with that complexion and coloring. At that time, around New York, she was a rarity and really caught my eye.

One morning I remember particularly vividly. Jimmy arrived with his friends as usual. To be sure, as the filly entered the room I drooled in enjoyment at the mere sight of this poetry in pulchritude. The little one smiled at me! I played the usual tune and was pleasantly surprised when Jimmy invited me to breakfast with them. We went to Glenn's famous restaurant which was only half a block across Lenox Avenue from the Touraine – only half a block, but the social gap was many miles.

This was the place where you could mingle with people like Marcus Garvey, the West Indian black nationalist who organized the Black Star Line (the first negro steamship line) among other gigantic projects slanted toward nationalism, or Francis Mills, the bronze stage star, W. S. Du Bois, Bert Williams, the great comedian who starred in the *Ziegfeld Follies,* and all sorts of negro intelligentsia. So I felt like a fish out of water when we entered. But this feeling was forgotten when the little lady looked into my eyes and said softly, "I enjoyed hearing you play." I couldn't believe my ears, and in rapid succession I dropped my napkin and bumped my head picking it up, which then caused me to knock over several water glasses. Our table became the center of attraction while I shriveled up and almost died of mortification. Susie (that was the beautiful lady's name) laughed merrily, saying, "I didn't mean to startle you into all of that action. Please forgive me."

I probably mouthed something inane trying to cover up my embarrassment. She didn't have much more to say to me until after breakfast. As we were leaving she handed me a phone number and whispered, "Call me when you get up. I really want to apologize properly for making you uncomfortable." That remark sent me home with my heart skipping to the rhythm of love, even though every now and then I would cuss myself for being so gauche. Nevertheless, later that day I phoned Sweet Sue and invited her to the movies that afternoon. I was delighted when she accepted, not that I thought she was doing anything but being kind. I was being cagey making our date in a movie theater, as I had no intention of being alone in any kind of private setting with her. For one thing, I couldn't trust myself not to tell her I loved her. Also, fellows like Jimmy would not like it a bit if a tooter tried to horn in on his private preserves. Still, I was intrigued.

Don't get me wrong. I liked girls. But I was also scared to death of them. There had been several episodes with a certain young lady who danced with *Go-Get-It.* She was hardly any older than I but far wiser in the ways of the world. Perhaps she didn't know the male was supposed to be the aggressor. The action began when she asked me to walk her home. As we started down the dark street she opened the conversation by asking me if I liked her. When I answered in the affirmative, she said, "Why don't you kiss me, then?" I gave her a quick peck on the cheek. Her next words were, "Oh, not like that, silly! Here, I'll show you how to kiss." And she did. One thing led to another very rapidly until right there on the warm sidewalk I found out why the boys and girls liked to play hide and seek behind the Odd Fellows Hall in Georgetown. What I never figured out was how everyone seemed to know what had happened when I finally got back to where the band was staying. I guess it showed on my face.

In later years I came to the conclusion that any fellow who didn't show any perceptible yearnings in that direction was considered fair game by les girls. The little dancer appeared to be so insatiable that I used to have one of the fellows in the band escort me home for protection. I never told him what and who I was being protected against, of course. But he probably knew.

But this time, with Sweet Sue, I was in love – in love with this little dolly and in love with love. It seems hard to believe that any fool could fall as hard as I fell for Sue. Although I remembered all of the stuff that Country had tried to tell me about women, still everything flew out of the window after meeting her. I even went to the library and read up on the great romances – Romeo and Juliet and so on – and tried to apply myself the way they did, to charm milady. Into what? I just wanted to be her slave and worship her. I wanted to place her on a pedestal. And she? The dear lady must have had some fun in the ensuing weeks with this clown who spent money like a country bumpkin, lavishing perfumes, candy, flowers and books on her.

But I started to tell you about Philadelphia Jimmy's lesson. You see, Sue was to be the catalyst in this matter, and evidently she was enjoying the play so much that she was in no hurry to see it end. One afternoon she phoned me, saying that she was sick in bed and would I buy a certain medicine for her – and also something for her supper, please. It was a bad winter day in New York, so of course I agreed to bring her the things. But natch. When I arrived she feebly called to me to come on in, that

the door was unlocked. When I entered she jumped out of bed
without a stitch on – and locked the door. Then it occurred to
me that she didn't seem sick at all. How right I was! Suddenly
we were involved in a wrestling match that made me feel as if
I had been attacked by an octopus. She only weighed about 90
pounds but she was all over me like a swarm of bees. Maybe
I've always been fated to be a pushover for the ladies. Anyway,
I lost.

After the balling scene, and when I came to my senses, Sue
was saying, "Now, you are my daddy, and daddy is supposed
to do what his baby wants him to do. Here," she said, handing
me some white powder. "What's that?" I asked. I had an idea
what it was but I wanted to make sure. "Cocaine, you idiot,"
she replied, daintily putting some on her little fingernail and
sniffing it up her nostril. As it dawned on me what her words
meant, I broke out in a sweat, then I grew cold. My thoughts
tumbled over one another. My first thought was, "Why did I
ever leave home?" Then I wished my mother or anybody
would come get me. And I wondered, "How do I get out of this?
God damn . . . God damn." All my life I've been deathly afraid
of three things: snakes, guns and dope. And here I had wound
up in bed with a dopie who wanted me to share dope with her.
These thoughts triggered my actions – my love ended as
suddenly as it had begun.

I leaped out of that bed, dressed as fast as I could and was
just about to leave the apartment when I heard the voice of
Philadelphia Jimmy. "Let the bastard go, Sue. He's too dumb
for us to use, anyway." Later, when I talked it over with a fellow
who I was sure knew all the answers, he laughed and said,
"Forget it! That's the way Jimmy recruits his willing workers."
Incidentally, it turned out that Sue was Jimmy's legal wife and
the other woman was just that – his other woman.

Lastly, there was Sweet Singer. To set the scene, I have to tell
you that Singer weighed about 110 pounds dripping wet. He
was the doorman in a Harlem joint on 133rd Street (known as
Beale Street) where I worked. The real name shall remain a
secret, but during the Roaring 20s this den of iniquity was
notorious. Fists, knives or gunplay provided the excitement

nightly, along with any other form of entertainment that the customer could pay for. You name it, and it could be found in the joint – or sent for. Any female entertainer who couldn't lift her skirt and pick up paper money from the table without using her hands never worked there. All of the waiters, bartenders and help were on duty 24 hours a day. That is, they were supposed to be available for various and sundry extra-curricular duties. And Mr Sweet Singer must have been no exception. He was such a warm, cultured gentleman. He greeted everyone with a friendly smile. "Hello there, Mr Jones – Miss Smith. Ah, here's our wonderful musician. Good evening, Mr Stewart," and so on. I grew to like this fellow, although I suspected he was left of center, sexwise. But there was no particular indication unless you looked askance at his rather high-pitched voice.

One night, while in my cups (I was still drinking heavily), I got into a heated argument with Singsing Sammy, the boss. After a few punches had been exchanged I found myself being escorted out of the place by none other than my pal Mr Sweet Singer. I wasn't ready to leave and decided to go back inside and explain to Sammy that there were no hard feelings and that I was sorry to have gotten out of line. But Mr Singer didn't agree with my thinking and suggested that I go home and sleep my load off. That's when I goofed. One word led to another, until Mr Singer said, "Quick! Look at that shooting star!" I remember looking up and, by golly, there was not only one shooting star but a whole gang of them, plus pretty lights and bells ringing. I saw and heard all of this from the ground. For a sensible moment I figured that my friend Mr Singer must have knocked me down. Then I passed out.

When I woke up I was in somebody's bed in somebody's house, and a woman I had never laid eyes on was putting cold wet things on my head. At first I thought I was having a bad dream because the lady was a giantess. Again, I swore off liquor. But she was nice to me and kept bringing me hot soup, coffee, cold towels and an ice bag. After I had revived sufficiently she told me that she was Mrs Singer and that I was there because her husband had told a cab driver to bring me to her rather than let me sleep it off in the gutter where he had knocked me. As I felt better I got up and started to put my clothes on, only to have Mrs Singer say, "Not so fast. You're not sober enough to navigate yet. Let me give you some of the old Indian remedy which I'm sure will make a new man out of you. Then you can go home." This sounded reasonable, and I was pleasantly surprised to find out that the Indian remedy was not a medicine at all but love, love, love, as she climbed into bed with me!

After my "cure" I dozed off until I was rudely awakened by a voice saying, "Wake up! Wake up, you son of a bitch! I can't kill a sleeping pigeon." These remarks were emphasized by the hideous 45 pistol Sweet Singer waved in front of my nose. I wondered why he felt he needed a pistol for me. After all, he had knocked me out so easily. I also fleetingly wondered why he was so angry with me for being in his bed when he was the one who had sent me there. Then it suddenly occurred to me that he didn't like his wife's having given me the "Indian remedy" . . . and, knowing his wife, it wasn't hard for him to recognize the tell-tale signs. Well, it turned out that, in fact, he was more able than most, since he was a woman also! I never would have guessed the truth, but years later he renounced everything, married and had two children. As a woman!

7

Around and About

Let me give credit here to another fellow who had much to do
with the way I turned out musically, my old buddy Happy
Caldwell. I've known Happy so long that I can't be exact as to
where and when we met. Those years run together but, to
venture a guess, I would say it probably was about 1923 after
I had left the Spillers' nest. Most likely we met at Smalls' Sugar
Cane on Fifth Avenue. That would be about right because I also
met Jimmy Harrison and June Clark there. They were the only
musicians in town playing "Western" style with the exception
of Happy Caldwell, who had grown up under the influence of
Joe Oliver and Louis Armstrong. Another reason that makes
me believe we met exactly at that time and place is because
right after we met we started rooming together. Hap started
teaching me the Western "get-off" style of playing, which had
a heavy accented back beat on the second and fourth bars.
When you soloed, it was called "taking a Boston."

Rooming with Happy was a terrific arrangement for a rebel
like me. When I had roomed in Mr Smalls's house with Bunky
Addison, he never let me forget that he gave me my first long
pants suit, nor would he ever stop trying to act like my father.
He was always saying, "Come on, get up," or "It's time to go
home." I had very little freedom with him. It felt like being
home with my mother – or even with Isabelle Spiller. But with
Hap, it was always as equal buddies. We roomed together off
and on whenever we could. One summer, it must have been a
couple of years after we first met, Hap had a suggestion. "We
ought to get out of this town for a while. Let's go to Atlantic
City. We can hang out on the beach, swim every day all day,

meet some fabulous broads and hear some of the best cats in the country. Everyone goes to the seashore for the season."

I went along with this program. We talked it up among the gang, saved our dough for a few weeks and then took off with Manzie Johnson, a drummer pal who had an old Essex or Maxwell car, vintage about 1919 I think. We planned to hit Atlantic City in style. The car wasn't exactly a Stutz Bear Cat, but riding was riding, to us tooters. In those days, before the Holland Tunnel had been created, you took a ferry to the New Jersey side and drove all through Jersey City, Newark, Elizabeth and Perth Amboy. And then Manzie changed our plans by saying, "Do you guys know Trusty, the piano player from Brooklyn?" Neither of us had ever heard of him, so Hap asked, "What about him?" Manzie answered, "I know he's got a job at the Smile Awhile Club in Asbury Park. All we have to do is be there when he gets in town next week and he'll be glad to have some New York bimbos to play with instead of picking up the local semis." That sounded reasonable to us, so we chugged on to the Park, had some food and went by the Smile Awhile.

Sure enough, Trusty was due to open the next week. All was well. I even knew the boss of the club, a West Indian Johnny, having met him through the Cuban fellow who had started the numbers game in New York (they called the game Bolito in Cuba). We started to look the town over, hoisted a few drinks here and there and were feeling no pain when disaster struck. We ran into Slim O'Neil, a young drummer who lived in the Park. He took us in tow, promising to show us the town, and some of the things I saw I'll never forget. Asbury was jumping with lots of clubs. For instance, a memorable spot was Gypsy George's, a big-time gambling establishment. Besides the usual poker, crap games, roulette, Georgia Skin, Bird Cage and Coon-Can games of chance, that was the place where, for the first time, I saw slot machines which paid off money if you won! Nickels, dimes, quarters, half-dollars and silver dollars – and that was the only one I ever saw that took five-dollar gold pieces! I'll always remember that dollar devil which sent our finances to hell. We tried to hit that beautiful elusive jackpot until all we had left in our pockets was "chicken feed" – jargon at that time for small coins.

One funny thing I've noticed, right on schedule whenever you were broke, you got hungry. And of course we were hungry by that time, as we had never stopped for dinner –hungry, broke, and with no place to sleep in a strange town. But Slim was equal to the occasion, telling us we could stay at his home and pay his mother after we started working. But first, we wanted some food. He took us to Aunt Minnie's, a big old house where a woman and her three daughters ran a combination rooming house and 24-hour restaurant. I can see it now. In a large room there were four tables, each about ten feet long, crowded with lively, loud-talking people eating breakfast. This was served starting at 5 a.m., and what food! Biscuits, corn bread, light rolls, fried apples, ham, bacon, sausage, scrapple, fried fish, steak, fried white and sweet potatoes, hominy grits, pancakes, jelly, milk, tea and coffee. All of this plus three eggs were served family style for a dollar per person, which was a high price in those days, but it certainly was well worth it.

Slim bought the breakfast and Aunt Minnie's oldest daughter, Cleo, fell for Happy like a ton of bricks – which figured, because she was a great big gal built like one of those legendary you-know-whats. Anyway, we were served with seconds all around as Cleo smilingly appraised Happy with that certain speculative gleam in her eye. Between talking and trying to see how much we could eat, it took at least an hour. When we tore ourselves away from that still groaning board, Cleo looked Hap dead in the eye, saying, "We hope to have you with us for dinner." Slim, who was a great kidder, said to the girl, "Yeah, and I bet you won't even use salt, Happy looks so sweet to you."

We kidded Happy a lot about his conquest, mainly because Cleo was about 5 foot 10 tall and with a girth to match. I couldn't say exactly about Hap, but he was on the small side. At the very most he was 5 foot 5, since I was taller than he and I was only 5 foot 6! But it turned out great later on, when they really became friends. We needed a pal like Cleo so we could depend on a square meal once in a while.

Trusty came to town all right, and we were hired. But, as

soon as he found out about how much we liked to blow, he was disappointed because he did most of his playing at the bar. The boss told him a few times that he was hired to play the piano, not to be host to the girls at the bar. But when these warnings had no effect we were all fired.

This recalls another team of buddies that were given their walking papers at another club for almost the same reason. Bobbie Stark and Benny Carter grew up in the same neighborhood in New York and they came to the Park together to work. But Bobbie drank too much, which led to a scene. They were fired and left Asbury. The reason they left town was because Asbury Park sure was no New York as far as walking off one job and finding another was concerned. A local piano player, Bill Basie, advised us that what we ought to do was try to snag a ride back to New York, since Manzie's Maxwell (or Essex) had long since given up the ghost, and it would be hard if not impossible to find a gig.

Basie was right, but we didn't take his advice, being ashamed to go back to New York so soon after all the boasting we had done about our great summer plans. No, we chose to hang on and see if anything would turn up. First we tried the joint where Basie was working, but it was too small for anything other than piano and drums. Yes, this is the very same Bill Basie who later found fame and became "Count" Basie, thanks to John Hammond. It never occurred to us that perhaps we could get a job washing dishes or pushing deck chairs on the boardwalk. Oh no, we were musicians. And many is the day we'd have to split a hot dog three ways! Finally we got a job at Shrewsbury Country Club, which lasted three weeks. This was just long enough for me to peer between the potted plants which hid us from the public and to see how the upper crust of the world lived. I observed lots of the same guys and gals that I had seen at the Gold Coast (a fancy saloon) and Sweet Lucy's.

Sweet Lucy was a combination of the famous hostess Elsa Maxwell and a madame with a down-home approach to the oldest profession. You reached her place through a 110-foot tunnel which went from the Gold Coast to what seemed to me like another world. I have read about such fabulous establishments in later years, and since then I've visited quite a few. But, to a kid, this place was like something conjured up out of the Arabian Nights. As I recall, the tunnel ended in a courtyard-like room with many doors, plus a balcony also with many doors. This semi-circular fantasy boasted a bar which ran halfway around the room and was broken by a fountain which had varicolored, ever-changing lights playing upon it. But perhaps the most astonishing sight was the donkey which cavorted from place to place like a tipsy kitten. Hap gasped to Slim, "What the hell is this? A real animal?" And Slim replied, "Oh, that's Jo Jo. He's the star of the joint."

There must have been no less than 30 assorted females there wearing gorgeous gowns, all sizes and shapes and colors. Some were like schoolgirls, others like grand dames looking down their noses as if they were toting lorgnettes. I stood taking all this in, when a heavy-set ginger colored woman in an ordinary house-dress stood up on something like a dais in the center of the floor and yelled, "Quiet! All right, now you been drinkin' my champagne. You been drinkin' my whiskey and using up the time of my girls. Now it's Lucy's turn. I got plenty of rooms. I got plenty of girls. Let's go. If you don't see what you want, ask for it! Tell me your name and I'll give you your hometown paper. I got second sight for a fool's delight. Yes, I'm the seventh daughter of a seventh son – and that's bound to get it from here to kingdom come. All right. Let the good times roll!" We took that as our cue to leave, because if Cleopatra in person had been available for ten cents we couldn't have afforded to snap her girdle. That's how broke we were.

We loafed around the Park and owed Mrs Slim many weeks' rent (which I must say she never asked for, thank God), and made it on hot dogs at two for a nickel when we were not invited by Happy's Cleo to eat – or when Manzie (the Rudolph Valentino type) was not called on by Sweet Lucy to solace some nervous society matron. Yep, we got by.

One night we were jamming at the Smile Awhile Cabaret – Bill Basie, Cecil Benjamin, Putney Dandridge (another terrific piano player), Jabbo Smith the trumpet man, etc. It was a big session with a lot of fellows. Someone said to me, "Hey, fella, you play good. I want you to meet my piano man, Bingie Madison. I'm Bobby Brown, I have five pieces and we work out of Newark." I guess I said, "Hi. Pleased to meet you," as Bobby continued, "We could use a good horn man. How about you joining us?" I countered with, "I'll make it if you hire Happy Caldwell on tenor. You see, we're a team and one doesn't go without the other." Bobby thought for a moment and said, "Okay. We'll drink to the deal." We didn't ask any details, just picked up our paper bags of dirty shirts and left early the next morning, Newark bound.

To me, the greatest thing about that New Jersey metropolis is its proximity to New York, and the greatest thing about New York is in the memory of what it used to be, musicwise. I suppose every place has changed an enormous amount since World War II, and I guess it really depends on one's frame of reference as to what a particular town means to a person. As for me, I'll take the years from 1921 to 1957 as the most rewarding and fun years. Let's turn back the clock. Getting back to Newark, it was then and doubtless always will be a small town. However, some exciting things happened.

For instance, I didn't know at the time how southern in most attitudes this burg was, but I found out. Soon after we arrived we went to work in a dance hall. I've forgotten the name of the place, but it was on a main street up above a theater. The unusual experience here was that we started playing at 8:30 sharp and each number had to be precisely one minute long. Sometimes we would get a request for a ballad tune and would only get as far as the middle before the floor man would blow the whistle as a signal for the next dance to begin. The girls were paid two and a half cents a dance and they earned around 40 or 50 dollars a week, which was big money in those days. A secretary or shop clerk only made, as I recall, about ten or 12 dollars working a six-day, 48-hour week. You can see that these girls had to stay on their toes. In the band room there was a big list of of do's and don'ts for us, such as

Don't take off more than two minutes an hour from the stand per man. Once you are in the club, don't go out for any reason.

Don't use the house telephone.
Don't come in if you are over five minutes late.
Don't take requests from anyone but the customers.
Don't talk to the girls.
Do say good evening to the boss when you arrive and also say goodnight when you leave.
Don't flirt with the girls.
Do report any girl who flirts with you to the floor manager.
Don't panic and leave the stand if there is a fight – just play the music louder.
Don't stop playing any tune if the lights go out for any reason.

Later we found out that a gangster owned the place. We called the joint the "Chain Gang," but we stuck it out for six months and I bought myself a purple suit (my idea of spiffy) with the extra money. By then we were well into summer time again and on to what we thought was a real good deal at Lake Hopatkong. That is, until we arrived there and found that we couldn't rent a room or a house within 75 miles of the job. It seems that we were good enough to play music and entertain these people but we were not good enough to rent a room, barn or stable.

However, Bobby had a month's contract and swore he would play it out. So he bought two tents and some stoves and we camped out behind the casino where we were playing. Then the fun began. You see, this was open, uncultivated country between the lake and a small stream where various animals came to drink. The first night we heard all sorts of strange sounds and the next morning the village storekeeper gave us the scoop about the local wildlife, the deer, fox, bobcats and so forth that had been seen in the vicinity. We felt a little apprehensive about being so close to savage animals, especially after another old codger in the store chimed in saying that he had seen mountain lions there! After thinking this over, Bingie calmed us with his opinion that the old man was just trying to scare us. I, for one, will never know if he was or not, because the very next night we were awakened by something prowling around outside the tent, making a lot of noise. We were concerned, but not too much, until a big black bear stuck his head inside the tent! That bear was welcome to the premises as far as Bobby's band was concerned.

I can still laugh at the speed with which we left the tent, the job and that part of the state. We didn't even wait to be paid! After returning to Newark we argued for the next few days about that bear. Some said it was a person in a bear costume intent on scaring us out of the area, because there were no bears in New Jersey and hadn't been for years. Others were just as positive that they had seen an actual bear. Bets were made and we called a newspaper and they referred us to the Department of Wildlife Conservation. They confirmed that, yes, bears were still seen frequently in New Jersey. And that was the end of that.

Back we went to the Chinese restaurant where we had worked before. It was less money but there were no bears. It was there that something happened which changed all my ideas about music. One evening Happy brought home a King Oliver record, and I'll never forget that tune, *Mabel's Dream*. This was the first time I had heard the duo of Joe and Louis Armstrong, although Hap and Jimmy Harrison had talked about nothing else when we first met. This record really proved what they said. Hap and I played *Mabel's Dream* until our arms were worn out from working the phonograph handle, the record was worn out and our souls were on fire. We were wild about that music!

The very next morning Hap and I left bright and early, headed for New York and determined to buy this and any other Joe Oliver records that were available. Where to look first? Why, Harlem, of course. No downtown stores stocked this kind of music. So off we went on the old Seventh Avenue subway, which clacked to the rhythm of our thoughts: "Gonna get the record, gonna get the record."

8

With Snowden

Here is another point in my life where luck played a big role. If I hadn't gone to New York to get that record at that exact moment, I wouldn't have run into Jimmy Harrison in the record store, and then I wouldn't have known that Elmer Snowden was looking for me, on Jimmy's recommendation! Elmer had broken with the Washington bunch (including Duke Ellington) and was slated to open at the Balconnades, a dance hall on 66th Street. Pops Snowden told me later that he had always thought I showed promise and that's why he wanted me for his new band. And I'm glad that he did. Because subsequently, through my playing with Snowden, I got to meet Louis Armstrong. And he liked my playing well enough to recommend to Smack (Fletcher Henderson) that I should be the cat to replace him when he went back to Chicago.

But I am ahead of my story. I went to see Snowden right away and was hired, although there was no opening for Happy. But I wasn't going to leave my buddy, so we decided to move back to New York and get a room together, as usual. I was thinking that, as soon as I got a chance, I'd quit and go play wherever there was a job for both of us.

Wherever you went those days, there was likely to be a band, and there were many good aggregations which at any other period of time would have received much more acclaim. For instance, there was the Kenny Roane combo – only six pieces, but everybody doubled, so his arrangements would feature a sax section or a brass section. He had such a tight, well-rehearsed, subtle approach to music that he was the inspiration for another little band which made people completely forget who originated the style. Actually, John Kirby was a carbon copy of the wonderful six-man group led by Kenneth Roane. Although both groups were outstanding and imaginative, Kirby had by far the best soloists. Then, almost at the same time, there was a seven-piece orchestra led by Banjo Bernie, whose fame on his instrument was legendary. Bernie's drawback, however, was that he couldn't control himself as a leader. Lots of times we would go to hear them break it up musically in some joint. Then, the very next night on the corner, the news would circulate that Bernie had skipped town again – and taken, in passing, the pay roll or the instruments!

Sam Wooding, Leroy Smith – these names were also among the wonderful full-sized bands of the era. But I had better stop naming bands and musicians. This might tend to confuse jazz historians who, human-like, prefer to think *they* know the origins and background of influences on this music. Sometimes what I read is quite a contrast to the way I remember the musicians and groups of the time. Millions of words have been written on the life and times in these United States during the Roaring 20s, and I'd like to add a considered look through the eyes of a jazz musician. This one gladly reflects on how beautiful the scene was made by those very necessary adjuncts to fun, women, and their companionship. And were there ever a lot of gorgeous women around! Yes, while this was the time of prohibition and rum runners, it was also truly the era of glittering glamor. The so-called tired businessman never had it so good, what with Earl Carroll, George White and the zestiest of them all – Flo Ziegfeld – all featuring the most beautiful girls on the stages of many theaters. Plus there was all that after-theater entertainment in places like the Strand Roof and the Ziegfeld Midnight Follies. And this was besides the many clubs featuring shows. The largest and best known were the Palais, the Plantation, the Club Alabam and the Cotton Club. The amazing thing is that all of these were doing great business at the same time.

One way and another, I was exposed to all kinds of establishments those days. And of them all, the Rajah's was most bizarre. I only became exposed to this operation by chance, as he catered strictly to people with beaucoups bucks. I was working alongside my buddy, when, as I recall, a party of six people descended into the club. We were damned sorry to see them fall in, as in those days the band kept playing until every last customer left. But Dago Frank, the waiter, was the epitome of obsequiousness. They ordered wine, so we began playing a bunch of show tunes in between our yawns. We might as well have been furniture for all of the attention that the party paid us, until one of the women called out, "To hell with that corn. Get the lead out of your ass and play us some blues! Doncha know the blues?"

We segued into some down-to-earth blues and the party got groovy, especially after one of the fellows put a 100-dollar bill on the piano. On and on we played the blues, and the piano became increasingly decorated with bills. Tens, twenties, fifties – by then we didn't even care if we quit or not. This was a bonanza night based on the blues. Happy Caldwell turned to Herb Gregory, our trombone man, saying, "Man, come on and wake up. Play some more blues! Keyhold blues, old blues, new blues, dirty red blues. With all of this dough in front of us, we're gonna play them blues until . . . until these folks say to stop."

The party finally broke up and one guy said to his woman, "Honey, why don't we go by the Rajah's; we'll go and take this horn man." She agreed, and off we went. This was a fantastic place akin to that fabulous joint in Jersey. At the time I didn't know what I was getting into, and actually I didn't care with all of this moola floating around. It had already qualified as one of my lucky nights.

There were all kinds of clubs in those days – nightclubs, cabarets, bars, bistros – and then this was also the time of the breakfast dance. These went over so big in Manhattan, especially in Harlem. Looking back, I recall Willie Lewis taking me to my first breakfast dance. It was held at Johnny Powell's Capitol Palace on Lenox Avenue. This sticks in my mind because it was the only time I know that Willie Lewis (my clarinet playing chum who got me the position with the Spillers) wasn't allowed to play. The bandleader, Willie "the Lion" Smith, would interrupt speculations of a group of musicians who would be signifying by saying in a loud tone, "Tonight is not the night for 'semis.' This morning the Lion's going to roar, but only with his own 'Cubs'." Then he struck the piano with a resounding striding into the tune *My Honey's Lovin' Arms*, cigar cocked at a go-to-hell angle!

At any rate, I am of the opinion that the custom of the breakfast dance goes way back in time, possibly back to the gold rush days in San Francisco, although those participants possibly wouldn't be considered professional entertainers in the same sense as the top-notch talent that memory recalls. We know, according to the files of the *Chicago Defender* (which is, incidentally, a great source of information), that the breakfast dance was very big in the Windy City back in the 20s, on the South Side. Although we cannot be positive what year the New Yorkers took up this dine and dance idea for the wee hours of the morning, I do remember in vivid detail and glorious color the years when the scene flourished. I suppose that in every metropolitan city there is a loose-knit fraternity existing between the various groups known as the "night people." This is a conglomeration of artists, taxi drivers, television and radio people, prostitutes, actors, musicians, adventurers and entertainers. The breakfast dance in Harlem was more than a social gathering. Everybody who was anybody was drawn to these events, and it reached such proportions that every club was trying to get into the act. Finally it died out from sheer over-exposure, and another delightful social outlet was gone.

But let me fill you in on that glamorous phase which existed for about five years in New York's Harlem. It is 4 a.m., cold and raining. 99.9 per cent of Manhattan is black as night, as the city slumbers. But the other little one-tenth of one per cent is brightly lit, the taxi cabs are honking, trying to get their passengers past the Stutz Bearcats and the Cadillacs. A group of copper colored chorines, giggling over something, would disembark from a limousine just as a bored-looking caucasian, elegantly clad, brings his Packard roadster up to the curb. It's cold out, but these customers are attired in their raccoon coats, so popular at this time.

This breakfast dance frolic continued getting more and

more popular until there would be as many as half a dozen – all over Harlem. However, the Bamville on 129th Street near Lenox Avenue, where we played, was perhaps the most popular. The clientele ranged from Jimmy Walker, that fun mayor of New York, to Dutch Schultz, the Bronx beer baron, to the usual Park Avenue types, as well as the little old ladies from Hackensack. At the Bamville one could be sure of the best bootleg whiskey in town, while thumbing your nose at Moe or Izzy (the best-known revenue agents in New York at that time).

As a rule, we could always spot any type of John Law. Most musicians know a cop or hood on sight, perhaps because the night life schools them to be quick and keen observers of human behavior. Actually, the only difference between the police and the underworld person is that, while one breaks the law, the other upholds it. And it does get confusing when they decide to switch sides! The point I'm trying to make is only a nostalgic comment on the attitude of the New York gendarmes toward prohibition.

The law-breakers and the law both could be seen at the breakfast dance. It was a market place for various and sundry merchandise, a platform from which many careers in the entertainment world were launched, a meeting place where the professionals could exchange information concerning prices and conditions in the various bistros where they worked. There was also an intellectual atmosphere which proved to be a large part of the attraction for some of the habitués. Poets mingled with politicians and kept women. It was where you could find out where to get an abortion or the best whiskey. Bookies and bootleggers congregated together, talking shop and ogling the pretty ladies, the beauties from all the chorus lines, both in Harlem and the Great White Way.

Let's join the ladies, God bless them! Let's languish in the realm of the "tall, tan and terrific," with thanks to whoever coined that phrase. It so aptly described the colored gals who were the showgirls, ponies and specialty artists gracing the Club Alabam, the Plantation, the Strand Roof and that famed Cotton Club. These females were the quintessence of pulchritude. These were the hopefuls who had been drawn to

New York like moths to a flame. Yes, New York with its Broadway, Gay White Way, and all the other posh nightspots was the most exciting ground for fame and fortune. Some of the ladies who didn't make it in show biz made it, instead, with the assistance of the ever-present Sugar Daddy. And lots of the beauties who did get into showbiz had their incomes augmented. These gals didn't settle for less than a *real* Sugar Daddy (at least, not until much later). A Sugar Daddy was the fellow who saw to it that his little mama was comfortable, providing furs, jewels, rent and everything that she wanted. He had to shell out big money.

Sitting up on the bandstand with your back turned, you could almost sense the arrival of an imposing covey of beauties. There would be a lull in the noise level of the conversation. Then, usually, this would be followed by yelps of "Darling," amidst other typical female sounds of the girls greeting their cohorts, just as if they hadn't just seen each other last week. I remember hearing one such entrance being cheered by the entire club. That was the night that the entire Club Alabam showgirl contingent fell in wearing an assortment of full-length coats of red fox, silver fox, mink and ermine. It had taken plenty of "sugar" for the respective daddies to provide the furs for this outing. Of course, sometimes the mink was rented or borrowed from a wife who was out of town. Also to be considered were the activities of the 40 thieves – a gang of fellows who did a thriving business in furs. Their special avocation was the spreading of wealth via unpaid-for furs, to the delight of many. Then, too, another division of the 40 thieves did a land-office business in almost-honest sales and resales. A gal couldn't be seen in the same fur twice, could she?

There was an amusing repercussion once when a woman had her mink "borrowed" without leave by one of the syndicate, who then sold the coat to a bartender. The bartender gave the garment to his sweetheart. At about 6 o'clock in the morning the three of them met – two girls and the mink coat!

We often could hear the ladies at a ring-side table, and I remember a conversation or two which would go something like this: Maude and Gladys were seated at a table for four, with their eyes glued on the entrance and commenting on virtually everybody entering. Maude would say, "Look, Gladys, there's Charlie! Isn't he handsome? Look at those shoulders! I'd like to lasso, hog-tie and corral him some rainy afternoon. And here comes Irma. What? You don't know her? Of course you do! Remember that party last month at Dashy's place? And the gal who drank all of the champagne and proceeded to make a fool of herself with Mr Sugar Brown? That's right, dearie, and in front of all those people! Oh, yes, you left before the party got rough. Never mind, I'll tell you all about it later. Here she comes!

"Hello Irma, darling. My how well you look this morning! Meet my girlfriend, Gladys. Gladys, this is Irma. Really dear, I've never seen you look so stunning. And isn't that a new coat? Aren't you lucky? Where did you get it? From Johnny? Well, all I can say is that Johnny man really knows how to please a girl. It's beautiful. Let's see the lining. Hey! Wait a minute! That's MY coat. Mr Lafitte bought and paid for this on Park Avenue, just last month. What do you know about this? Why you . . . ! You'd better get your ___ out of my coat before I do something drastic. Oh, no you don't! You're not going anywhere, not with MY coat. Take *that*, hussy and – ouch! Can't you be a lady? You're not hustling at Hazel's. Now, stop it! Help! Help!" And the band played on.

This was typical of the not uncommon diversions that made the dances famous. Yes, the combination of beautiful women, free-spending men, luxurious gowns, furs, good booze and fellowship made these scenes so colorful. To name a few names, I remember seeing at the breakfast dances people like Libby Holman, Ethel Waters, George Dewey Washington, Mildred Bailey, Cole Porter, Legs Diamond, Battling Siki, Jack Johnson, Milton Berle, Gilda Grey, Ann Pennington and many more show-business and sporting people, all joining in making Harlem jump.

The fun ran into the large hours of the morning, like 11 or 12 noon. You might have noticed that I haven't named any musicians who were around up to this point, and the omission was deliberate, because everybody and his brother would be there. The reason is that this music was a catalyst for 90 per cent of the breaking down of the social barriers. In a good smoke-filled room, such as Bamville, with any luck one could spot luminaries such as Carl Van Vechten, Babe Ruth, Alelia Walker (the first colored millionairess) and Col. Hubert Julian (the "Black Eagle," who became famous for his flight to Europe which finished before it started – in the Harlem River), interspersed with fledglings from Philadelphia's mainline, the Piping Rock set and so forth. All rubbed shoulders with the ribbon clerks and their counterparts from Brooklyn and the Bronx.

At some point in the morning there would be the period which commonly became known as the "all on." It was a kind of impromptu jam session of talents, and everyone or anyone who had that inner conviction that they were good enough could do a turn. This wasn't simply for the plaudits of the audience. No, everyone enjoyed showing what they could do. Then there were the theatrical bookers, agents and such who soon found out about these affairs, and they would be there on the look-out for new talent. John Malin, the female impersonator, would have a battle of wits with Jackie Osterman, another quick-silver mind. And they could trade quips and insults for an hour, convulsing the crowd with their rapier-like thrusts of humorous remarks, concocted on the spot, just to cut one another down.

Another duel which continued for years was a friendly feud between Milton Berle and Willie Bryant. Together, these fellows were so great that once a big-time agent offered Bryant a rather large-sized pot of money if he would leave Harlem and take on another identity – say, be a Cuban or claim to be Jewish. Willie was light colored and his features aquiline enough to have easily "passed." I have often wondered what Willie's life and career would have turned out to be had he taken the offer.

Yes, the Bamville days were fun, but the downtown clubs grew concerned about the business all these clubs were drawing, and some newspaper columnists started a whispering smear-type attack on Harlem. This caused apprehension among the Broadway producers. Ziegfeld, Georgie White and others warned their casts not to go to Harlem and learn the new dances. "Stay away from uptown or get fired," was the injunction. And they started staying away.

In my opinion, American jazz dances always have been and continue to be created by the Negro. The Eagle Rock, the Turkey Trot, Walking the Dog and all the dances, with the possible exceptions of the tango and the waltz, came directly from the colored brothers and sisters. The Charleston, the Shimmy, the Black Bottom and so on were all conceived by the Negro but were attributed to everybody but the folks who invented the dances. Another passing thought: even though tap-dancing has become passé, I wonder if Gene Kelly, Fred Astaire and the few other stars famous for dancing ever realized the debt they owed to Dancing Dotson, John Bubbles, Johnny Wiggins, Tip, Tap and Toe, Chuck (of Chuck and Chuckles), Baby Lawrence, Bill Robinson, Eddie Rector and other great dancers and style originators of that period.

That's another phase of Americana that I personally miss – the dancer's jam sessions which used to go on nearly every night downstairs under the Rhythm Club. You could see Pete Nugent of Pete, Peaches and Duke and Bill Bailey (Pearlie Mae's brother) watching Arthur Bryson, of Russian dance fame, challenging Dewey Weinglass on that dance. After that, Peg Leg Bates would demonstrate to Big Time Crip how to execute some of his fantastic one-leg dancing. Other nights, there would be a battle between Snake Hips Tucker and his protégé Snake Hips Taylor. And I might mention that there was always a large audience of dancers, watching and learning how the great ones did it.

With the downtown pressure on, the scene changed to smaller clubs again – places like Happy Rhone's on Lenox Avenue at 143rd Street. By the way, it was said that Happy was the person who created the foot cymbal employed by drummers. The Nest on 133rd Street did most of the breakfast dance business. However, for a while Smalls' Paradise would jump due to the waiters, who not only created the Charleston but would also serve drinks while dancing with a tray on top of their heads! The real people in the know made the Nest their playground. In fact, 133rd Street, right off Seventh Avenue, became the mecca for the sophisticates. On 133rd was Pods' and Jerry's, where Billie Holiday started. There was also Gladys Bentley's (she was a male impersonator) and Clark Monroe's Uptown House, too. All these clubs on 133rd Street were in the same block between Lenox and Seventh Avenue. The street would be loaded with characters. There was the man who would stuff yellow ten-dollar bills down the bosom of any girl who would permit him. Lots of girls didn't just let him – they would scramble to get to him.

It seems to me that television has supplanted and eliminated personal creativity along with all those wonderful places that adults once went to for amusement. There used to be all those pool halls, vaudeville and burlesque theaters, and so many dance halls and nightclubs. Almost none survive. These spots were important because these were the places where neophytes could listen and learn. Maybe that is the reason the caliber of entertainers seems to have slipped, too. Strange that no one seems to be aware or care that there are some actors who can't act, musicians who can't play and singers who can't sing. Yet they demand and receive enormous stipends when they don't even know how to walk on or off a stage! This may be sour grapes, but these are the thoughts I have been thinking and wanting to say loud and long.

Did I mention that I was working in the area, too, with Snowden? We were playing at the Nest right in the heart of all the action. Being with Snowden was another learning experience. In this band there was Walter Johnson on drums, and what a great swinger he was! And there was Freddie "Steeple Head" Johnson, a very fine piano man, plus Prince Robinson, an outstanding clarinet and tenor sax man who never received the recognition his great talent deserved. Historians to the contrary, I believe that Snowden always had one of the best outfits for its size in New York, at least during that period, just as he had had in Washington.

Tooting with the band at the Nest Club, I had ample opportunity to observe more bizarre events. One of these was a Mr Gunion, who became well known by having reservations made for ten or 20 people, and precisely at 2 a.m. Monday morning his private spectacle would begin. First would come the waiters bearing dinner in a silver service. From Sherry's or Pierre's on Park Avenue his chauffeur or private waiter would then stagger in with booze by the case for his guests. About 2:30 a flowery male would flutter in, checking the table, the food and the liquor, and finally came over to the bandstand. After telling Snowden what the mood of the evening was to be, he would pass out brand new twenties and fifties to everybody in the band. Then the scene was all set.

People who were not in the know would be startled when a nondescript little man would come in bringing his party – of women only. Usually there would be a complete assortment of types: blondes, brunettes and redheads in all sizes. Once he really startled everybody when his party of nine "girls" included a nun! That night there was also a Chinese, a Dutch maiden and an Indian lady wearing a sari (which was the first time most of us had ever seen a sari). And I don't remember what else. They had probably come from a costume party, but they almost didn't get in that night. The doorman balked at the girl in the nun habit.

When Mr Gunion entered the doors would be locked and the place closed to the public. Meanwhile, Mr Gunion's party would get under way. Dinner would be served and we would play the dinner music which had been selected, mostly sweet tunes dripping with sad nostalgia. Then his table would be cleared, which meant we would switch to Broadway show tunes. Mine host danced each female around the postage-sized floor once or twice. Then his servants would pass out the champagne for everybody, including the band. Then the real evening began. Playing cards would be brought out and strip poker would be the order of the morning, with the music getting softer and softer and the lights growing dimmer as the girls took off their losses. After our Mr Gunion had won all of the clothes (and I'll bet he played with a marked deck), he'd yell, "Let's have some action in this dump!" The lights would be turned up and each gal would do a solo dance – in the nude! The first party we played for him (and there were many), I was that flabbergasted, never having seen so many bare bottoms, at least not at the same time. Then came the finale, which was a mad Charleston contest. After that we would all pack up and leave, tired, drunk and with a pocket full of money.

By the way, Mr Gunion was a real person but that was not his name. Gunion is Harlemese for any big spender. This leads me to wonder what ever happened to those days? And where are the Mr Gunions to throw parties like those?

Another memorable and interesting vignette of the Nest Club is the story of a girl I will call Honey Bun, because that was not her name. Here's a description of this gorgeous gal, the better to put you in the mood of the happenings. Honey was a dancer, about 5 feet 8 and with a build most dancers only wish they had. She had long tapering legs and queenly proportions. And to this lovely figure add a pear-shaped face, burnt orange in color, which made a perfect setting for her deep-set green eyes. Honey conducted herself with so much decorum that, in those days of frenzied abandon, she stood out like a sissy in a YMCA. She didn't drink or smoke and wouldn't sit with the patrons under any circumstances. One night, while Honey was doing her spot in the show, a young man sat staring at her with intense fascination. This was not so unusual, as the girl was perfection in her art. But this fellow attracted attention by the way his body followed her movements. There he sat, seemingly mesmerized like a cobra being charmed by a fakir. Anyway, we all noticed the usual attempt made via the waiter to coax Honey over to his table. We looked knowingly at each other when Honey shook her head "No."

The scene developed further when the young man went over and tried to sit down at her table, because Honey took off for her dressing room like a frightened doe. That could have been the end of this episode. But this lad whipped out his wallet, plucked a bill, tore it in half and sent the waiter back to her dressing room with half a bill. Maybe this technique worked in reverse. Honey stormed out and flung the bill into the poor fellow's face, and the entire club hear her say in a voice that left no doubt, "You take your money and buy some sense with it. I only dance in this place. I don't sit and entertain strange men. I am not for sale at any price." Then off she flounced back to her dressing room, as the guy left in such a hurry that he didn't stop to pick up the half a bill which she had rejected. We were amazed to find out it was a 1000-dollar bill! That was the first one I had ever seen and, in fact, I hadn't even known there was such a denomination.

The story doesn't end there. In fact, it actually ended many years later and thousands of miles away from 133rd Street. After the episode with the 1000-dollar bill the fellow came almost every night, sat alone and just stared at her. He tried everything: big baskets of roses, and one night he sent a chauffeur who tried to hand her the keys of a beautiful Locomobile. Honey threw them on the curb. When the other girls tried to talk to Honey, saying she was crazy not to accept these would-be gifts, she only replied, "I'm not for sale." Honey finally quit the club, and I didn't see either her or her admirer again until I chanced upon the man in Europe many years later. Then I dined with him and his family. That is, his wife, Honey, and their three children!

I can't remember exactly how long I was with Elmer Snowden, but I do recall the various places we played. As I recollect, when I first joined him we were playing the Balconnades. Then we went to the Kentucky Club, which is the same club where the schism between Snowden and Duke Ellington had occurred earlier. I never knew what happened between these two fellows. All I know is that they arrived in New York with Pops Snowden as leader. And then, at some point, Duke took over. After the Kentucky Club we did a short stint atop the Strand Roof on Broadway, followed by a back-home tour to Washington, Baltimore, Norfolk and Philadelphia. Then Snowden got the nod for a new club in Harlem. It was the Bamville, and we did so well that, when the owners, Mal Frazier and Johnny Powell, bought a smaller but more chic club, we were ensconced in the Nest.

In that setting the band really began to attract attention, and pretty soon we, too, had a second line of musicians who came by every night to hear what we were playing. Now, the term "second line" originated in New Orleans and referred to the kids and others who followed funerals to the graveyard. They tagged along because the custom in Louisiana at that time was to have a brass band accompany the deceased to the burial ground, and was an elaborate indication of the person's status. Once the body was interred the band started swinging all of the way back home, to the delight of the kids and music lovers, who enjoyed the return session enough to banish any grieving.

However, the second line that I refer to has nothing to do with funerals. Really, we are referring to admirers, the musicians who came to listen and learn. That was one form of second line. And then there were the females of the big-band era who composed our second line. I don't mean to imply that only girls were in the audience, because there were lots of fellows who were just as avid fans. Only they were not nearly as pretty to us. When we were on the road making the big jumps, we used to pray that we had a chance to meet a lady from the second line. And that, after the dance and grabbing a bite to eat, for some reason the bus would be held up long enough for us to a snatch a little loving before being cussed out by the bandleader for delaying our departure!

Getting back to Snowden's second line, they came from all over New York, and it was an understandable curiosity because Snowden's music was quite different from the usual. For instance, he had a lot of Jelly Roll Morton tunes in what he called "the blue book." When these competitors would show themselves coming through the doors, Pops would pretend that he didn't see them and just mumble under his breath, "Get out the blue book, number 7," and off we'd go. By then our line was somewhat different. We had in the band at that time Bob Ysaguirre on bass, Walter and Freddy Johnson as drums and piano, Pops leading us on banjo, and the front line was Te Roy Williams, trombone, Joe Garland, alto and baritone saxophones, with Prince Robinson playing tenor saxophone and clarinet. Anybody who was around at that time will tell you what a wonderful band it was. Pops's dedication, imagination and approach all contributed to our great sound.

We rehearsed after the job. And it didn't make any difference what came up during the evening. If we were supposed to stay and woodshed, by God, that's what we did. I remember one night when I got high and was kidding Freddy Johnson real hard about something or other, whereupon he wheeled and gave me a right fist square in the chops. A lost tooth was the result, plus a busted lip. This sobered me up. When I went to Snowden to tell him all about its having been my fault, how sorry I was and that I would finish out the evening, but would like to be excused from rehearsal, he commiserated with me. Then he said, "As for rehearsal, you'll stay, of course, split lip or no split lip. Don't forget there's a little boy around the corner who is dying to rehearse with us." Knowing this was true, I just had some more whiskey and made the rehearsal.

It does seem as if I was involved in a bit of violence here and there, which usually found me on the receiving end, getting my lumps. Rarely did I get into a fracas by throwing the first punch. And still, there were a few set-tos that I won. The most memorable one happened like this. I was playing in Bobby Brown's band on the notorious Gold Coast in Newark, New Jersey. At that time, thugs, pimps, con men, bootleggers and smugglers and any other variety of underworld flotsam and jetsam could be found in a neighborhood of about six square blocks. Their presence naturally drew their female counterpart. I recall names like Battle Cook Sue, Dinah the Dutchess, Hattie Hoe Down, etc.

My shining night began when a pal of Bobby's was thrown out of the Casaba Club by the bouncer, an ex-prizefighter named Jack Jarvis, called The Angel in the ring. Bobby, who fancied himself a good man with his dukes, stood up for his friend. He was promptly flattened by The Angel. I remonstrated, with no real intention of getting into the act. I just didn't want to see my leader get zapped. When I tried to talk to Angel, he replied by throwing a right fist in my direction, which I was lucky enough to duck. Then, in sheer panic, I countered with a fast left to his stomach and a desperate right which landed smack on his jaw! His knees sagged and he went down. To my surprise, when he got up I was glad to hear Angel say there were no hard feelings, and we had a drink together. I was the hero of the night in the unforgettable Casaba Club!

But, getting back to Snowden, I couldn't bear to leave the group without further reminiscences. I mentioned how we played the Jelly Roll tunes, such as *King Porter Stomp*, *The Pearls*, *Winin' Boy*, the *Jelly Roll Blues*, plus some other great number such as *Bass Ale Blues*, etc., from Walter Melrose's catalog (a Chicago firm). Incidentally, we got our songs right from the source, the publisher or the tunesmith, and then Snowden changed everything but the basic melodies of these songs. We would work for hours on a voicing for the instruments. Sometimes we would have a clarinet lead or perhaps a baritone sax. Anyway, each arrangement was individually styled. Then, to the fury and consternation of other would-be copiers, nobody professed to know the name of whatever we were playing. Our stock reply was, "I don't know. Ask Pops." And when Pops was questioned, he'd say, "I don't know. Ask Prince. He bought it." No, sir, no one ever knew what was in the blue book but us.

The period of time starting from Saturday night, 9 p.m., to Monday morning, 11 or 12 noon, was about as grueling as anything one can imagine. We'd play Saturday night until 4 a.m. Sunday morning. Then we took a little time off before beginning the matinee dance, which started at 3 p.m., running until 8 in the evening. Another short time out for dinner, and back to the stand for the Sunday evening session, which continued right into the breakfast dance, which generally broke up about 11:30 to 12 noon on Monday. No wonder we had to rely on Top 'n' Bottom, gin, bourbon, scotch, champagne and such. But we enjoyed every bit of it, or at least we thought we did. Besides, all you had to do was keep stomping out that beat of wild jazz, keep slinging down that good stuff right out of someone's bathtub still, keep moving and grooving and living and loving it all. It helped that we were all young then. But it's not too surprising that, with this exhausting pace, some of us didn't make it into middle age.

9

With Henderson

I'm sure there's more than sufficient psychological evidence to support that old adage "imitation is the sincerest form of flattery." When Mr Louis Armstrong erupted upon the New York scene, I was one of his most ardent admirers. And, after all these years, I still am. I tried to walk like him, talk like him. I bought shoes and a suit like the "Great One" wore. Once, when he made a personal appearance at the Savoy Ballroom, I got so out of this world between his blowing and the booze that was flowing that the floor man put me out of the ballroom – and I was working there at the time! The way it happened is that we (meaning just about every young trumpet player in town, including Ward Pinkett, Reuben Reeves, Jabbo Smith, Tommy Morris, etc) were all clustered on the other bandstand, drinking whiskey out of Coca-Cola bottles. Every time Louie hit an impossibly high note on an ending, crash would go a bottle! Probably I was doing more than my share of bottle-tossing. Another time, Ward, Gus Aiken, another trumpet player, and I emerged from a bar and thought it would be a good idea to go across the street, stand under the King's window and serenade him. We had just gotten started when Whitey, the cop on the beat, discouraged us by saying, "Get the hell off the streets before I run ya in."

There were so many fellows showering Satchmo with unblushing adulation that I didn't think he knew me. I was *that* surprised when he walked into the Nest Club that eventful night. It started out as just an ordinary evening until Snowden spotted them: Big Green the trombone man, Buster Bailey and Old Dipper (Louie). Incidentally, Louie has had more nicknames than anyone else in the game, which to me reflects how truly affectionately he is regarded. At any rate, Snowden spied them before I did and called number 9. Number 9 was a pop tune of the day called *Oh, Katharina*, and the way Snowden called the tunes was a code for the men in the band. If he had said number 9 in the yellow book it would have meant the same tune, but we would have followed the head arrangement. The way he called it that night meant that I was supposed to play as long as I wanted within the stock arrangement, set my own tempo and show off. It's an experience I will never forget. And I must have played pretty well because Louie and the other fellows in Henderson's band took to dropping in from time to time.

To keep the record straight, I'd like to explain the social attitudes of musicians in those days. In the early 20s, the hierarchy or top rankers had little to do with fellows lower down the scale. The Clef Club clique were the aristocracy, with fellows such as Luckey Roberts, Chris Smith, Ford Dabney, Will Vodery and Tim Brymn. They were the bigwigs who played Miami Beach, Piping Rock, Bar Harbor and all the other posh resorts where society gathered to follow the sun. That was long before Meyer Davis and others took over the society work from the Negroes.

Next in importance would be the bands of burlesque musicians. Men like Gonzelle White, Julian Arthur, the Spillers, Jazz Lips Richardson, Mamie Smith and other well-known acts of the time comprised this collection. They were very important due to their year-long contracts, traveling all over the country. Other big names of the time were Arthur Whetsol, the first trumpet who rejoined Ellington after touring with Al Jolson; Bill Basie, piano (later better known as Count after he left Gonzelle White); and Louie Metcalf, a trumpet man who at that time accompanied Johnny Hodges and who did the same pantomime as Jolie (Al Jolson). And Jolson had copied Bert Williams, the originator of blackface pantomime!

Now we get to the newer members of that select fraternity. In my opinion the Chicago counterpart of Fletcher Henderson was Doc Cook. The opposite of Chicago's Dave Peyton and Erskine Tate would be New York's Sam Wooding and Billy

Fowler. There weren't many bands of over ten pieces around during those days, but what few there were really had little to do with the rank and file such as us.

Another group were the regular working musicians who played the small clubs, the neighborhood joints, the penny-a-dance halls, etc. This was my metier and I loved it – particularly the dance halls. What a proving ground, a sounding board and a school all in one! During the 20s every hamlet had its dance hall and the big cities all had dance emporiums. Dancing was in vogue due to Vernon and Irene Castle. In New York alone I remember the Roseland, which was tops, and Fletcher Henderson, who played there, was king. There was also the Balconnades, the Brooklyn Roseland, the Arcadia and the Empire Ballroom. In Harlem the Savoy flourished along with the Renny, the New Star Casino, the Rose Danceland on 125th Street and other smaller places. My first penny-a-dance hall job in New York was on 14th Street. There was that place in Newark we called the Chain Gang, where I played for several months. Later I worked a place on 86th Street and also at the Rose Danceland (before Jelly Roll Morton took his band in). All of these places were a real education, what with the changes of tempo from a waltz to a tango to the one-step. Then the orchestrations were in any old key, just as the arrangers had written them before placing them with the music publishers. Added to this, you had to be alert, since each dance could be only about a minute and a half long so that the house could make money on the turnover.

Right now, we are at the Nest Club, where I was playing with Elmer Snowden's band on that special night of nights with the events which led to my playing with Henderson. It was a day or two after that group had come to hear us. The telephone in the cloakroom rang and the attendant came to the stand saying it was for the kid (meaning me). I went to answer, wondering who could be calling me on the job, half afraid it was my mother calling from Washington with some sort of emergency. I couldn't believe it when a voice said, "I've got a job for you, Pops" (we all called one another Pops in those days). I thought I recognized the gravel voice, but I think I said,

"Oh yeah? Where is this job?" The guy laughed and said, "This is Louis and I want you to take my place with Fletcher. I'm going back to Chicago." It really was Louis Armstrong!

To say I was stunned would be an understatement. I answered, "Okay," and hung up. When I returned to the stand, Te Roy Williams asked, "Bad news, huh?" And everybody was all ears when I replied, "Naw, it was some joker who said he was Louis Armstrong trying to b.s. me." Then Pops Snowden asked what he said. When I repeated the conversation, they all broke into joe giggles and laughed like crazy. All that is except for Prince Robinson and Snowden, who didn't look too surprised. I remember Elmer's saying, "Well, if it's true, you had better take it."

No more was said and we started playing. I began to have a feeling like the youngster dreaming about getting a fabulous bicycle he has longed for and is afraid to wake up and find out that it's only a dream. Something within me told me it was true. But I still couldn't believe it. New York, at that time, was loaded with a lot of good trumpet men. To name a few, I recall Tommy Ladnier, Ward Pinkett, Bubber Miley, Horace Holmes, Jabbo Smith and Eddie Allen, and there were so many others.

Anyway, the next night Fletcher came in and told me it was true and wanted to know when I could come to rehearsal. I told Smack I'd let him know, but I also told Snowden I wouldn't think of leaving him for Henderson or anybody else. In the ensuing argument I went over all of my reasons for staying, such as being in love with Snowden's band, that I wasn't sure I could read their music, I didn't own a tuxedo, and, besides, nobody could replace Louis's power and high notes. Pops heard me out patiently and then said, "All of this may be true, but you'll take the job anyway. I'm firing you for your own good and it's up to you from then on." Sure enough, he paid me off at the end of the week and said, "Well, so long. I hope you do well on your new job." I still didn't believe him until the following night when I reported for work and found another trumpet player sitting in my place. Pops called me over and said, "Listen, you thick-headed s.o.b. You get your butt over to the Roseland and tell Fletcher you are ready to rehearse."

That's how I took the job with Fletcher Henderson, but my heart wasn't in it. I liked his band all right, but I had the feeling that the man wasn't born who could follow the King – and I still feel that way.

In the band at the time were Don Redman, Buster Bailey and Hawk on reeds; Russell Smith, Joe Smith and Big Charlie Green in the brass section; Charlie Dixon on banjo; Kaiser Marshall on drums; and Bob Escudero on bass. My relations with my new compatriots were pretty good on the whole, except for that certain reserve with which established big-time musicians usually greeted youngsters, which is and was justifiable. You had to prove yourself before you were accepted, and I was just turning 18.

Unfortunately, Big Green, my trombone section mate, was very unfriendly. He would play all sorts of devilish tricks on me. For instance, he turned the valves around in my horn while we were out for intermission. Or he'd mix up the music in my book. Smack sometimes called out ahead the set we would be playing when we returned from intermission, and after having carefully gotten the music ready it was a drag to scuffle trying to find it again. But I got wise to this fellow and would stick my parts in my pocket. That took care of that problem.

The truth is, and I can tell it now because nobody cares, Big Green rode me out of Smack's band. He sat right behind me, and when I first joined he told me, "Boy, you know I drink plenty of gin. Now, if you want to get along in this band, see that I have my gin!" I agreed and I would have gone along with almost anything to make good. But I soon found out what I had let myself in for. This chap drank at least two quarts of gin nightly! After about two weeks I got tired of paying his big tab, and that's when all the tormenting started. I couldn't have stuck it out as long as I did excepting that I was spared when we went on the road. This took the heat off.

Now Big Green really was a big bruiser and it took some courage to joke with him. He was 6 foot plus, his manner was rough and loud, and he always appeared ready for a fight at the drop of a wrong word. Charlie was slightly cockeyed, and the more saturated he was with his bathtub gin, the more his eye seemed to move all around in his head. He became even more frightening when he'd brandish his six shooter, which kept company with his gin in his trombone case. All of the younger fellows were slightly wary of the big one's moods, and the more potted he became, the less we would have to say to the man, not wanting to get shot.

But the inevitable had to happen and it came about like this. We played a matinee at Princeton and the students were most cordial with their liquor, so, when we started back to New York, Green told Bobbie Stark to get the hell out of his seat on the bus. This time Bobbie had enough whiskey in him to speak up to Big Green, saying no seats had anybody's name on them. This shut the big boy up and he took another seat, but kept mumbling to himself, "I'll fix his wagon! Just wait until this bus gets to New York." We hoped that Big Green would go to sleep and forget all about it, but he kept sipping and mumbling until we pulled up to Roseland. Then Bobbie made a bee line out of the bus and we breathed a sigh of relief that there would be no bloodshed. Big Green strutted up the backstage stairs, saying, "Where's that little smart ass? I'll show him about fooling around with Trombone Cholly" (Trombone Cholly was Big Green's own nickname for himself). There was a showdown all right, as Bobbie suddenly dashed down stairs with a cannon no one had never seen him with before, yelling, "You don't have to look for me, you cockeyed bastard!" That ended *that* particular situation.

However, as soon as we started at Roseland the following season, Green opened up on me again in a most diabolical manner. He began heckling me on the bandstand. This was easy when you consider that Henderson's book was written around Louis's endings and the interplay between Hawk and Louis. All Green had to do was wait until I had a high note to make on an ending. Then he would mutter something to the effect that he didn't think I could hit the note, such as, "Well, I'll be an s.o.b. if he doesn't miss it." This rattled me so much that often I *would* miss the ending note. Everybody would look at me and grin, maybe with sympathy, but it looked like malice to me. This got on my nerves so badly I hated to go to work.

Luckily, Charlie Dixon told Green to cut out the heckling and Fletcher overheard the conversation. Then the whole story came out, including the gin pay-off. From that night on I was invited to live at Smack's house, because he said he realized that an 18-year-old just couldn't take care of himself. Later I found out that Miss Lee (as we called Mrs Henderson) had written my mother in Washington, telling her that she would keep an eye on me. This she did, as much as possible.

However, Green continued his feud in a more subtle way. Lots of nights there would be peace on the bandstand. But as soon as the railing in front of the stand was filled with big-eared musicians (everybody in the business came to hear the band, which had innovative arrangements, and to try to pick up some pointers) Green would either "accidentally" poke me in the back with his slide, or drop his mute or something – anything – to distract my attention. Later I was to have a similar experience in the Duke Ellington band (Cat Anderson was the heckler this time). This just shows that history does repeat itself, but I was older and handled it better. But earlier I was naive enough to react in the expected manner. I goofed off and I told a big lie, that I had to go to Washington because my mother was ill. And I left. That's how Charlie Green ran me out of Smack's band.

I don't recall how long I was away, since my solace at departing from the job was hitting the bottle. I do remember leaving my horn in a locker at Roseland and my clothes at Smack's house. Everything else that happened I've conveniently blocked out of my memory. After a period of traumatic blankness, somehow I found myself talking with Mrs Henderson in her home. She said, "I've decided the best thing for you is to get out of New York. Here's a ticket to Xenia, Ohio, where you will enroll at Wilberforce and play in Fletcher's brother's band." I tried to explain that my mother would not like me so far from home, and that's when Miss Lee told me she had been in contact with my mother all of that time and knew I had lied about going home. Furthermore, I learned that both my mother and my father (he was living in Newark) were agreeable to the Wilberforce idea and concurred that something had to be done about me. My drinking had reached a danger point.

Xenia, Ohio, was the nearest town to Wilberforce University. Zenia, look out: here I come!

10

At Wilberforce

If I had any fears about my exile being Dullsville, I was reassured after being met at the depot by the McCord twins, Castor and his twin Joe (short for Jobeatus), who wore a bearskin coat. In rapid succession, Joe tossed my luggage in the car, gave me a big drink of corn squeezings (corn whiskey), ran over a chicken and informed me that I was to live at the Country Club, as the Kappa house was called on campus.

Back in the roaring 20s, a campus without a terrific band was considered square. The youngsters of that era insisted on having dance music around. Now, Wilberforce may not have had the highest scholastic standing or the best football team, but its band was the greatest in the country. Or so the fellows kept telling me.

This first introduction to my new life gave me the clue that I would spend more time having fun than studying. The slug of booze made me choke and sputter with tears in my eyes, and I thought if they'd made that corn whiskey any stronger no bottle would hold it! It occurred to me that maybe Wilberforce University, despite being a church supported and endowed school, was also a swinging place.

After a long lurching drive over dirt roads between rows of tall corn, eventually we pulled up to a dilapidated two-story frame house. One of the fellows remarked, with pride in his voice, "Here's the Kappa house where we stay," and Jobeatus, the fellow in the bearskin coat, chimed in, "We call it the country club." Freddie Jenkins ran down the steps to greet me, and I was encouraged about the band because Freddie played good trumpet. Then I met Henry Hicks, who really ran Horace

Henderson's band. He was more conservative and it was reassuring to hear his Alabama drawl as he told Joe to stop lying about how great the band was. Actually, it was a pretty fine group. On trumpets there were Freddie Jenkins and Shelton Hemphill; Castor McCord, Jobeatus McCord and Quentin Harrington were on saxophones; Talcott Reeves was on banjo; Lavert Hutchison was on bass; and Bill Beason was on the drums. This was a real fun bunch with something always happening to make one laugh. For instance, there were the winking episodes, but first I must explain what the word "wink" meant during that period, in our vernacular. It was employed as a slang phrase which came from the word hoodwink, and we used it to mean that someone had beaten somebody out of something. For example, when you would take the trouble to hide your last clean shirt and discovered, on getting on the bandstand, that another brother was wearing that shirt, that brother had winked on you.

One gimmick which we used at the little country stores was to choose a guy to put on the drunk act, and it went like this. We would all pile out of the cars and into the store, immediately spotting whatever was handy to eat – sardines, crackers or whatever. One of us would have just enough money to pay for a few sodas, and, as soon as he handed the money over to the storekeeper, in would stagger a loud individual, yelling, "That's my money, mister. He can't buy that stuff with my money. I was asleep and he robbed me." The rest of the fellows would mill around creating excitement, meanwhile snatching everything edible in sight. We rustled many a snack that way, but once it backfired and we had to cut it out.

Here's what happened that time. Most of our gigs were in the Midwest, and on one of these raids a guy "borrowed" a whole ham and was gleefully licking his chops in anticipation of a great feast as we drove along. But he was not so happy after we'd gone abut 50 miles and discovered that, in his haste to wink on the man for the ham, he'd left his sax sitting by the gas pump. So we reluctantly drove back for his instrument. The storekeeper met him at the door, saying, "Somebody stole a ham from me. Fair's fair. And when I see my ham you can have your horn." Moral: no more winking. It wasn't worth it.

Life on the campus was real free and easy, with mostly parties, rehearsals and playing on the occasional job that came through about once or twice a week. Needless to say, going to classes was not obligatory. We honorary Kappas didn't pay rent so we didn't care much if we worked or not. The only thing we really needed money for was food, and when we didn't have money we managed. Sometimes we raided the school's kitchen, where several of the fellows had girlfriends working, and there was always plenty of food to be picked up from the farms that covered the area. Jobeatus knew all of the chickens for miles around by their first names. Or so he said. Let me not forget the crap game that Jimmy Bell, the trumpet player whom I replaced, ran in what was supposed to be an abandoned farm house, off campus. That was just in case you felt lucky. We never felt lucky as a group but sometimes we'd pool our small cash, and Talcott Reeves would generally win something for us. As for schnapps – any liquor – Uniform and another guy we called Red ran a still right outside the campus jurisdiction. If you brought a gunny sack of corn, you could get a pint of lightning via the barter system. Naturally, the farmers for miles around contributed unknowingly. As you may suspect, there was very little if any time spent in study. However, we did get together and woodshed some great arrangements, which as I recall were all head arrangements.

I hadn't been there long before Hicks ran into the house yelling, "F.A.C.Q." Everybody jumped up and ran to the campus which was about a block away. I didn't know what it was all about, but I soon found out when I saw 20 or 30 seniors carrying paddles and running in the same direction. F.A.C.Q meant some new guys were about to be initiated, so you'll need no further translation, will you? ("Fresh Ass, Come Quick"). That was how I first met Ben Webster, who was one of the initiates. He was let off from the ceremony, and I'm positive it was because the guys had him play sax instead. Later, though, when we were both with Ellington, he denied that he was able to play the saxophone at that time, so maybe my memory is not accurate on this score.

I recall a few trips. Sometimes we would all go way up to Detroit to hear Smack, who was really good to us. He would always give Hicks or Little Smack (Horace) gas money for our jalopy so that we could get back to school. He also gave some arrangements to Horace which he was supposed to copy and return. Somehow, I doubt he ever did.

As I try to recapitulate, I become more and more aware of the tricks that time plays on my memory. For instance, I have no real remembrance of how long we were at the "Force" or even how long I was with Horace and other bands. On the other hand, I recall so many things that happened, we must either have spent several years together or we lived very fast, with events crowding each other out. My memory includes one particular auto trip with us slipping to the very edge of Cotton Top Mountain on the way to Buckley, West Virginia. The road was all yellow mud, fully six inches deep. We must have been a sight crammed into Horace's brown Chrysler touring car, complete with side curtains, and two spare tires on top just to keep Cass McCord's baritone saxophone company. Nine of us with horns and baggage and spare tires in a car built for seven!

Jobeatus was the envy of us all. Where he got his bearskin coat I'll never know, but he sported it all winter, to our chagrin and envy. Later, we were all more prosperous, and Joe was the first to buy a car, with Hicks and Cass following suit. I still have to laugh at Little Freddie Jenkins as he slopped around in the big bear coat that he bought, an exact replica of Joe's! Although he was a comic sight, the personality which was so tremendous with Duke Ellington in later years had already begun to peek through.

After a while the money bug hit Horace and we began to range further and further afield. Our route had been mostly in West Virginia, Kentucky and Ohio – roughly a 300-mile radius. One spring the group headed for Michigan, Indiana, Pennsylvania and all of the major towns in those states, which was a real big thing for all of us. We were seeing new people, hearing new musicians and enjoying the carefree life which was so much fun for youngsters during that era.

One exciting trip was to New York where we had a nice

engagement at the Bamville club for most of the summer. It was great to meet all of the younger musicians and have a reunion with Benny Carter, who had made great progress since we had last heard him at Asbury Park. Upon returning to the Force, it didn't come as a great surprise when Hicks told us Benny was joining us. He would arrange for and lead the Henderson Collegians when Horace was not on the job. That was double okay with us, as we were intrigued with the full sound of four saxes in the section. Then, too, Horace was away from the band more and more on some mysterious business. Luckily, we had Uncs – Herschel Bayless – who was our combination prop man, band boy, driver and business manager. We especially leaned on him when Horace was away. Sometimes we wouldn't know where he was or when he'd return. We'd go on and do our gigs and then, in the middle of a dance, sometimes Horace would walk in, sit at the piano and start playing as if he'd been with us all the time. This caused the fellows to think that Little Smack didn't care, and the break happened on this memorable occasion.

Battles of bands were in, and some promoter in Detroit got the bright idea of pitting David against Goliath! The mighty McKinney's Cotton Pickers, led by Don Redman, cast the gauntlet by challenging the Henderson Collegians, led by Carter, to a showdown at Graystone Ballroom in the Motor City. Then, the promoters who had conceived the idea used all of the known tricks to play the event up as a grudge contest between two outfits. As I recall the episode, Horace didn't figure in our plans, but did arrive to play with us. Back on campus we rehearsed like crazy and came up with a set of six or seven tunes that we felt were real blockbusters. Strangely, I can only remember the names of two of these: *Rhapsody in Blue* and *King Porter Stomp*. We had had the Don Redman arrangement of *Rhapsody* for quite some time but had never dared to play it before. For the occasion, we applied ourselves diligently and, section by section, spent many hours getting the correct nuances and dynamics letter-perfect. Benny Carter performed miracles as he drilled us. Then, to really cap the climax, we practiced bobbing in rhythm on the two out-choruses of *King Porter Stomp*. Whoever came up with that idea couldn't have dreamed up a more exciting finish, as the combination of motion, screaming brass and pulsating saxophones tore up that Graystone Ballroom. The crowd roared, whistled and demanded more, more, more. So we had to repeat the out-choruses four times! As far as McKinney's Cotton Pickers were concerned, there was no contest. And we had won the cup, which Benny Carter still has in his possession.

We were quite set up when we snagged a six-week engagement at the Savoy Ballroom in New York City. This spot was the most sought-after job in the country for negro orchestras at that time. We were only a college group, after all, so this was a fantastic break. I had played there a few years previously with Leon Abbey's Savoy Bearcats. This time, however, was especially momentous for me, and here is why. It was there that I met Marguerita Elizabeth Benson Slaughter, who was one of the 50 beautiful hostesses employed there. I had noticed this little doll wending her way through the throngs of fellows that hung out on the campus at 135th and Seventh Avenue during the day. My opening gambit with this young lady was to describe to her the local campus scene and just how she had crossed the street to avoid the fellows – and even the red coat she had been wearing! After this initial meeting, it took several years and the persuasions of Benny Carter before she did finally consent to marry me. But that was later.

Meanwhile, Little Smack was champing at the bit to make the big-time like his older brother. He wanted a beautiful new car, which just couldn't be on the kind of dough the Collegians were making. So Horace figured a way out, which was to rent a car. That, however, led to trouble when the band's money became involved – there wasn't enough left over to pay us. Horace, perhaps, would not like this reference to the past but, in all fairness, I have to tell it as it was. Anyway, this all happened when we were kids. Since then, we've all changed – for the better, I'm sure.

Sometimes, there was another kind of unpleasantness, especially when we would finish playing and there would only be one restaurant open. That joint would almost invariably be off limits for us. The small American flag painted on the window with the inscription "100% American" emphasized that only caucasians were welcome.

Once we had the opportunity of making one of those restaurant fellows look as small as they made us feel most of the time. Here's how it happened. We played a policeman's ball in a town in Ohio which shall be nameless. In this business you never know when you might return to a place. During this particular ball, all of the officers got juiced. When we played *Home, Sweet Home* the chief himself felt the night was too young and the music too beautiful for us to stop without a few more dances. He very politely asked Horace to play a little longer. Little Smack told the chief we were sorry, but that was all. The chief then grew insistent and offered to pay us for the overtime, but Horace still shook his head no. The officer grew angrier and red-faced, demanding to know why these boys dared to refuse his wishes and his money. Henry Hicks stepped in to try to avoid trouble. He told the chief the facts – that we had driven 400 miles to get there and had found no place willing to serve us dinner. Besides being tired and hungry, we still had to drive another 100 miles before we could get food and sleep.

I guess this was the first time this man was actually brought face to face with the facts of being a Negro in his part of the country in the 1920s. You could almost see his thoughts parade across his face. Then he answered, "I'll take care of everything. Now, how much will you charge to play another hour?" We looked at each other, not really wanting to do anything but collect the dough they owed us and get out of town. Hicks spoke up, however, quoting a figure, and said, "I know you are a responsible man. We'll take you at your word when you say you'll see to it that we eat afterwards."

We played the extra hour, then packed up wondering what the outcome was going to be. We didn't have long to wait because, when the chief saw that we were ready to go, he told us to follow him. He led us to a nice looking place, right down the street. I noticed the usual American flag on the window and felt sure they wouldn't serve us. The place was crowded with people from the dance, a real small-town gala night. Sure enough, when the proprietor (who happened to be a Southern

European type) saw the first black face, he rushed to the door
in order to tell us to stay out, I guess. However, the chief caught
him by the arm, saying, "Wait a minute. I want steaks for my
friends and I want them right away." The little boss turned
green and stuttered, "But . . . but . . ." The chief, ignoring him,
continued, "And not only that. Tell your boy I say to get down
to the Armory and turn the heat on, because they're staying in
town overnight and I want them to be comfortable." It surely
did our hearts good to see this foreigner wilt perceptibly and
almost fall on his face, bowing as he said, "Yes, sir, Mr Bob. Yes,
sir."

Come to think about it, maybe the restaurateur ran the
town's gambling joint or something illegal? Some months later
I spent several hours in the pokey for demanding service in
another town in another state, and, by some strange quirk of
fate, the man who called the fuzz on me was a foreigner of the
same extraction as the restaurateur in Ohio!

We were dead tired one evening after driving down to
Louisville, Kentucky, playing a dance and driving right back to
Cincinnati. I was conked out in a real state of collapse when
someone knocked at my door. I was furious at being disturbed
so I yelled, "Get the hell away from that door and let me sleep."
But the knocking continued so I had to get up. I was really
amazed to see that it was Fletcher. The last we had heard, he
was somewhere down South. It turned out that there had been
an accident involving the Smith Brothers, Joe and Russell. It's
been so long ago that I'm not sure, but it seems to me that Joe
had the crack-up and Russell had to stay where it happened to
take care of Joe. This left Smack without two trumpet players
for an important date at the Graystone Ballroom in Detroit that
night.

As he told me the story, I began putting on my clothes. I went
down the stairs, picked up a quart of whiskey and cuddled into
the rumble seat of Fletcher's Packard roadster. I sipped for a
while until I pulled the top of the rumble seat down. When I
woke up it was night and we were in Detroit. That was the first
time my eyes were really opened to the tremendous power
Coleman Hawkins had on tenor saxophone. He would take the

lead on the ensemble out-choruses, and, believe me, he topped that band with as much force as a strong trumpet player. This little interval didn't end when we finished the dance. We had some food and took off for the next stop, Louisville. But again, I slept until they left me off back in Cincinnati.

Looking back on that episode, I figure that Smack liked my refusing pay for that gig. It wasn't that I couldn't use the loot, but because I still considered myself a member of the band. Perhaps that explains quite a few things that otherwise would be unexplainable. For instance, it was soon after that occasion that he asked me to return to his band again – permanently. And when I returned, both he and Miss Lee insisted that I come back to live with them at 228 West 139th Street.

It became obvious they thought I had matured. Instead of being treated like the new kid, now, quite frequently, I was given the role of liaison between Smack and the band. This happened especially when it was something unpleasant Smack wanted no part of. He would pass those chores on to me or his wife. Neither Miss Lee nor I minded being given these duties because Fletcher was a wonderful person. His wife was always ready to do his bidding. As for me, I was truly flattered at the honor, and this time I thought I'd stay with Smack forever.

11

Smack and McKinney

When I returned to Fletcher's band it was at the height of its popularity, perhaps due to our network broadcasts from Roseland. We went further and further afield on our summer tours, all over the northeastern part of the country, touring the coalfields of Pennsylvania and the New England territory of the Shribman brothers for weeks with no layoff. This was very different from the previous limited excursions to play dances in places like Louisville, Lexington and Cincinnati. Now we had become regular attractions in swank places such as Castle Farms in Cincinnati, the Palais Royale in Buffalo, the Graystone Ballroom in Detroit and many other big-time spots including country clubs. Of course, in between the weekly engagements there would be the one-nighters, and we ran up and down the scale of clientele from a tobacco barn to a beautiful ballroom. One night we'd dine in splendor when we played a high-class hotel and the very next evening, a mere 100 or so miles away, we'd be lucky to fill the inner man with hot dogs. We really didn't mind as long as it tasted good.

As a matter of fact, Smack's band was the eatingest band I've ever known. We'd get a big kick out of trying to see who could eat the most. Jimmy Harrison and Coleman Hawkins were the ringleaders in this and I tried to keep up with them and the other real trenchermen. I can still hear Jimmy now, saying to Hawk, "Bean, I'm kinda petered. I guess I'll have to have three sirloins to make me feel good tonight." And Coleman would reply, "That's the trouble with you – you don't eat enough. Look at you! All skin and bones. Why, I aim to have half a cow, at least! Three sirloins, indeed! What are you trying to do – save your money and starve to death?" Then Jimmy would laugh and say, "Hold on, hold on. After I eat them, then I'm going to have my dinner." They could go on and on, kidding each other about who could eat the most.

The first time I heard them, I thought they were only joking. But when we arrived at the restaurant, I found out they really meant it. A typical meal after work would consist of a half dozen eggs, a triple order of ham or bacon, a toasted loaf of bread, plus fried potatoes, jelly, coffee, pie and perhaps a meat sandwich – just to keep the sweet taste of the pie out of his mouth, as Jimmy used to explain. Hawk would go right along with Jimmy and the rest of us would follow as best we could. Don Redman, Kaiser Marshall, Buster Bailey, Little Joe Smith, Charlie Dixon – in fact most of us were the type of heavy boarders that restaurant owners loved to see hit town. I soon fell into line and in one summer went from 155 to 180 pounds. And I was only 19 years old at the time.

Those were the days of running up and down those bad roads at 75 and 80 miles an hour. We traveled by auto, Smack leading the pack in his ever-present Packard, buying a new one every year. Jimmy Harrison drove a Pontiac; Joe Smith (of the trumpet playing Smiths) enjoyed his Willys Saint Claire roadster; Kaiser Marshall had a Buick which unfortunately was involved in an accident and didn't last long. I remember that Buster Bailey was driving at the time of the accident. Don Redman also had bad luck. He bought a brand new Cadillac and only owned it a few hours, as I recall. We were playing a concert at the Renaissance Ballroom when Don drove up in this beauty of a car, which we all admired. In the middle of the concert someone rushed into the theater to tell Don that his auto, which he had parked in front of the theater, had been smashed up. A total loss!

Our meeting place, whenever we left town for a road trip, would be in the vicinity of the Rhythm Club at 132nd and Seventh Avenue, which was where all the tooters hung out. We'd have a real second line of spectators when we'd line up, then count heads and roar down Seventh Avenue heading for the ferry to New Jersey. Now that I've become mellowed and cautious, I marvel that any of us lived as long as we have: flying up and down the roads with no sleep, on ordinary country roads, no freeways or beltways, through the little cities and hung over on whatever we had had to drink the night before (and these were still prohibition times, with all alcoholic beverages being suspect as to content).

To illustrate what I mean about flying, let me tell you about one incident. We finished a dance in Louisville, Kentucky, and since there had been no word from the booking agent as to where the next date was, Smack said, "Well, let's get on to the Apple." We lit out immediately, as everyone was anxious to get home. We drove all day, almost without stopping. From Louisville to New York is a goodly distance, and you can imagine how pooped we were when we arrived at Fletcher's house on 139th Street. As we drove up, Miss Lee ran down the steps, saying, "Fletcher, what in the world are you doing in New York? You're supposed to be playing in Lexington, Kentucky, tomorrow night. Didn't the agent get the word to you?" Smack's only reaction was to say, "Yeah? Is that right? Well, fix us some food and we'll hit the road." And we did just that. We ate and went right back on old Route 1.

Then there was the time we were playing the Show Boat in Pittsburgh, which was a real big deal for us. Firstly, the Show Boat was a real riverboat anchored in the river with gambling and a Cotton Club-type show with a cast of 60 people starring George Dewey Washington, the noted baritone singer. And secondly, because the early part of this particular tour had been very wearying, naturally we welcomed a lengthy engagement. But our pleasure was cut short when only a week later we arrived on the job one night and were greeted by marshals who served the entire band with a summons. We were all named individually in a million-dollar suit by a booker who was suing us for breach of contract. Personally, I thought it was some kind of joke or publicity stunt until I went to get my horn off the boat and was told there was an injunction against removing any instruments. Of course, nothing ever came of the suit and the fellows in the band didn't even have to appear, but that lovely engagement was unfortunately curtailed.

Another episode I'll never forget was the time we left New York to play a dance on the eastern shore of Maryland. I knew the town, having frequently played there as a kid with Ollie Blackwell. When we arrived I thought it was strange not to see any colored people standing around the corners, as usual, but I didn't give it much thought. We started playing and after a few numbers I suggested to Bobbie Stark, my section mate and drinking partner, that we should get some Coca-Cola and go into the men's room to fix up our evening's refreshment (which at the time was gin and Coke). We hopped off the stand during our break and went to the soft-drink stand. Right then, if I had had my wits about me, I would have sensed the tension in the air. When we tried to make small talk with the colored fellows who served us, they'd only reply in monosyllables. Bobbie said disgustedly, "I guess these so-and-sos are just dumb," as we walked to the men's room.

When we reached the door, an officer stopped us, asking, "Where y'all going, boy?" to which quick-tempered Bobbie snarled, "Don't call me 'boy'! How big do men grow in your country?" The law man replied, "Yer jes' a boy to me – boy." He gestured, "It's broke down. Iffen ya got to go, dere's de yard." That's when something warned us to leave. I grabbed Bobbie by the arm and led him back to the stand. Later on, I had reason to be glad that I did.

No sooner had we returned to the bandstand and sat down when a woman accompanied by a big red-faced man came up and demanded, in a strident voice, "Do y'all know *Pink Elephants*?" Nobody answered, so she came right up to me (I sat on the end) and repeated the question, only this time she prefaced it with the traditional, "Boy." I yelled to Smack, "The lady wants *Pink Elephants*, and he answered, "Play it and we'll follow you." We actually didn't know the tune, but somehow we struggled through something like it and heaved a sigh of relief. We needn't have bothered being relieved, because the woman came right back. She thanked me, saying, "Blackie, that was all right. Now I want you to sing *Pink Elephants*." Everybody looked at Smack and Smack grinned as he said, "Sure, go ahead and sing it, Rex." I made up some kind of words and we did a few minutes of ad lib nonsense. We were sure that was the end of *Pink Elephants*, but there was still more, later. Meanwhile, the trumpet section was tired of blowing dry and started hiding behind their music stands to sip on their gin. If Fletcher saw us, he didn't say anything.

It was only about 20 minutes before quitting time when along came Miss Pink Elephants with her boyfriend. This time they were both loaded for bear – they were loaded with whiskey for sure, and evidently I was to be the bear! As long as I live, I'll remember this scene. The man spoke for the first time, saying to the woman, "Ain't you seen enough of your little nigger?" The woman replied, "Naw, this little nigger is okay. Didn't he play and sing *Pink Elephants* just for me? Why, I bet he'd even dance like a pink elephant if I ast him, wouldn't you, boy?" I tried to be diplomatic as I answered, "We'll gladly play it again for you, ma'am," but the man interrupted and yelled, "Nigger, I don' give a good God damn iffen you're glad to play or not. When my woman tells ya to dance, ya dances! Ya heah?"

Without further talk, the band struck up, you guessed it, *Pink Elephants*, and I did a dance – my first command performance. Right after that we packed up and cut out of Cambridge in a hurry. Down the road apiece we stopped to gas up. The colored attendant asked where we were coming from and when we told him he almost turned white! He said, "My gawd! Didn't you know they lynched a man there just two days ago?" This explained why we hadn't seen any colored people on the streets and why we couldn't use the men's room. The only mystery – and I still wonder to this day – is why the woman was so keen on *Pink Elephants* and how she could be satisfied with our innovative version.

Fletcher's trumpet section at that time consisted of Cootie Williams on first, my buddy Bobbie Stark on second and me on third. Bobbie and I were very compatible and we hung out together, both on and off the job. Bobbie played solos with a lot of velocity and feeling. I never could understand why his artistry didn't receive more acclaim. We both did our job on the stand but I can look back now and see how the two of us must have made Fletcher's hair stand on end with our pranks.

Bobbie's main weakness was his inability to get to the job on time.

One night, at Roseland, we started playing as usual at 8:30 sharp. But there was no Bobbie. The whole band watched for his entrance, wondering what the story would be this time. There was a crisis brewing because Smack had warned Bobbie that the next time he was late he was fired. The minutes dragged on and still no Bobbie. Then, all of a sudden, there was a commotion in the crowd and along came Bobbie with a cab driver, lugging a huge grandfather clock right across the dance floor. This sight stopped everything. The band doubled up with laughter and was unable to play. The dancers noticed our amusement and joined in. The manager, Mr Burgess, ran from the office and, when he saw the tableau, he broke up, too. Bobbie just stood there not smiling or saying a word, just holding on to his clock that had neglected to chime him awake. Milt Shaw, who had the other band, struck up and the diversion was over, but it was a funny, funny scene. No, Bobbie wasn't fired.

This next little recollection involving Bobbie Stark happened long before he married and settled down. We were playing the Roseland on a long-term engagement and became friendly with many of the patrons on a first-name basis. So it was no surprise to me when two couples began saying hello and making conversation every time we left the stand. They became regulars and pretty soon it was obvious that the girls had more on their minds than music. They would dance by the bandstand, apparently just enjoying themselves, until they got right in front of Bobbie. Then that feminine telegraph would start beating out the message "Here I am." Bobbie tuned in on the wavelength, which led to an exchange of telephone numbers. It turned out that Mary was from the Bronx, Arlene lived in Brooklyn. And the first time they had seen Bobbie and another brother (no, not me) the die was cast. These young ladies had fallen for the fellows. This posed a problem if you know anything about race relations back in 1928. But love found a way in subway crowds and on park benches for a few hand-holdings, a quick hug or kiss. And that was that.

But all of the restraint broke down when we had to leave to go on tour. First stop, Baltimore, Maryland. Driving down was uneventful despite a drenching rain, and we had just checked into the hotel when the door opened on an amazing sight. Looking like fugitives from a minstrel show or kids celebrating Hallowe'en, there were Mary and Arlene. They were a mess. Mary's blonde hair framed her dark brown made-up face and Arlene was equally grotesque; her make-up was black and had streaked into her red hair. This was a scene to be remembered, and the love-smitten girls, doubtless being oblivious to their hideous appearance, greeted Bobbie and the other swain with, "Daddy, dear, see I got here rawt long wit youse" in a pure Brooklynese accent (or was this pure Bronx?), which didn't help matters a little bit. We all broke up, we shouted, we laughed, we rolled on the floor. And the spell was only broken when the desk clerk said, "Fellows, I don't know what this is all about, but I do know this is Baltimore and you ain't checking these women into this here hotel. And I don't care if you say they's your mother!"

Then there was the evening when we were in higher spirits than usual due to its being Bobbie's birthday, so at intermission we sat on the stairs behind the scene at Roseland, sipping gin and Coke. Coots started kidding Bobbie about some girl and Bobbie retorted by kidding Cootie back, making fun of how green and country looking Cootie looked when he had first arrived in New York. I sat back, egging them both on, hoping that in the heat of their argument they wouldn't notice how often I was hitting our communal bottle. They didn't, and if I had left well enough alone there'd be no story. Anyway, they traded insults jokingly until it was just about time to return to the stand, when Bobbie told Coots, "Yeah, you're just a country boy lost in the big city." I remember I was coming up the stairs and I chimed in, saying, "Bobbie's right, Coots." The next thing I knew, I was desperately clinging to the stair railing, trying to keep my neck from being broken. Coots had knocked me down the stairs. After all that guff from Bobbie and I had hardly said a thing! I didn't even know he was angry.

I realize that I've mentioned being knocked about a few

other times, but generally I only received what I deserved. To be honest, the antagonism usually came about either because I talked out of turn or was being stupid. Over the years I managed to talk myself out of several jobs and into several life-long enemies. I'll tell you about these as they happen.

Since the time Danny Doy had gone to Europe, it had always been my ambition to go there, and I nearly managed this for the first time with Smack. It was during a memorable gig when we were breaking it up at Connie's Inn that Smack was cabled an offer for a European tour. This caused Tom Rockwell, his manager, to ask advice from Irving Mills, who responded with a bill of goods. He offered to get us booked into the Cotton Club first, which was to be followed with his helping with the European tour. Neither had any real chance of happening because, as some of the guys told Smack, Mills, being Duke's partner and manager, didn't want the competition.

The fact is that Henderson had a fabulous group and really was competition for Ellington. Fletcher and the bunch of star musicians with him only lost one band battle to my knowledge. That was when Jean Goldkette literally kept us off the stand at Roseland Ballroom most of the evening. It happened because a deal had been made for Smack to play Goldkette's Graystone Ballroom in Detroit for two weeks while the Goldkette Victor band recorded in New York, then the two were to join forces in the Roseland. So Goldkette had the say, and he said, "No, no band battle."

People who didn't hear the Henderson band in person are misled by listening to the records which the band made in those early days of recording. To begin with, at the time there was an unwritten custom among record people that no negro orchestra should be allowed to record anything that wasn't blues or hot stuff. This decision was for purely economic reasons, as the record fathers figured that blues and jazz or anything else a colored band might play would appeal only to the minority. It occurs to me that the element of chance was also an intriguing factor, as nine out of ten times the tune that the artist or bandleader had the highest hopes for flopped. However, it often happened that the little ditty that was cooked up on the spur of the moment as a filler to complete the session took off and went into orbit.

I remember once back in 1929 when John Nesbitt, a great trumpet player and an even greater arranger with McKinney's Cotton Pickers, was commissioned by Smack to make a special score on the tune of *Chinatown* for our outfit. Nesbitt came through with a spectacular, out-of-this-world swinger, and we tore into that music with such a vengeance that, wherever we played, dancers screamed for more. On the strength of such acceptance we could hardly wait to get back to New York to record this blockbuster. However, when the long-awaited recording date finally took place, by some strange quirk of fate *Chinatown* proved to be merely a second-rate performance. To make the fourth side we just threw in a riff version of Fats Waller's *Honeysuckle Rose* and, amazingly, this was what became a Henderson classic!

By the early 30s the recording business had really become big business, and research produced a much better quality of sound reproduction. This resulted in a shortage of skilled personnel to do the intricate jobs of monitoring, mixing sound at the proper levels and so on. There were fellows sitting at master controls in the glass cage who cared nothing about music, knew even less and, in the opinion of many musicians, should never have stopped driving trucks or whatever it was they had done before.

This particular record date was noteworthy from more aspects than one. After a lot of top level discussion it was decided that Henderson would record something musical and beautiful. Most historians either were unaware or have forgotten to mention that Henderson had 35 or so special and lovely waltz arrangements in the book, and that these were featured on all dates. Anyway, for this momentous break with tradition in recording, we set out to prove something, and that is what we did. It was on this date that Don Redman's *Whiteman Stomp* was produced. This work was revolutionary in concept and was so far ahead of its time that even 40 years later it still commands respect, especially since Paul Whiteman's own record of the stomp falls flat when compared with the original.

The other side of the record was a ballad, *Dear, on a Night Like This*, and there's a little story to be told. This lovely melody was orchestrated to highlight the wondrous talents of our first trumpet, Russell Smith. Here I must digress just a bit so that you can get the picture, or otherwise only another trumpet player would grasp the drama of the incident. In those days the top playable range of the trumpet was considered to be high C, but Smith possessed such perfect stamina and control that he could play to high F, G and even A, far above the average. And he could play legato, sustained tones way up on these lofty notes. We made what we thought was a perfect take the first time but, on hearing the playback, smack in the middle of Russell's high and muted solo, just 16 bars before the end, we heard a foreign cluster of sound. Brows furrowed, frowns replaced our satisfied smiles and everybody looked around with unspoken questioning glances. Then bedlam broke looose as we wondered what the hell it could have been. Smack jumped up from the piano and headed for the control booth. But before he got half way the engineer met him, saying, "That's too bad. That noise in the studio ruined a perfect take. Was it someone's chair moving? The drummer's foot pedal?" Fletcher replied that it must have been in the record equipment because it was quiet as a mouse in the studio.

We tried it again, hardly breathing or moving. We were stiff and it showed in our playing. But, despite our efforts, there was that shuffling noise again and again. I've always supposed that the inexperienced engineer twisted a knob to the right instead of the left or some such. But Russell never played his solo as perfectly, and we never did another cut as good as that first ruined one. In disgust, it was decided to let the last take go. This was just the sort of problem that prevented Henderson's band (and others) from being recorded to best advantage.

During these years when I was back with Fletcher, I felt that I was mature enough to think about settling down. I'd been courting Margie, whom I'd first met when I was still with Horace. She was the first girl I'd ever wanted to marry, but I was too shy to ask her to be my bride. Benny Carter, like the good friend he was, played Cupid for me and helped me to win her. Was I ever thrilled when he told me he'd talked Margie into saying yes.

Some months later, not too much after the episode with Bobbie and the clock, I asked Smack for a raise in salary. I had just found out I was scheduled to become a poppa. As chance would have it, about the same time McKinney made me a good offer which I felt I had to take due to the forthcoming baby. But my heart stayed back in New York with Smack's band. In fact, during the short time I played with McKinney, about 11 months I think, I still played with Henderson whenever I could. We'd go into New York to record and, as soon as the date was over, you could find me at Roseland, sitting in. When a promoter had both Henderson and McKinney as well as Ellington do a short tour of about six cities, I played nearly every set!

At the time I joined McKinney, he also hired Benny Carter, Elmer Williams (the tenor sax man) and my former nemesis, Big Charlie Green, on trombone. He told us, "We do things differently in Detroit and I want to tell you the rules. First of all, there's a 25-dollar fine for being late." We all nodded in accord and he continued, "The fine for not being well groomed is 10 dollars." Someone said, "Okay." Then Pop added, "I don't allow anyone to carry weapons under any circumstances." Then I saw Green frown and I knew it was because, despite his 6 feet plus, he actually felt undressed without his 45 automatic and didn't like this at all. McKinney concluded, "If I ever catch any one of you fellows with a bottle on my bandstand, I'll ship you right back to New York. Understand?"

We all acquiesced and went home to pack. However, on arriving in Detroit, everything seemed to go wrong. Elmer Williams lost his bag, so we had to stop and buy him a shirt. This made us late to meet the fellow who was to drive us somewhere southward in Michigan, to join the band. Then we had all hassled with Green when he insisted on stocking up on gin, just in case the town was dry. All of this made us at least an hour late leaving Detroit. Pop McKinney was all frowns when he met us at the gate, saying this being late wouldn't do at all in his outfit. I suppose Big Green was trying to ingratiate himself with the boss when he agreed heartily, handing Pop a bottle of gin and his pistol! McKinney stood there in amazement for a moment. Then he handed Green back his possessions, two weeks' salary and train fare home.

There were lots of different styles of running a band, and while I've heard people say this leader was an ogre and that one was too casual, the fact is they all managed to have a dozen or more fellows turn up on the job, dressed in uniform, instruments and music on the stands. Every person had to utilize his personal method to achieve this goal.

Chick Webb had a habit of cursing out his sidemen when they riled him. His secret was that he also made them know that they could have the shirt off his back if they needed it. Count Basie was an easy-going leader, but had Marshal Royal to carry the big stick. Benny Goodman became notorious because he developed a fixed stare which musicians nicknamed "the Ray." In my experience, there were few real no-nonsense leaders. Let me name two: Benny Carter and Don Redman. Pop McKinney commanded respect and his rules were very definite. Mal Hallett believed that a drink could solve most differences, while Cab Calloway wanted to settle things with a fight – he'd invite the problem man to go outside. And although Ellington seemed to be oblivious that the men had a way of wandering on and off the stage, anyone really observing what was happening would note how seldom any of the fellows were absent. He never really fired anyone, but he had a way of giving the freeze by not letting the fellow solo at all or calling him to do solo after solo at breakneck tempo or something else to make him look bad, until the man would quit. I've heard Fletcher Henderson being critized for his seemingly lackadaisical attitude. Nevertheless, for years he kept together some of the greatest jazz musicians of all times.

During this period, Pop McKinney watched me shuttle from his bandstand to Smack's, until he finally said in an outraged tone, "Rex, who the hell do you think is paying you? Where's your loyalty?" Certainly he was right in asking me. The truth is, my loyalty was with Smack and I was soon back in New York with him.

12

The Inside Story

There's a whole lot of chicanery and maneuvering in the music business that the public never suspects. I've mentioned the great rivalry which developed between Ellington and Henderson, and it wasn't pure circumstance that, while one went up, the other passed out of the musical picture. During the late 20s most knowledgeable music lovers conceded that Fletcher had by far the best orchestra, the best soloists and the best musical arrangements. To put the record straight, there are the unexplainable quirks of fate and the questionable half truths on some past occurrences. This train of thought is due to a lot of faulty reporting about those days.

At first, from where I sat, it looked as if Smack could win the competition. He was chosen for one of the most important jobs that a colored orchestra ever had – that of playing a Broadway show. Unfortunately, Vincent Youmans's *Great Day* didn't prove to live up to its name, or even to live, for that matter. But I didn't know of any other Broadway musical with a 95 per cent white cast which had a colored band in the pit. The story is frequently told that Fletcher replaced Duke in *Great Day*. That is just not the way it happened. Irving Mills tried his best to keep Smack out of *Great Day* so that he could build Ellington, but it was Vincent Youmans himself who chose Henderson. We broke in the show in Long Branch, New Jersey. This I remember especially well because I took time out from dress rehearsals to honeymoon there with Margie. From there we went to Philadelphia. We were qualified for Broadway despite the claims of critics in later years after *Great Day* had opened in Philadelphia. Nevertheless, we did open in New York at a theater on Columbus Circle for a short run. I was there, playing in the band.

I have often read statements by music historians which indicated that Henderson's band lacked precision and intonation. This is not true, despite occasional sloppy performances. Somewhere in the vaults of some record company there may still exist recording gems which the Henderson band made and that were rejected because they were considered too perfect musically for a negro orchestra of those times! I mentioned recording a tune called *Dear, on a Night Like This*, and the best version, which was never issued. That number and Don Redman's *Whiteman Stomp* are evidence of the sound that the band could produce when allowed to do so. Also, few people remember how extensive and beautiful Smack's waltz book was. No band of that era could cut the group playing waltzes.

Henderson might have maintained his advantageous position but the cards were stacked against him. This was mainly due to his own temperament which was basically not competitive enough even to seek out a manager like Ellington's, who had the connections to all of the important outlets for work. The good engagements were concentrated in the white theaters and the big white clubs. Since Henderson was never able to get a manager with effective ties to the scene where the real money was, he became a victim of the times.

During the seven or eight years I was with Smack, we played all sorts of places outside of the Roseland. They ranged from afternoon house parties at Princeton or Yale to an Easter morning breakfast at Sherry's on Park Avenue, but the dances we used to enjoy the most were the battles of the bands. We would finish up at Roseland and take off for Harlem, playing at the New Star Casino against Billy Fowler or Fess Williams. In later years it would be the Savoy or Rockland Palace, playing mostly against Chick Webb or others of that caliber.

Among the unforgettable battles of bands were those in New England, and most of the time we wouldn't know who was to be on the opposite stand. We had friendly rivalries with Rudy Valee, Mal Hallett, Guy Lombardo and many others, including Glen Gray's Casa Loma Band. I guess, of all the road bands, the Casa Lomas were our best buddies. We'd often exchange musical arrangements and always chatted and drank together. In fact in an emergency, such as someone being late or perhaps having too much to drink, his opposite number would fill in for him. That's the way it was until one night when we both were playing the senior prom at the University of Pennsylvania. The first part of the evening went smoothly until after the intermission, when Glen and the boys played their half-hour set and we picked up from there. Somehow, our old-time friendship got fractured when the students wouldn't let us stop playing for the rest of the night. That was not our fault, but the Casa Lomas left without even saying goodnight.

My return to Smack's band had opened up another era for me, but unfortunately it ended suddenly and painfully. All that goes up must come down, and my final departure from the band I loved came about like this. In a desperate attempt to compete with the characters who, drawn by the smell of money, had invaded the band business, Smack had two bookers working simultaneously. A situation developed in which Fletcher, also drawn by the smell of money, had commitments to be in two places at the same time. There was a southern tour booked by Reese Dupree (who wrote the standard *Shortnin' Bread*) and a dance job in Reading, Pennsylvania. At any rate, due to these conflicting bookings, Smack took a pick-up group to Pennsylvania for two weeks and sent us (the regular band) on the two-week southern tour.

Since the days when I had lived with Smack, we were close, and he chose me to act as nominal leader of the band anytime he was off the bandstand socializing or collecting the money. At any rate, this time Mrs Leora Henderson, Smack's wife, went along to collect the money and I was to help her, call the tunes, and stomp off. As I recall the tour, we started in Philly, played Washington, Norfolk, Charlotte, and then hit the deep, deep South – Augusta, and Cuthbert, Georgia, which was the home of the Henderson family. After we left Norfolk the tour became an increasingly hostile fugue of disappointments, starting with being stranded for gas in a little hamlet because the operator of the only gas station didn't like the idea of Mrs Smack being in a bus with all of us. Mrs Smack was very light in color and he took her for white. Then we got stuck in red clay up to the hub caps outside of Birmingham, Alabama, which was not too bad excepting that we didn't exactly care for the aim of some teenagers who broke the window of the bus. But then we had good fortune because, just as our white bus driver from New Jersey was stepping out to do battle, the sheriff sauntered up and drawled, "It's all raight to have fun, boys, but don' carry it too fur."

Of course, we had become accustomed to the ordinary hazards of the region on previous trips, but we didn't know how to handle Miss Lee's dilemma when we stopped at a nice, clean looking place that had clearly marked "colored" and "white" rest rooms. As the guys surged out, Miss Lee just sat while the owner and his wife argued over which door she could enter. That was a tough one. Finally, the man sidled up to our bus and said, "Scuse me, ma'am, but is you white or is you colored?" Miss Lee drew herself up to her full height and replied, "Sir, I am a Negro and I am proud of it." The man grinned sheepishly and said, "No harm meant, ma'am, I jes' wanted to make you welcome." And as he walked away, he muttered, "I tol' you she was jes' one of those light nigras."

In general, the tour was a fiasco, a complete bust. Underpublicized, under-attended, we wound up in Columbus, Georgia, virtually stranded until Sam Stieffle sent a bus to bring us up to Philadelphia, where Smack had arranged a hasty opening at Stieffle's Pearl Theater. That bus ride was unforgettable. I don't recall the mileage but I do know that we hightailed out of the South in unbelievably quick time, stopping only for gas and other essentials. We made that trip on cold sandwiches and soft drinks.

As happy as we were to return to civilization, still we suffered at the Pearl, where the shows started at 10:30 in the morning and ran continuously until midnight. The Pearl was a part of the "around the world theater tour" which Ellington, Henderson, Lunceford et al played as the red-hot attractions in the Harlems of that era. The only drawback was the way that the theater owners worked us – five shows a day, each one an hour and 45 minutes long. This was considered normal, but if the people really flocked to see us they would make us do as many as eight shows a day. There have been times that I played the last note of a show and then heard the stage manager shout, "Half hour – half hour to the next show."

Besides that, we had two broadcasts which were done at a studio and also two midnight shows which ran until 2 in the morning. All of this took its toll, and whiskey flowed like snow in a blizzard. Our tempers became scraped and sore. This was the mental climate of Fletcher's orchestra as we limped into New York for an opening that very evening, at the Empire Ballroom right across the street from the Roseland Ballroom. We had closed Philadelphia only the evening before and that morning had had to do a long-deferred record date. There was a lot of grumbling amongst the guys. Who could blame them? How much abuse is the body supposed to stand?

The record date was just so-so, but that night all of Broadway knew Smack was back on the scene. We really blew and then some. As a matter of fact, most of the truly great organizations could have been called "money" bands (the name came from the fact that you could bet your money that the band would play well). What I mean by that is that when the musicians reached the point of almost complete collapse from a hard trip, lack of food, sleep etc., a small ember of pride in performance would spread. Within minutes, the flame of creative improvisation would be soaring to exalted heights – a money band, playing, blowing just for the love of it all.

That fateful night at the Empire, Fletcher was asked to do a benefit the following night for the Scottsboro Boys. We just couldn't believe Fletcher was serious in accepting and asking us to donate our services after all we'd been through for the past month. Although musicians as a rule seldom argued with the boss, without any thought I said, "I'm too tired to make anything but bed." Of course, all the rest of the tired men chimed in, "Me, too. No benefit." There, I had done it again, and I didn't know until 30 years later that the young man whose request was denied blamed me for the non-appearance of the band and never forgave me. I'm afraid I would do exactly the same thing again, even knowing in advance the unfortunate results for me.

It was only a few nights later when Hawk said, "Smack, have you heard Red get off? He sure is playing great!" Red was a trumpet player and, knowing how the gossip system worked in that band, I started feeling sorry for Bobbie Stark. As a rule, no one ever praised anybody outside of our band unless it was cut and dried that that musician was about to join us. Poor Bobbie was fired and hired at least twice a season. I hated to see our section break up, especially just when we had sworn to save our money to buy identical camel's hair coats for next winter. I guess I had the shock of my life when I went to Smack to plead for Bobbie and Smack said, "That's very nice of you to talk for Bobbie. But he's not leaving – YOU are!"

Yes, I was fired, but not for the reason he gave me. He told me that I was playing too loud and that I was trying to take the band away from him. On the first score, when I joined him he had told me to try to play like Louis, which meant play above the band, so this complaint was illogical. The other was more so – it was he who had put me in charge of the band. Not only had I never asked for the job, I didn't even receive extra money for doing the front-man bit. No, the real reason was my speaking out against the benefit and embarrassing him.

As it turned out, my being fired by Fletcher led to my short-lived career as a bandleader at the Empire Ballroom. At first, it looked like he had done me a favor and I thought I was ready for the responsibility. But later I wasn't too sure. Running a band is not that easy and there's no doubt that I made more than my share of mistakes.

13

My Own Band

I felt I was dreaming when Richard Decker of the Empire Ballroom told me, yes, he'd like to have a good stomp band for a few weeks. So, despite making less money – only 55 dollars a week instead of the 85 I'd been getting from Smack, I was happy. I stopped drinking and smoking and started planning my band.

At the inception, the group proved to be the right music for that ballroom, located in the heart of New York on Broadway between 51st and 52nd streets. The original contract was for two weeks and we remained 14 months. We worked very diligently to make the band a good-sounding musical group and rehearsed enough to make impressive arrangements out of the free lead sheets and piano copies we latched onto. Very often it was broad daylight when rehearsal broke up.

Out of these sessions, too, many a tune was born. *Blue Lou*, *Stompin' at the Savoy* and a few others that became famous in later years were our creations. Edgar Sampson, who was chief arranger for the band, would listen when some fellows set a riff. Then we'd all fool around, straining to make it complete as we worked out a bridge or release. By the time the band broke up we had ten or so numbers which were originals, played only by us. But of all that music later attributed to Sampson and Goodman and Webb, I am particularly sorry that I was not given credit for the bridge of *Stompin' at the Savoy*. How I regret not having that standard included in my ASCAP catalog!

In the band there were a few musicians who became quite well known. We had Sid Catlett on drums for ten months, and he only left because of his long-standing custom of spending

Christmas with his family in Chicago. There was Edgar Sampson playing first sax and doubling on violin. In fact, all of the saxes doubled on violin, including Rudy Powell, who allowed me to coax him into playing clarinet solos. The other alto saxophone man was Allen Jackson. The rest of the personnel were George Thigpen, first trumpet, Ward Pinkett, second trumpet, Nelson Hurd on trombone, Noel Klukies on tenor and Freddie Skerritt on bass.

One day, when we were first rehearsing for the job, the pianist didn't show up. I was at my wit's end trying to find a good piano man willing to work for the $22.50 a week that I was able to pay. While I was standing on the corner asking another musician if he knew of a piano man for me, a young kid said, "I play piano, mister. Why don't you try me?" I looked the lad over. He looked about 14 years old. I asked him what tunes he knew and the kid replied, "Anything you know I'll play with you." We went to the rehearsal room and sat young Roger Ramirez down. He played great piano all right, but perhaps is better known for his composition of *Lover Man*. We were both happy that he joined my group.

This period was the height of the Depression, in 1933, and I had the bright idea of supplementing my meager salary by taking over the men's room concession in the ballroom, not realizing that my biggest problem would be hiring competent and honest help to staff the room. Decker, the boss, had no objections to my renting the room. As a matter of fact, he lowered the price for me, and again I tried to build something out of very little. Many a night I'd mop up the joint and do whatever had to be done after we had finished with the music for the evening.

Every now and then something would come up to make me think that I was on the right track, musically speaking. One evening a very big figure in the business, let's call him Mr Booker, came to the Empire and remained most of the evening. The next day my phone rang, and it was Mr Booker wanting to know if I was signed with anyone. When I told him I was a free agent, he made an appointment for the next day in his office to discuss his managing the band. This made me feel as tall as a tree and as happy as a lark. At last, I thought, I could stop scrounging for arrangements, stop praying for uniforms, stop, stop, stop, and just blow my horn.

I was at his office right on the button, timewise, and while I cooled my heels for about an hour I had plenty of time to gaze around and assimilate the splendor of his office, which seemed to me more like the inner sanctum of some oriental potentate than an office for doing business. Finally, the first secretary told the second secretary that Mr Booker would see me now. The gentleman was very affable and within five minutes I was on my way out, clutching a multi-paged contract which I was to sign and return to my benefactor. All of the way home on the subway, I kept trying to recall what the great man's conversation had been.

Right now, I ought to explain a curious quirk in my mental processes, which is a retention block that I develop when I am under great emotional pressure. For example, when I stood before the minister to be married and he asked the customary "What is your name," I couldn't remember my own name! Once, in Australia, before 6000 people, I just could not remember my starting note on the tune *I Can't Get Started*. To my dismay, this dreaded phenomenon just pops up from time to time. So forgetting the interview with Mr Booker didn't surprise me too much.

It was after I got home and started to study the contract that I couldn't believe my eyes. Of course it was in legal language and at first it was all Greek to me. But, as I plowed on, it dawned on me exactly what the document said. These were the terms. The party of the second part (that's me) was to furnish from 10 to 15 musicians, in good standing with local 802 AF of M, for any occasion indicated by the party of the first part (Mr Booker) at any price compatible with union scale. That part was all right. I was also to be responsible and pay for arrangements, uniforms, deportment, all publicity costs, traveling expenses, etc., and for this the party of the second part was to receive 50 dollars a week for 50 weeks a year plus 25 per cent of the net profits. I asked myself what profits I could hope for, after all these expenses, so I never bothered to return the contract, and it was some months before I realized that I should have gone along with the set-up and crawled before trying to walk.

One of my pet theories was that the public would like a real vocalist with the band. I had once suggested to Smack that he hire Cab Calloway away from Marion Hardy's Alabamians, the band that brought him to New York, but Smack told me that he didn't want any singers with the band. And it would be okay with him if I just played the horn and left policy to him. I'll admit it was fresh on my part, but not two years later Cab Calloway was Fletcher's competition! That was, as he said, *his* problem.

Now that I had my own band, I took my own advice. I sent for Sonny Woods, whom I had heard in Pittsburgh. Although some of the fellows in the band looked at me as if I was crazy, the combination of a Morton Downey-type crooner's voice backed up with muted brass and violins proved to be just the change of pace that the dancers loved at the Empire Ballroom. The band rocked along, trying to sound like Smack when we swung, and like Leo Reisman's society band on the ballads. Then Mr Decker put us on the radio three times a week. We did half-hour broadcasts from this popular ballroom. We apparently built up a fair audience as far as Washington, DC. Ike Dixon, a Baltimore bandleader who also booked dances in the area, wrote me asking for my terms for a two-week tour.

I knew how limited I was as a business man and turned the request over to Decker. He shopped around, and, when he found out it would be impossible to replace us for the kind of money he was paying me, he turned thumbs down on the tour. Instead, keeping us as the house band, he brought in many of the famous groups of the day as attractions. I remember Ozzie Nelson, Rudy Valee, Guy Lombardo, Bert Lown, Joe Haymes and others of that ilk. They drew the crowds and we developed a following from being heard in that company.

Finally, Decker permitted us to double at the Lafayette Theater for one week. My recollection is that I celebrated my 27th birthday that same week in 1934. Although we rehearsed like crazy, the opening show was almost our closing, too. We were as scared as rabbits and, when the curtain went up, we went up in fright. This audience was the most critical you could find and, if they didn't like you, you could be booed right off the stage. I had seen it happen. Luckily, I had the foresight to give the opening eight bars to Big Sid as a drum solo, and they swung into the tune all right. The audience was very encouraging and I thought to myself , "So far, so good," as I announced the next number, which we had spent a lot of time on.

We lined up in semi-darkness across most of the stage with megaphones to sing *Talk of the Town*, in glee-club style as I had seen the Casa Loma band do. The sax section had the introduction on violins and Sonny Woods stood on stage left. He was supposed to have a baby spotlight on his face, but disaster struck when the electrician goofed the cue we had rehearsed with him. Instead of slowly lowering the lights so we could get into position, he entirely blacked out the stage just as I finished the announcement. This created a long pause as we scrambled to our places. Evidently the electrician became panicky at his error and completely forgot to turn on the fluorescent light, which was supposed to sell the number. Amidst the confusion, the violins repeated the introduction, and in the dark we heard Sonny Woods's high tenor quaver out the first line of the song, "I can't show my face." Somebody in the audience yelled, "That's right. I sure can't see your face or nobody else's." That set the crowd off. They roared with laughter, and I was petrified until Ward Pinkett picked up his trumpet and improvised a perfect eight-bar introduction, allowing us to get into the tune. Then the audience settled down to listen. But, for years after, the phrase "I can't show my face" haunted me.

We did well that week for a new band, but I was due for a surprise. When we finished the last show I picked up the pay roll, signed a receipt and was just about to leave the office when the girl said, "Mr Stewart, haven't you forgotten something?" I couldn't think of anything and told her, if she meant about the union dues, I'd pay those myself when the representative came backstage. I noticed he was always backstage when a show closed. While I was back in the dressing room, sure enough, the union man came in as I was paying the fellows. He said, "I guess you had better let me do this for you, Rex." I replied that I knew how to handle it and thanked him, but I wondered why this chap was being so helpful. I kept on paying the musicians their money, being very careful to keep the union portion in a separate pile. When I finished, I handed the correct amount of tax to the union man. He took it, gave me a receipt and then asked, "Where's the rest of the money?" I had no idea what he was talking about and said so.

Then I had a real eye-opener as he explained, "Do you mean to tell me that you don't know? Nobody told you about the arrangements? Why everybody knows that X number of dollars are to be handed to me. Regardless of the contract, a certain percentage goes to the association – never mind who they are. And I get something for my time and trouble. Ask anybody. That's the way business is done. Now you can call it anything you want – insurance, kick-back or whatever. But if you don't take care of business, you're going to be out of business!"

I told him, nothing doing, and he replied "Okay, if that's the way you want it. That's what you'll be doing – nothing." I never could be positive, but after that hassle a lot of things went wrong enough to break up the band. The first evidence came quickly, as Decker told me it was all right to go ahead and tour the band, as he had found another group that he wanted to play for a month, starting right away.

I realized that by trying to protect my integrity (and the money I had earned) I had cut my own throat. But just in case Decker wasn't involved and really did plan on our returning to the Empire, I got on the phone and booked us for dances in Washington and Baltimore for the following weekend. The jinx, or whatever it was, followed us right on to Washington. When we got ready to play, we discovered all of the music had disappeared. We had apparently left it in a taxi, but it was never found, although a reward was offered.

Aside from bad luck, subsequent events have continued to prove that, try as I may, I've rarely been able to conform with the accepted image most agents, bookers or critics have of a negro musician. I'd just as soon have it that way – kind of a "be true to myself" attitude.

By the time my dreams of having my own band expired, I was quite fortunate to have made a considerable reputation as a cornet player. And this seems a good time to comment on the fact that I didn't always play cornet. Although my first horn was a cornet, after I reached New York I noticed all of the musicians were playing trumpet, so I yearned for a trumpet, too. Besides, I felt like a rube carrying my horn around in a green cloth sack. One night I ran into John Mason, one of the partners of the team of Mason and Henderson, who had been my bosses on *Go-Get-It*. He asked me how everything was going and I told him my troubles about wanting a trumpet and somehow not being able to get one. Mason took me to a pawnshop and bought me a trumpet! To add to my surprise, he tested various instruments until he was satisfied with one. I had never known that he was a trumpet player. I was proud and happy to have a friendship with John Mason for many years thereafter. Later he came into proper recognition with his song *Open the Door, Richard*.

In the period between the demise of my band and joining Luis Russell, I freelanced around New York, playing a lot of dances with Luckey Roberts in Tuxedo Park, Bar Harbor and at a Dupont estate in Wilmington. Generally I kept busy and was making more dough than I had with the band. At that time, too, I had the unique experience of playing solo in a sequence at Radio City, and I admit to being scared to death by the huge stage. Every time I entered and exited, it seemed more like walking the last mile on the way to the death chair, but it was a wonderfully profitable experience which lasted three weeks.

My stay with Luis Russell was much like my job with a few other bands which I don't think I have mentioned before. It was while I was with Billy Paige that I first met Earl Hines, before he migrated to Chicago. For a time I played the Savoy Ballroom with a group led by Leon Abbey. Later Alex Jackson, a great musician, formed a band in New York and I went to Cincinnati with him, where we played a club called Land o'Jazz.

Probably the most important thing that occurred was while I was playing with Luis Russell: I wound up with Duke Ellington. Here's how it happened. It all started in Irving

Mills's office, where I had gone to get paid for my first record date as a leader. Duke Ellington, who was with Mills, came in and we exchanged the usual musicians' pleasantries. Then Duke said, "Man, I've been waiting for you to join my band. How about coming home? You know we're homies." This was a reference to our both being from Washington, DC. I was no longer the green kid who had arrived in New York some 13 years earlier, and quickly countered by asking about the pay. When he told me 75 dollars, I refused the offer. It was common knowledge that all of Smack's key men were paid over a 100 a week, and he knew I had played with Fletcher. At that moment I was earning 95 dollars a week with Russell, and I was sure that a big-time band like Ellington's paid everyone more than he was offering me. Although I was no longer with Henderson, and despite the Depression, at that time good musicians commanded high salaries. And, as much as we made, there has always been a wide differential between the going price for white and colored musicians. I had no intention of lowering my salary. So I told Duke, "No thanks."

However, I guess Ellington either didn't believe me or had been prepared all along to up the ante because, when I arrived home, Jonesy, Duke's valet, was standing at the bottom of the stairs. I lived on the second floor and, as I approached, I could hear Jonesy yelling up to my wife, "Tell Rex that Duke says everything is okay and to be sure to go to Ben Rocke's to be fitted for uniforms tomorrow." Jonesy didn't know me, so we passed one another on the stairs. But there was almost a collision with Paul Barbarin. He had been standing in my doorway talking with my wife, had overheard Jonesy, and was doubtless speeding down in a big rush to tell Luis Russell that I was negotiating with Duke.

At that time, the Russell band was working a two-week engagement in Brooklyn, and this was only the first week. That night, as usual, I was there to work on time. Actually, I felt a great closeness to Luis. His mother was from Panama and my wife's mother came from the very same town. They were such close friends that Russell's mother brought my wife from Bocas del Toro as a child. So, needless to say, I was more than upset when Luis handed me my money with only the terse words, "Don't get on the stand!" I wanted him to know that I had refused Duke's offer, but he didn't give me an opportunity to tell my side of the story. After that, despite my wife Margie's pleading with Luis, he was adamant, and I went with Dumpy. In the final analysis, that was just about the best thing that could have happened.

14

Random Thoughts

Joining the Ellington entourage meant travel by Pullman and a decent bed to sleep in every night, even if frequently this was just our usual Pullman berth on the railway siding. Nevertheless, it was a welcome contrast to so many years of hard travel. None of us will ever forget the many traumatic nights spent on creaking cots with springs so low to the floor that the bed bugs often didn't even bother to creep up. Oh no, they'd just hoist themselves up from the floor or descend upon a brother from the ceilings! Along with these discomforts there was the constant hazard of the "moonshine" which caused us to have an ever-present hangover. It severely dimmed the perception of the driver, which resulted in many accidents on the road and death sometimes being the victor.

The fellows would moan and groan over the hardship of traveling in a beat-up bus a thousand miles a week, dashing from perhaps Old Orchard Beach in Maine to Hershey, Pennsylvania, then on to Pittsburgh the next night, with no chance for a bed or rest or bath or anything else but that damn bus. Then our next stop might be Chattanooga, Tennessee, and on to Oklahoma City. This particular trip actually took place while I was with McKinney. The wind-up would have been in Detroit, his home-base, and, come to think of it, this was more than a thousand miles of travel. One fellow I recall had become so accustomed to the jolting bus that it was days before he could sleep in his own bed! This hard travel was accompanied by the constant diet of, choose one: cold hamburgers or the hastily snatched, overdone hot dog. Sometimes we were offered "axle-grease fried chicken" or dried-up ham sandwiches on even more dried-up bread.

It occurs to me that we musicians must have been a hardy lot, or how else can one explain the survival of so many of my confreres who lived the hectic life of one-night stands? But some of us were not so hardy and just couldn't keep up with this merry, mad pace. They fell by the wayside, either leaving the business when pressured to do so by family or when their health began to fail and they had to quit. Others played on until that fatal automobile crash ended it all, and for many the traumatic insecurity engendered by the conditions within the profession led them into drinking in a fashion that could only have one end.

The musico who survived the ravages of those million one-nighters, the insufficient sleep, the incredibly bad food and all the rest of the unpleasantness that accompanied "the good old days" browses now through the moth-eaten scrap book and wonders what happened, and why. I join them in their bewilderment. I have lived to see the motion picture theaters grow from 100 or so capacity to vast palaces which seated thousands, then pass from the scene. Vaudeville grew from a few scattered dates to great chains with routes that extended across the entire country. If an act was good enough, they could work 50 weeks a year. Alas, these circuits are no more.

I also was a part of the beginnings of the dance-band tours and here, again, the pattern repeated itself. The tours are no more. Why? I ask. Is this progress? What great social upheaval, what tremendous sociological force acted as a catalyst to turn the people away from the pleasures of dancing, the theater and the movies? I think the answer is television, and I think the world is a lesser place without those sources of entertainment.

Among the legendary figures who couldn't hack the scene, perhaps the best known would be Bix and Charlie Parker, Charlie Christian and Jimmy Blanton. They've been much written about, so I propose, instead, to mention just a few of the others who either fell by the wayside far too soon or who have never received proper recognition for their gifts: Bubber Miley, Chu Berry, Big Charlie Green, Miff Mole and Davey Tough. These fellows are just a sampling – there are many, many more.

Jack Hatton was the first, as far as I know, to put all sorts of things in his trumpet bell to alter the sound – flower pots, bottles, etc. It changed the pitch and sound of the instrument long before mutes were made commercially. It is possible that this ploy might have influenced Bubber Miley. But I don't intend to deny that Bubber was a pioneer, the originator of a new sound on trumpet and cornet: that unique growl. This is how he claimed he happened to develop his distinctive trick. He came from a very religious family who often attended services at little obscure churches, perhaps only a store front, where people had meetings and sang. He was captivated by the sound their singing produced and tried to emulate this sound. What he came up with was the growl.

As I said earlier, Bubber played so well that at one time he was hired to add to the sound of a white band. In those days there was no such thing as a mixed group, so he played while hiding behind a scrim. That was before he went with Duke. After joining the band his growl became an integral and important part of the Ellington jungle sound. Nevertheless, for some reason he was in and out of the band I don't know how many times. This was all in the years before I joined the band so I don't know what happened. But he started something original and lasting. Any trumpet man in the Ellington band was obliged to learn to growl in the Bubber manner. And, of course, what Ellington's men did was emulated by other musicians. Bubber's influence was enormous.

Chu Berry was a big bear of a man and, as a matter of fact, he resembled a great big teddy bear. He was always in good humor and never had an unkind word to say about anyone. His given name was Leon Berry, his home town was Wheeling, West Virginia, and he hove onto the Harlem scene with his tenor saxophone. While he lived, he loved the life of a musician, late to bed and even later to rise. His favorite hangouts were Tillie's Chicken Shack on Lenox Avenue and the Victoria Cafe on Seventh Avenue, where they used to serve good barbecue. Later he'd frequent the Woodside Hotel along with the fellows with Count Basie's band when they lived there. Chu loved to talk, drink and eat, and if he could do all three while playing he was in his particular seventh heaven. As I remember Chu, he never was one to stand in awe of Coleman Hawkins. On a session he'd blow chorus for chorus with "the great one" and never once would he let up. One remark he made which I'll always recall was, "Shoot! I know Hawk's the greatest but he can't hold down but one job at a time, so I'll just keep on blowing and maybe I'll get that other job that he can't take." He would have at that, with his full rich tone, but Chu was killed in an auto accident in the early 40s.

Charlie Green hailed from Omaha, Nebraska, and, aside from his trombone playing, he was perhaps the strangest musician that I have ever known. The first time I saw Charlie, he was playing with Fletcher Henderson at a dance up in Harlem, the New Star Casino. This big and brawny fellow must have measured 6 feet 4 in his stocking feet. He was a roustabout type of fellow who didn't walk like other musicians, but loped along at a fast pace like an Indian brave. I suppose with his bronze coloring and hair he was, indeed, the descendant of some tribal forebears. That figures, since he always proved that he really couldn't take "firewater," even though he put away vast quantities of the stuff. When Big Green was feeling good he'd give you a big smile, and then you could see acres of gold-filled teeth in his mouth. But when he raised his voice it was a roar something like he was calling cows from way across the prairie, and rafters would shake. Still, I have seen him stop in the middle of Seventh Avenue on a cold, rainy night to pick up a stray cat or dog and bound homeward with it, cooing all the way. This was the other side of Green, and I guess it actually matched the inner portion of the man because, as loud as he yelled and as often as he invited a brother "outside" to fight, somehow nothing ever happened. His trombone style was different from all of the other fellows around town at the time, and about the only description that I can pass on with any certainty would be to label it a circus moaning-type of approach – guttural, simple, loud, but with definite overtones of the holy roller influence. That was Big Green, who toted a big pistol which he wouldn't shoot and drank enough whiskey to sink a battleship until it finally sank him. Yes, finally all that firewater got to him and he was found in a Harlem doorway, frozen to death.

Then there were a lot of fellows who never got the recognition they deserved. Another trombone man, Milfred "Miff" Mole, was, in my opinion, the most significant and at the same time most sadly neglected figure in the entire spectrum of jazz music. Many is the time I stood in front of the Roseland where Miff was appearing with Sam Lanin (Lester's older brother) and heard older musicians say, "That Mole kid is impossible! Why, he plays the trombone all wrong, jumping octaves, slurring when he should be sliding and ragging when he should be playing background." How wrong can you be? It was Miff's eccentric style that was copied and became the sound to try to duplicate. He was the man who actually turned his instrument, the trombone, around!

Dave Tough was a white Chicago lad and, any way you considered him, a hell of a drummer. Not only did he have good hands (all drummers will know what I mean), but he also had that inner sense of rhythm that has to be born in an individual, since it cannot be acquired out of books. Besides these attributes, Tough had a quality of perception that put a lot of drummers to shame, as he always sublimated his ego and played only for the soloist. His problem was reverse discrimination. When Dave first began coming up to Harlem, he had a hard row to hoe with the Harlem musicians. They'd let him sit in at Smalls' or the Savoy, but he was more welcome at the lesser joints such as the Mimo, the Bamboo Inn, etc. But, after he'd leave the drums, most tooters would find something else to do rather than drink along with him. This was sad, because I knew how much Davy wanted to be accepted uptown.

His rejection was partially due to his romance with a cute little colored gal whom most of us knew and respected very highly, although at the time we did not approve of their affair. And another large part of Dave Tough's motivation for being up in Harlem was because he liked the food, the easy-going life and especially the people, whom he said were not hung up with all of those neuroses. In any case, Dave was one of the few individuals who never hedged an iota on the racial question. He married the girl, with the resulting stigma that accrued to him at the time. It was the cause of his losing many jobs with the better orchestras. But Dave didn't care and proved that he was as tough as his name. He was a survivor.

Things have changed a lot since those days. Along with the musicians who left the scene too soon, there are a lot of other missing ingredients. I am speaking about dancing. You may well wonder what a chorus line has to do with reflections about jazz. The explanation is simple. Dancing, singing and/or playing an instrument in the same environment created a healthy rapport between these arts and forged an unbreakable chain of reflected creativity. We were all in show biz together.

I recall a type of theatrical show that had its vogue in Harlem but exists no more. At one time both the Harlem Opera House and the Lafayette Theater featured lines of dancing girls. These fillies of the ensemble were not merely decorative, they were the dancingest females in the world. They possessed a style which was not based on precision like the famed Radio City Music Hall Rockettes of New York, nor the ballet-influenced routines of the wonderful Tiller Girls of England. On the contrary, they created and executed steps which Bojangles, Astaire and other world-famous dancers would be proud to exhibit. What made them so outstanding was the ability and verve with which they beat that stage to a frazzle. This is not to imply that the chorus lines were the entire show, but I do say that their dancing held the usual melange of low comedy, singing and other acts (ventriloquists, jugglers, acrobats, etc.) together, so that the production jelled as a show should. There were many organized choruses on location in places such as the Grand Terrace in Chicago, the Royal Theater in Baltimore, the Howard Theater in Washington, DC, the Pearl and Dunbar Theaters in Philly. But there was no doubt that the true queens of terpsichore were the girls in Ristina Banks's number one chorus. Wherever you are, Ris, we still salute you.

The road was an institution of learning: learning to accept being away from home and all that that entails. It's hard on the ladies. And for all men who earn their living traveling on the road, there is at least one problem they have in common. The traveling salesman tries to solves it by hieing himself to the nearest bar. The bald truth is that every fellow is looking for a little intimacy with a woman. Where do you find one in a strange town? For the musician, the solution is simpler by the very fact that he *is* a musican, with all of the attendant glamor of being considered a celebrity, worldly, sophisticated and free with money. The females gather around a bandstand and are ready, willing and eager to make a date. Or at least that's the way it was when I was on the road.

To be honest, every stop on a tour didn't always turn out to be a holiday, as sometimes there would be great gaps in our search for a dame. Those nights, Tricky Sam used to be funny when he'd sing in his frog-like voice, "When the dance is over the hall is always clear!" This philosophy had to do with the front of the bandstand, which was filled all evening with flirting, questioning females who would vanish like Cinderella after the dance. To tell the truth, this was the exception not the rule, and usually there would be some amorous encounters. The ladies seemed to think musicians were romantic figures, almost like a movie star, and they wanted to know us.

Despite our traveling many uncomfortable hours, we had to project enthusiasm, tired as we were, and we usually did. But sometimes we had to pack up right after the date and start out for the next gig. To be factual, all of the fellows had little black books crammed with addresses and telephone numbers of fillies from coast to coast. But having so many friends in so many places sometimes tended to produce problems, some of which were humorous and others not so funny.

One of the comical incidents I recall was the time that we finished playing a dance just as the heavens opened all of the way and it was a veritable torrent. As we bee-lined it back to the hotel some of the brothers left with great glee, since they had made out at the dance. Others, not so fortunate, were morose because all that they had was an empty hotel room or the ever-present poker game. No one was going to venture out again in all that rain. Personally, I was neither fish nor fowl, as I did have a date but she had not shown up, and I wondered if the rain had killed my evening. So, taking a vantage point where I could spot my little lady if and when she arrived, I had a bird's eye view of a most fascinating sight.

The quietest member of the band sped past me with a very attractive yearling in tow. Evidently he was so enthused that, on reaching his room, he forgot to pull down his shades. So I saw him bring out his grog and embrace his chick at length. Then he went in the bathroom to shower. His little cutie, meanwhile, draped herself on a couch near the door, which was partially open. Lights, camera, and the action began. Our leader, obviously a wolf in wolf's clothing, was adorned in an elegant dressing gown. He strolled down the hall, passed the room and did a double take. He leaned inside the door. I couldn't hear the words, but the gestures told the story. Sure enough, his magical urbanity melted away the young lady's token resistance, and they disappeared from my sight. I thought to myself that there would be hell to pay, and I was so right, because when the quiet one emerged from his shower and found no girl, he let out a bellow of rage that was heard all over the hotel. As a matter of fact, I could hear him from the stairs where I stood.

It was amazing to me that he should have taken it so hard as, after all, she might have gone to the lobby for cigarettes or perhaps was merely vising in another room. But no! His crystal ball told him that he had been had and he was furious. Next he scurried up and down the hall, knocking on doors, yelling, "Wilma, Wilma, come on out baby. Wilma, where are you hiding?" As the commotion intensified, guys in various stages of undress came out to see what all of the noise was about. Every door opened but one, and, as I stared fascinated, I soon saw why. Brother Wolf's window was raised slowly and, in all of that rain, a small figure crept out on the balcony clad in what might be considered rain attire in Tahiti. The poor lamb had on only her slip! And then the door to that room was flung open, too, as the wolf decided he should let his room be checked to avoid suspicion. But, needless to say, the unlucky brother was not apt to look on the balcony. I don't know what happened next because finally my charmer turned up and, as I escorted her to my room, I mused over the vagaries of human behavior.

It was rough all over the country to find a place where a guy and a gal could get together and let nature take its course, but

Boston, as any real traveler can affirm, was a real blue law, puritan town. It frequently happened that the gendarmes arrived and broke down the door, hauling every tub off to the pokey. Even a fellow's private digs where he paid rent was not immune to this type of embarrassment. Sometimes a horny landlord or a jealous boyfriend chose to call the cops – anonymously, of course. I remember a period when guys who were caught in flagrante delicto were forced to marry, right then and there! However, where there was a will, we fellows found a way.

Despite the social attitude of the time, which frowned on interracial friendships, there was an amazing amount of mixed dating and marriage, even though the couple suffered a lot of slings and arrows from both sides of the fence. Part of the problem was that most of the clubs we played catered to white audiences only, so those were the only ladies we met while working. Of course, off the job I should also mention that there was another flock of young females, mostly colored, who tended to hang around our hotel and backstage, hoping to cadge a drink, a meal or just be near the glamor of the musicians. Yes, there were girls.

Back at the ballroom, I well recall a time or two when fate ignored the blue laws and current mores. The spark that would leap from a baby blue-eyed sister to a brown-eyed brother started a chain reaction that transcended race, creed and color. She flipped, he flipped. Love and lust had a way of by-passing the traditions. Yes, even in Boston!

William Saroyan is a gentleman whose writing efforts have always struck a responsive chord with me. He wrote – and I hope I quote correctly – that, to know a man, one must know his women. That is a profound observation. I must confess that I am amazed to have all but forgotten so many lovely females I have known. Well, a gentleman never tells, and besides it might sound like bragging.

I found the ladies when I was a young boy, and I do recall being simultaneously in love with Portia, Virginia and Ardrianne! Portia let me carry her books home from school for her; Ardrianne let me kiss her once at a kid's party; Virginia couldn't stand me in spite of my offering her my turtle, my candy, my ginger cake or anything else I had. Naturally, I loved her most of all – a normal attitude for a kid of eight, or even 80, perhaps. Later I was so enraptured with my horn that, for several years, girls were not in the picture. Then, while with *Go-Get-It*, nature or puberty took its course, and I was a sitting duck for that aggressive charmer whom I remember only as Little Bits, a dancer with the show. Between Little Bits and my next fling, there was a long dry spell sans sex, and I didn't even notice the lack. There had been an episode or two – Sweet Sue and Sweet Singer's "wife". And then, while I was with Billy Paige's Broadway Syncopators, there was Kitty, the dancer who wanted a man's watch.

Here's the rest of that story. She was a dancer in the show, and I looked at Kitty and she looked at me. After the first week I was courting, and after the second week I had moved in with her. How happy I was to hook up her gowns, bring her coffee and run errands for my Kitty! And, of course, there was all of that lost sex-time to make up for. I was so happy, knowing I was a man at 16. I even had my own woman. But paradise did not last long as my Kitty became more demanding than my young body could stand. Obviously she wasn't too happy with the situation and decided to break off the affair. Her method was a classic. She begged me to buy her a watch, and there was nothing unusual about that excepting that she insisted on having a man's watch. The very next night, one of the male dancers in the show called me over and asked, "How do you like this watch my old lady gave me?" I recognized it and stammered, "It's nice." He went on, "I'll let you in on a secret. You won't be seeing Kit anymore. We're leaving for Philly at the end of the week, so see that you don't bother her in the meantime." It seemed that the fellow meant business, and I was worn out of love, anyway. I just went to the bar, and reflected while I had a drink.

Evidently I was too good a fish to leave unhooked permanently, though, because in about six weeks Kit called me from Philadelphia, telling me she had broken up with that other fellow, she was sorry and she missed me so. If I loved her, why didn't I come down to Philly? I didn't rise to the bait, and told her to forget it, from now on my only romance would be with my horn, and that a horn didn't need a wrist watch.

It turned out that Kit was quite an actress, too. She hung up doing some real-sounding sobbing. Tears have always affected me, so after thinking about her for the rest of the evening I broke down and called her back. That's where I made my mistake. Within minutes I was on my way to see her. That old Pennsy couldn't get me there fast enough. She met me, we had breakfast, we made love and the only thing that seemed wrong was that she didn't take me to her home. The reason was, she said, that her mother was quite "sanctified." No matter, then. I spent my money having fun with her until it dawned on me that I didn't have train fare back to New York. I blithely kissed her goodbye, rode the train as far as Trenton and got off, not knowing a soul in the town. As I slunk down the streets, I cursed my pride for not asking Kit for train fare. Fortunately, a milkman making deliveries took pity on me, and I lugged cases of milk the rest of the morning to earn fare to New York. The moral to that story is, always keep train fare. At any rate, Kit married the other guy after all and wound up with a batch of children.

Then there was Romazina, whom I'll never forget because of her unusual name. She was an unusual gal, too, and even the circumstances of our meeting were bizarre. I was in Gimbels department store buying some shirts when, from out of nowhere, a woman grabbed my arm, saying, "Come on, John. Hurry or we'll be late." I was about to tell the woman that she had the wrong party when she winked, and I noticed a floor man coming toward us. I allowed her to steer me to the street.

On reaching the corner, she said, "Whew, that was a close one." And I thought to myself, "What a well-stacked little beauty!" She was about 5 feet 1, 32-20-34, with that rich red-brown mixture complexion that is seldom seen. Add to that a heart-shaped face with big brown eyes and a retroussé nose. Romy poured out a torrent of explanations without drawing a breath. She was a student at one of the better-known universities, her home was Martinique, New York was fun – especially the stores, which gave her a big kick when she could have something lovely without paying for it. Also, since I had been so nice about rescuing her, she wanted me to have one of the expensive ties that just happened to get into her purse. And did I know where she could get some black rum?

Of course I knew where to find Rum Negrito. And, if I hadn't known, I'd have made some myself. Before the rabbit could get out of the briar patch, there we were a-swinging in love. There were only two problems. One was to stop Romy from clawing me like a tigress when making love. And the other was to discourage her light-fingered excursions into the wonderful world of department stores. I finally solved the first by buying her some cute little mittens, which she adored, because when she put them on we were both alerted to her mood. The other problem came to a head during the Christmas season, when my little one went shopping without a nickel and returned with all sorts of goodies for me – undies, jewelry, etc. Then the plain-clothes man entered the scene. We both spent a few hours in the pokey until her counsel bailed us out and whisked Romy aboard a ship without even letting us say goodbye.

It was fun while it lasted, but thinking about Kit and Romy leads me to wonder if like attracts like – or is it opposites who tend to find each other? I had my share of kinky ladies, whatever that means.

Is it possible that we musicians just naturally tend to be a colorful and mysterious variety of homo sapiens? I suppose eccentrics abound in all strata of society. Yes, it is true that a few musicians did wind up for short or long periods in the loony bin. And there were plenty of odd manifestations among the ones who were otherwise quite sane. There were the fellows who felt lost without their lucky charms. I remember that Ben Webster had a special "lucky" ring that forever went into hock. Big Green didn't consider himself dressed without his gun. Dizzy Gillespie is a fine trumpet player and composer, but he elected to act the clown as a gimmick. To be honest, it has worked well for him so I can't knock it. And here's another one. There was a guy that felt he had to wear red socks all the time, even with his tuxedo! And there was the chap who presented an immaculate appearance, but his predilection for black shirts caused much comment on the corner where his musician chums gathered.

Coleman Hawkins amazed me when I played on Broadway with Fletcher. I couldn't believe my eyes when I saw Hawk pay two dollars for a cake of soap, which in those days was a ridiculous amount of money. As I recall, soap was usually about five cents a bar. What was really strange is that he used this expensive soap only to wash his face. The rest of his body had to make do with the ordinary cake. Another thing about Coleman that gave us a real yock was the time when we played a soft-ball game. Everyone came in old clothes and sneakers. But Hawk, on third base, was nattily attired in his boiled tuxedo shirt and patent-leather shoes!

Duke Ellington has been much written about and some of his foibles are rather widely known, such as his refusing to ever again wear a garment with a missing or loose button. And, as natty an appearance as he made on stage, backstage it was something else. Duke relaxed in a bathrobe of unknown origin with tired slippers to match, and on his head would be the inevitable stocking cap.

15

I Join Duke

Now it is 1935, I joined this fabulous band, and I had ample opportunity to learn at first hand about Duke and the other Ellingtonians. To be absolutely truthful, I didn't think much of the band when I joined, perhaps due to my receiving what I considered low pay. To my way of thinking, this was the band which had played the classiest spots such as the Cotton Club, made movies (*Check and Double Check* and *Belle of the Nineties*), plus playing all of the top theaters, etc. It seemed to me the salary ought to be a lot higher. Then, too, I didn't like their tempos or the music they played.

I recall one tune of that era that they recorded called *Rude Interlude*, which caused much commotion within the Rhythm Club set. Some of the guys thought it was great; others said it was just a bunch of noise. Chick Webb and Jelly Roll Morton almost broke up their friendship over *Rude Interlude*. Chick argued that the tune was unmusical and didn't swing, but Jelly Roll was equally positive that it was a beautiful mood piece and stated publicly that Duke was on the right track musically because he wasn't afraid to experiment. When I heard the record, I wanted to puke, it was so distasteful to me. And for once I mentally sided with the "Webb," which was a switch for me as I usually was only amused by Chick's strong opinions on music. In later years I am sometimes reminded of Chick's attitudes when I've read criticism by people who tend to be just as dogmatic in their remarks. The difference would be that Chick could play the hell out of drums and had first-hand experience and feeling, whereas the critics had none.

Now I was part of the Ellington organization and Duke

explained the various benefits of being with the band, among which was the glamor of Pullman travel. He stressed the many precedents the band had set, the style, setting and uniforms that he paid for, the bonuses which he gave yearly, plus the wonderful presents which Irving Mills gave every Christmas. So I thought, we'll see. But as soon as that train pulled out of New York, I began to feel like I didn't belong. I guess the clothes those guys wore made me feel self-conscious. I had a good 60-dollar tailored suit (pretty good money in those Depression days), but that wasn't in the same league as an 85-dollar Macintosh straight from Hollywood, nor did my conservative Boston shoes seem to belong in the company of the specially made shoes most of the fellows wore. I was really puzzled at my own feelings, because I had never been one to care what I wore as long as it was clean and neat. In fact, I hated to appear "sharp" ever since the days of joking at my expense over the purple suit. Whenever I could, I'd have some chum wear a suit or shoes for me, just so they wouldn't look too new! (I wonder how Freud would analyze that?)

Meanwhile, back on the train, my eyes bulged at the amount of money in the poker game. Now, I had been around for quite some time and had kibitzed at a lot of the ever-present poker games at the Rhythm Club, the Band Box and other places where the musicians frequented. And I had played poker in Smack's band, Horace's band and so on, but I had never seen so much folding stuff flowing in a private game since my days with the Spillers. And the people who played in those games were big celebrities, headliners. This was just the fellows in the band and the pot often came to hundreds of dollars. Most of the time there'd be two tables – one an unlimited stakes game and the other a 25-dollar table stakes game. They called the first one the Big Top and the small game the Side Show. Duke and Ivie Anderson were the rulers of the Big Top; they not only had the card sense and skill, they also had the money to make a faint-hearted player turn down the best hands when they decided to put the old pressure on. The Side Show was the personal bailiwick of the unholy twins, as we called Sonny Greer and Otto Hardwicke, whose apparent greatest ambition in life was to break up the game in the Big Top. And, in all of the years we played, I only saw that happen twice.

We arrived in Chicago early in the morning, went directly to the Ritz Hotel up on South Parkway and registered for our rooms, and continued on to the State and Lake Theater, in the heart of Chicago's Loop section. Up to now there'd been no rehearsal, so I wondered what music was to be played, but I didn't really worry because I was certain Duke wouldn't give me any real responsibility – not right away, at least. Time moved on until, at last, there I sat for the very first time in the brass section of the great Duke Ellington orchestra, completely bewildered. The stage was blacked out while Sonny Greer's timpani roared like a pride of hungry lions in the jungle. Then came the somber strains of *East St Louis Toodle-o* from the sax section, evoking a mental image of a giant python slithering up on the lions. Next came a sound which could be likened to a baboon cursing his mate; that was Cootie making the opening statement via his growling trumpet. This scene started behind a scrim and, as each sound came into focus, it would be embellished by a corresponding baby spotlight directed to the section that the sound came from. This lasted for about two minutes and it built up, chord upon chord, section upon section, until a giant dinosaur shuddered in the ecstasy of conquest. This diminished into a murmur with the chattering trumpet of Cootie slyly insinuating promises of sensual adventures to come. A fraction of a second of complete silence, and – wham! – came the Ellington tune *It Don't Mean a Thing if it Ain't Got that Swing*. Before the audience could catch its breath, the Ellington juggernaut was rolling in high before another captivated crowd of music lovers. Applause, applause, applause.

On to the next facet of this multi-jeweled entertainment. There was another band number. As I reflect back on those years, it may have been *Stompy Jones*, written and dedicated to Richard Bowden Jones, the greatest prop man, valet and light-board operator that any traveling band ever had. Jonesy was untiring, alert and utterly devoted to the band, especially to Duke.

Above: Rex's maternal grandparents, Angelina Fawcett Denby Johnson and George Johnson; below left: Rex as a young man; below right: Rex's mother, Jane Johnson Stewart

Willie Gant's orchestra at Smalls' Paradise, 1924 (left to right): Billy Taylor, Willie Gant, Ward Pinkett (behind), Happy Caldwell, Rex Stewart, Mainzie Johnson, Fred Skirrett, Joe Williams, Johnny Lee, Son Adams

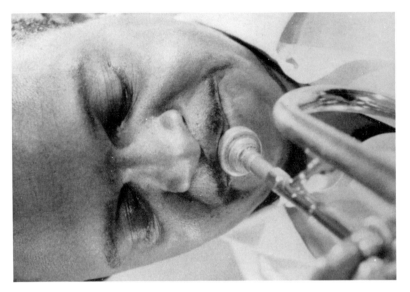

Two early portraits of Rex

The Ellington band on stage, with dancers from the show

Above: The Ellington trumpet section: Rex, Cootie Williams and Artie Whetsol; below left: Rex, Harry Carney, Ivie Anderson and Hayes Alvis at the microphone; below right: Rex taking a solo

Above: Members of the Ellington band (back row, left to right): Sonny Greer, Fred Guy, Rex, Cootie Williams, Tricky Sam Nanton, Juan Tizol, Lawrence Brown (hidden); (front): Johnny Hodges, Otto Hardwicke, Harry Carney, Wallace Jones; below: Rex with Sonny Greer, Tricky Sam Nanton and Jimmy Blanton

A signed photograph of the "Blanton–Webster" Ellington band

Rex after he had left the Ellington band

Above: Rex and friends at the Milan Hot Club, May 1949; below: Rex with Sidney Bechet and Earl Hines at the Victor studios in Chicago, 1940

Above: Rex Stewart and his orchestra, 30 July 1945: Brick Fleagle (guitar), Dave Rivera (piano), Rex, Earl Bostic (alto saxophone), Junior Raglin (bass), Cecil Scott (baritone saxophone), Tyree Glenn (trombone, vibraphone) and J.C. Heard (drums); below: Three of the Henderson All Stars: Paul Webster, Emmett Berry and Rex

Rex's cabaret card

A late portrait of Rex

Above: Rex with his daughters Regina and Helena; below: Rex cooks for friends in Geneva

Rex at Condon's club in Greenwich Village

Rex with Henri Chaix (left) and (right) Jacques Bisceglia

Above: Rex with a quartet; below: Rex shortly before his death

Before I continue, let's look back into an average day for Jonesy. We are leaving for Detroit on the Detroiter, which was a crack New York City train. We'd just closed the Roxy Theater in New York and were headed for the gin mills or home. But not Jonesy. He had to stay right at the theater until the transfer company picked up the baggage. And what baggage! Sonny Greer had six huge trunks for his clothes, timpani, cymbals, vibraphone and drums. Ivie carried three trunks, one each for stage gowns and street clothes and a special trunk for coats and shoes. Then there were the trunks for scenery and the light console. The microphone and sound system were in separate trunks. This was only the beginning. Still to come would be the three uniform trunks, the shirt trunk, instrument trunks, plus the personal trunks of each fellow. Duke also carried five personal trunks and an especially made trunk for his shoes! Oh, I almost forgot the music stand trunk and the trunks for music. As these were not the ordinary traveling trunks, Jonesy would pitch in loading the trunks. Since the express men worked by the hour, it was up to R. B. The quicker they loaded, the sooner he could get some much-needed rest.

It was also part of his duties to get everybody aboard that train on time, a chore necessitating a lot of running from one part of town to another, checking and double-checking the various after-hour spots, conditions of sobriety and overall awareness of train time. This action went on in every town, rain or shine, balmy or blizzard. R. B. J. was Johnny on the spot, Duke's A number one chargé d'affaires.

There was a lot more to Jonesy's job. After we hit a town, he'd help set up the stage and lights, then check the linen, send out the costumes to be pressed or cleaned, and inspect Ellington's wardrobe and try to anticipate what the Duke would want to wear, which was a chore by itself. Then Jonesy was free to cat nap until we arrived with our shouts of "Jonesy, where is this or that?" "Can you find some coffee?" " Hey, R. B., get us a sandwich." And, above all of the din, there'd be the stentorian roar of the boss, "Jonesy, where in the hell is that jacket I bought in Chicago? You know, the beige one?" When that voice sounded, R. B. dropped everything and dashed off, mumbling,

"Geezus X Christ, I ain't but one man." But what a man he was! He loved the band and worked and worked until he dropped dead in LA many years later.

I got so involved that I forgot to continue telling about my first date with Ellington. The stage show went on. Let's see, after the two numbers came a dance group, someone like the Four Step Brothers or Tip Tap and Toe. I'm not sure who it was; it could have been one of so many. I do recall that next on the program was something slow, maybe *Black and Tan Fantasy* or *Mood Indigo*, both of which ended with a black-out. The next thing I knew, the lights came up and Duke was making his usual flowery assortment of well-chosen words, introducing Spencer Williams's composition of *Some of These Days*. I was so absorbed wondering what in the world Ellington would do with this tune that I didn't hear him call my name.

The band went into an introduction that sounded like the *William Tell* overture, and I was trying to figure out what was supposed to happen when all of a sudden Cootie nudged me with his elbow and said I was on! Duke stood at the piano giving me his well-known "show me" smile. The tempo was way up as I edged to the microphone, tentatively trying to find out what key they were playing. Then, as my ear and fingers coordinated into the melody, Duke left the piano and whispered to me, "Sing the next chorus and play two out-choruses. You know, like Louis." The only words I could come up with were "Some of these days . . ." mumble, mumble, scat, mumble, scat. Then, at the finish, I hit a high C and held it. But the band then hit a series of chords which I had to scramble to find notes to fit. After what seemed like hours of this, I hit an altissimo A, the band for once made the same chord, and I was home free, covered with sweat that poured out from everywhere. That was my initiation into Duke Ellington's band and, if I expected any praise for getting myself off the spot Ellington had put me on, I was certainly mistaken. Nobody said a word and it was years later when I mentioned the episode to Duke that he told me, "I wasn't concerned. I knew you could do it. That's why I picked you for my band."

Duke, of course, I had known since I was a boy. The first time

I remember meeting him might very well have been our last. On a hot summer day I was wistfully fooling around the YMCA swimming pool and fell in. I was pulled out by an older fellow who has not only forgotten all about the incident but swears he can't swim! That was Ellington.

The next time our paths crossed there was an event which we both recalled in later years with much amusement. At the time, my family had moved to Georgetown, another section of DC. And the big social event was the Saturday night dance. All of the little kids would shinny up the fence to peep in the windows of Odd Fellows Hall to watch the locals enjoy themselves. I was surprised to see Duke plunking away at the piano with some other fellows. This chance encounter sticks in my mind for several reasons. Principally, I guess, because it was the first time I had seen Eddie Ellington since I lived down the block from him on 12th Street. Then a fellow named Tobin amazed all of us kids by playing a C-melody saxophone that night. It was the first time we had even seen a sax. The climax of the dance was the funniest scene because we heard them play the customary *Home, Sweet Home*. And the next thing we knew, the fellows in the band were making a break for the street for safety, and Duke led the parade. And I don't blame him. The fellows in Georgetown played rough. In those days, all too often you had to fight for your money, especially if, for any reason, a crowd failed to fill the hall. I don't remember exactly whose band it was, but I do recall that Otto Hardwicke was playing string bass, Duke was on piano and Tobin was on the C-melody sax, while a fellow known as Stick-A-Makum was the drummer. He was a hero in our eyes as he stuck by his drums that night.

I really became aware of Ellington when I graduated from Policeman Johnson's kid's band and started hanging out with the other tooters on the corner of 7th and T streets. Louis Brown the piano man, Doc Perry, Elmer Snowden, Sam Taylor the pride of the Southwest bootlegger set, and many other musicians hung out there, including Stick-A-Makum.

Now, I have read many stories about Duke and his early beginings in elegance, but here's one that's never been told, to my knowledge. It was the custom back home to really extend yourself on Easter Sunday morning. Folks who as a rule paid no attention to their clothes got all spiffed up for that occasion. To a large extent, this was a Protestant town and it would take a more serious scholar than I to explain why the end of Lent would have so much significance to the colored people. In any case, there were always parties galore, dances and, of course, the annual Easter promenade, for which everyone planned months ahead vying for the compliments that would be their reward.

In those days, the fashion in DC was to have a tailor-made suit with some feature that no one else was wearing. One memorable evening Ellington astonished everybody by strolling up to the corner attired in a shimmy back herringbone suit (this was shirred and pleated in the back). To all of the style-conscious musicians, Duke was considered the epitome of elegance from then on.

The next time I saw Duke he was playing with a group of piano players at Convention Hall. My memory is a bit dim as to which other fellows were in the huge aggregation. There was the great James P. Johnson and a few others. I remember Emory Lucas because he was a friend of my family.

Since those days I've read that Ellington started his career at the Poodle Dog playing the *Soda Fountain Rag*. But I go back farther than that, back to the days when Duke was the king of Room 10 at True Reformers Hall.

I had been in New York about two years before the Elmer Snowden band with Duke Ellington arrived on the scene. When we met again there was a kind of moist reunion. Not a big-time thing, as I was still a kid to Duke, Sonny, Elmer and Toby. In fact, I didn't become accepted as an equal until I played with Fletcher Henderson a few years later. When I joined the Ellington band, there was the usual outcry from the trade magazines and dyed-in-the-wool fans, just as there was when he selected Lawrence Brown. According to these aficionados, neither Stewart nor Brown fit, and could only destroy this perfect instrument. I must confess that I could identify with this feeling later when I heard that so and so was joining the organization. But Duke always knew what was best for his band, I've found out.

Lawrence Olin Brown played a golden-toned horn which long ago catapulted him into the select hierarchy of creative innovators. Larry, in appearance, resembled the Baptist minister who has wandered into the wrong place seeking converts more than he looked like the popular conception of a jazz musician. He was a handsome man, always immaculately dressed. And his personal life bore no relation to the image his horn conveyed. He neither drank nor smoked, he used neither slang nor profanity; and he seldom bothered to smile except through his instrument, which expressed all of the emotions ranging from savagery to tender, sensuous love for humanity. That's the Lawrence Brown that we used to call "Rev" – short for Reverend.

There were many fascinating and intriguing nuances contained within the individuals themselves, over and beyond the public image of the band at that time. For instance, another man in the trombone section was the unforgettable Joe "Tricky Sam" Nanton. He was the epitome of earthiness when he soloed on his trombone, but quite the opposite in private life. He was a keen and pungent observer of human foibles (including his own) and a witty philosopher who wore Brooks Brothers suits long before they became popular. And he was a virtual storehouse of facts and figures about scientific and sociological matters that constantly amazed me. In short, Tricky was the thinker, the reader and a complete chameleon. Years later, after being advised that continuing to drink booze would be fatal to his health, he just shrugged off the whole thing and went ahead having his ale whenever he felt like it.

Then, rounding out the trombone section, there was Juan Tizol from Puerto Rico, whose pure white countenance made him stand out like a blob of sour cream in the middle of a bowl of black caviar. He had arrived in the United States with Marie Lucas, an outfit playing light classics, and at first seemed a strange choice for Ellington. But he truly was a very important cog in the Duke's wheel, because he did all of the extractions of Ellington's voluminous writing efforts. This was no easy chore, as oft times Duke would attempt to write things that really couldn't be written! Then Juan would scribble a facsimile and spend hours interpreting what the boss intended. Before leaving Juan, this seems to be a good place to puncture another myth about the band. For years, musicians and the public were allowed to think we achieved those spectacular musical effects by osmosis. But such was not the case. Almost everything we did was written and was the result of hard work plus research colored with imagination. And it was Tizol, with his extensive musical education, who was frequently the catalyst.

After I grew accustomed to the stage routine, the dance book was the next problem, because there was so little continuity in the written arrangements. You had to sit in the band, listen, and ask many questions before anything made sense. I'll explain. In most orchestras the starting point is the upper left-hand corner of the music, and you proceed right down through the pages, sections A-B-C-D, etc. But not in the Ellington band. First of all, there seldom was a count-off, down-beat or anything like that to indicate the tempo. Most of the time Duke would start playing a sequence on the piano (that was to let us know what tune we would play). This might be a few bars or it could go on for a minute. Then he'd look up toward the band and play a progression which indicated when to start. Nobody explained this to me and it didn't help a bit when I looked around to see what music was on the other guy's stands. Everybody memorized their parts. In this band you had to. Without Cootie guiding me from number to number, I really would have been lost.

I've noticed, though, that, the better the band, the less reliance the musicians have on written notes. By that, I mean that well-schooled men could retain their respective parts in their heads – and I'm talking about a large quantity of music. I generalize because I first saw that in Smack's orchestra, later in Ellington's group and again, years later, when I played society music with Lester Lanin in New York.

After two months with Duke I was still constantly being made aware that I was a junior member and as such was not entitled to the privileges of the older members. And, although I felt that there was a lot of justice involved, still I reasoned that

I outranked some of the fellows and was on a par with others, because I had been the featured, if not the starring, player with the first of the big-time orchestras. So now that I'd proved I could carry my own weight with Eddie, as I had always called him in Washington, I tried to explain all this and suggest that I was entitled to a raise. But he'd only get that spaced-out look on his face and say something vague like, "We'll get together." Things went on like this until, one day in a theater, Otto asked me if I wanted to buy his trunk for 75 dollars, which was a bargain. He wanted to sell his so that he could buy a new one costing 200! I told him I'd think about it, knowing full well it would take a miracle for me to send money home, maintain myself and also to buy a trunk for 75 dollars when I was only earning 75 dollars a week, notwithstanding his earlier promise to pay more.

I tried to get a 75-dollar advance loan from Jack Boyd, who had recently been promoted to band manager after Sam Fleishnick left. But Boyd told me, nothing doing. Next I kept the money I was supposed to have sent home and tried my luck in the poker game, the so-called Side Show where the stakes were much smaller. Now, to me, stud poker is perhaps the greatest card game devised by man. There's room for everything from bravery to cowardice, and tragedy to humor. A good player can and will beat a lesser player in the long run. Then, on the other hand, even a Nick the Greek can be the loser if the cards do not run to him. This night, everything went against me. If I had a pair, someone else had three of a kind; if I low-dragged aces back to back, another guy would win the pot with two pairs or a flush. So after a few hours I was broke. The combination of frustrating circumstances overwhelmed me and I became more and more morose and unhappy.

The next morning, boarding the train on the way to the next town, I looked high and low for Ellington. However, when I finally found him he was in no mood to discuss anything. He got that glazed expression in his eyes which he had a way of doing to avoid a discussion. But I told him anyway that I wasn't going any further on this salary. Duke merely grunted something and pulled his hat down over his eyes. The insouciant nonchalance of this gesture was just too much for me to take in my lousy mental state, so I got my little horn and my two suitcases together, told Jonesy to forward my mail to New York and started to get off the train. I was halfway up the platform when Tizol came up behind me and laughingly said, "Hey, wait a minute, man, where you going?" So I told him, "Back to New York on the next train out." Then he advised, "Don't be a damn fool. If you want to quit, give two weeks' notice. Do it the right way and Duke will pay your train fare."

That made good sense, especially as it dawned on me that I had lost all my dough in the poker game and was in no position to go anywhere. As I stood there wondering what to do, the porter yelled, "All aboard," and at the same time Juan said, "Get on the train. You'll get more money. Why, Rex, Duke likes you. Just you wait until he wakes up and then ask him again for that raise." Sure enough, Juan was right, because while I was sleeping Duke shook the curtain of my berth, stuck his head in and said, "Now what was that you were saying Fat Stuff?" (that was Duke's private nickname for me). I told him my beef about needing more money and right there he gave me a 25-dollar raise, starting that very week. And he also remarked that, from now on, I was to have a lower berth because, if he had to pay me senior money, I might as well have all of the privileges.

On reflection, and I've given this a lot of thought, Ellington is the most complex and paradoxical individual that I've ever known. He is completely unpredictable, a combination of Sir Galahad, Scrooge, Don Quixote and God knows what other saints and sinners that were apt to pop out of his ever-changing personality. The above are the facets which he permits to be observed. Deep down under this facade there is the devout man, the one who reads his Bible every day and the caring family man who never forgets for a minute the ones he loves. And, at the same time, rarely did he forget or forgive anything. I could go on and on trying to describe this indescribable man, but the narrative would suffer, so I'll return again to my thoughts about the band.

One of the best things about joining the Duke's organization was that my boyhood buddy, Billy Taylor, joined about the same time, playing bass fiddle. Billy's parents and my mother had been friends in Georgetown ever since I can remember. I guess we met when I was about eight years old, and we grew up together sharing many kid experiences, like swimming, fighting, hooking pies off the pie wagon and "borrowing" fruit from the neighbor's trees.

There was one such incident that I always laugh about when I think of it. One hot summer day Billy and Stewardie sneaked out to Rock Creek to cool off, with Billy's little brother, Teddy, tagging behind. Since the Taylors lived on 27th and D streets, we took the most direct route, straight between two cemeteries, which we didn't mind as long as it was broad daylight. There were just the three of us, and we cavorted for hours, only pausing to push a hunk of night soil (human excrement), a floating log or a water moccasin out of the way. Ordinarily, we wouldn't have stayed as long as we did because we'd have been lured home by hunger. But little Teddy, evidently trying to prove that he belonged, had brought along a paper bag of boiled white beans. We heated them in an old tin can, then we went back to more swimming.

The sun was going down and Teddy was almost in tears as he pleaded with us, "Come on, let's go home." We didn't pay much attention until we heard a strange noise which came from somewhere nearby. Then, abruptly, all of the sounds of crickets, birds, etc. stopped. It seemed as if everything was listening. We, too, held our breaths, staring at Teddy, who was pointing at something which we could barely make out, something white at the very top of the big tree. Teddy yelled, "Oh my, oh my. Now will you guys come on home! What is that, Billy? Billy, please tell me what's that, up there in the tree." Then whatever it was let out another unearthly sound, a cross between a cow mooing and steam escaping from a boiler. Billy looked at me and I looked at Billy. Then we took off. I bet Superman or Flash Gordon would have had competition that evening, as in nothing flat we grabbed pants, shirt and shoes, and without even putting any clothes on we jetted up that creek bank, straight through those cemeteries and down 27th Street. The closer we got to Billy's house, the faster we sped, ignoring poor Teddy's wails of "Wait for me! Wait for me!" All of this loud commotion drew lots of people to their doors and they saw the spectacle of three lads tearing up the street, clad only in their bathing suits.

A little bit later on, Billy got us both a job at the swank Army and Navy Club as bus boys, which is actually the first job I'd ever had. I don't remember what we were paid, but I do remember enjoying a cup of coffee, a beverage I was not allowed at home. And I recall a dirty trick that was played on me by the captain of waiters. It happened like this. We quickly caught on to our duties as bus boys. Then the manager of the barber shop asked us if we'd like to earn some extra money shining shoes after we had finished the other job. Billy couldn't, because his dad was very strict with him – he wasn't allowed to sell papers or shine shoes. And neither was I, for that matter. But when I thought about all the goodies, the apples on a stick, the cakes and cookies I could earn, plus hoping I could save up enough for a baseball mitt, I was for it. Getting back to the nasty trick, there was this red-headed captain who didn't like the way I spoke, nor did he care for the way I'd answer right back when spoken to. So he rode me in a kidding way and would mimic my speech. At first I didn't catch on, until Billy warned me to watch out for this guy and that I should try not to speak so proper. My manner of speaking must have been unusual because the fellow started calling me "Perfessor," which I should have ignored. But no, old stick-his-foot-in-it Stewardie had to pop up with "The word is '*pro*fessor' if that's what you mean."

Well, that did it. I had made my first of a lifelong string of enemies. And, when he found out that I worked in the barbershop, he'd come in, get a shine and never pay for it. I went along with this the first few times, hoping to erase the past friction between us. Then I decided, "Nuts to this! Everybody else pays so why shouldn't he?" When I told him he owed me a nickel, he gave it to me. Then the very next morning he got his revenge when he walked up to me, holding a brown whiskey bottle in his hand and saying, "Want to smell something good?" "Sure," I answered, and took a deep whiff. Next I found myself getting up from the floor. It had been concentrated ammonia! Maybe there's a moral somewhere in the story, but I never found it. Anyway, soon after that Billy and I went back to school and I never saw the guy again.

Now I was really delighted that my old buddy Billy Taylor joined the Duke too, although at first I was apprehensive for his sake because there already was a bass player – Wellman Braud from New Orleans. I worried about how the two basses would get along. First of all, no orchestra that I'd ever known carried two bass players. Then, too, I had noticed that most musicians from New Orleans considered themselves far above anybody that wasn't from "home." But it turned out that I was completely wrong in the case of Braud, because he took us both under his wing and was as helpful as anybody could possibly be. He told us all the scuttlebutt, past and present, approximately how much salary everyone made, where the band had played and all sorts of interesting things. It was just the kind of information we newcomers needed to begin feeling like we were really part of the band.

Mr Braud was a very interesting man, and thinking of him reminds me of the passage of time since we first met. I was in my late 20s at the time I joined Duke and Braud must have been about 43. He commanded considerable respect, partly because he was older than most of my contemporaries and the fellows who hung out at the Rhythm Club. I used to see him there resplendent with his gold-headed cane, his immaculately tailored suits, always set off with a vest of some exotic material. All of this added to his bearing, which reminded me of an elegant military man.

However, once I saw him lose his dignity when he chased John Kirby down the block and broke that beautiful cane over John's head. It turned out that Kirby had borrowed a bass fiddle from Braud and refused to return the instrument or pay for it. The years have passed, but this gentleman, who appeared like a patriarch to me when we first met, seems not to have aged a bit. Rather, it is as if I grew older while Braud did a Rip Van Winkle, remaining unchanged. Is there something about bass players which encourages longevity? I think of the triumvirate

– Ed "Montudi" Garland, George "Pops" Foster and Wellman "Pickador" Braud (this was my private nickname for Braud, which started when Robert Ripley mentioned him in *Believe it or Not*) – who all stemmed from the same background and were born about the same time. I wonder if there is any possibility that the vibrations of the instrument could cause an inner sense of well-being that manifested itself in a form of serenity enabling them to rise above the average man, and escape the wear and tear on their bodies which afflicted the rest of us musicians? They sure seemed to have outlived the average band man, who, sadly, didn't endure the adversities.

For instance, when we were doing seven or eight shows a day, eating always was a problem. Usually there wouldn't be a restaurant near the theater which we were allowed to enter. And there seldom was enough time to get to the ghetto where we could be served and make it back for the next show. Braud liked to cook and sometimes put on a pot of his Louisiana home fare for our meal. His specialties were smothered pork chops, and red beans and rice. Occasionally, we bought pots and sterno and other paraphernalia to do a little cooking backstage. Braud and I were the major chefs but sometimes that didn't work out successfully. I'll never forget the time we were on stage and we could all whiff the strong smell of onions burning. Someone was supposed to watch the pot; I think it was Jonesy. Whoever it was forgot and we were responsible for a small fire backstage. The manager gave us stern warnings not to cook backstage again. Then we'd practically have to mutiny to get Duke to arrange for catered food to be sent in.

Braud wasn't the only man in the band from New Orleans. There was that soaring clarinet and tenor saxophone player Barney Bigard. Many a time I've heard him quickly lapse into a French patois when he met a friend from home. They had their special lingo that kept us out. But here is an instance when the "home" boys didn't stick together. Bigard loved to play pranks. During one performance Braud decided to make a quick switch from his string bass to tuba, unaware that his fellow player from Big Easy had filled the tuba with water. Braud blew a cascade of water on the sax section. It was only fair that it was Barney who caught most of the deluge!

Barney was among so many of us who were inspired to create melodies during those Ellington days. He has written enough tunes to entitle him to membership in ASCAP. Among his credits are *Mood Indigo, Minuet in Blues, Saratoga Swing, Saturday Night Function, Clouds in my Heart* and *Barney Goin' Easy*, which later became *I'm Checkin' Out, Go'om Bye.* I have no doubt that there were many others which he sold or gave away.

Having known and worked with these two fine New Orleans musicians, but not to denigrate either of them in any way, I think it is time to speak up and say that I, for one, am pretty tired of the New Orleans legend. It's about time somebody refuted that canard, the self-aggrandizing story that the music we know as jazz was born in New Orleans. The East Coast was surely settled earlier, with all of the diverse ethnic groups which we are told contributed to making the musical art form. It would have been unlikely that the East Coast waited until after the Louisiana purchase to evolve a folk music. This to me is unbelievable and illogical and, I believe, motivated by pure chauvenism. Let us not forget that this same music was regarded as only background sound in whore houses, and was calculated to stir the so-called baser instincts during the early 1900s. This is the same rhythmic syncopated free-style music which only became acceptable after the parasites discovered they could make a buck out of it!

I think back to my boyhood in Washington and recall hearing the many musicians who were playing ragtime and funk and other forms of music which were the forerunners of jazz. None of these people were influenced by anyone from New Orleans, as far as I know. Indeed, they didn't have a chance to hear the New Orleans sound, as they never traveled that far afield and this was before radio and popular records appeared in the 20s. Some of these early musicians are complete unknowns today. There was a trumpet player in DC, Dan Johnson, nicknamed "Georgetown," who was so great that every band who heard that horn wanted him to join. I shall never forget the Wilmington Bell Hops and Mose Duncan's Blue Flame Syncopators, who were out of Baltimore, as was Ike

Dixon. The Hardy Brothers represented Richmond, Virginia. There was Pike Davis, another wonderful trumpet player, "Baltimore," the greatest show drummer of his time, Allie Ross, the violin prodigy; and Catherine Perry, another violin great. I mention these names because they deserve belated recognition and also to show that there's something wrong with our haphazard approach to jazz history. There were a lot of other great musicians you will not read about anyplace else – probably because they can't be tied in with New Orleans.

And, I suppose most important, we who lived in Washington, Philadelphia, Baltimore and so on didn't hear and weren't influenced by the New Orleans style. Somehow talent emerged in those parts anyway. Who would like to explain away the enormous, unusual and irreplaceable talent of my boss, Duke Ellington?

16

The Duke and his Men

Slowly the picture started to emerge. Not only did I perceive vast new vistas in music, but, to my amazement, an entire new spectrum of emotional experiences unfolded. The voicing, the texture of this band thrilled me. It was then that I understood why Duke had hired the musicians that he had. For example, each sound, each instrumental intonation, had been chosen for a specific place in the framework of the ensemble. After that had been done, the master would, by trial and error, polish, mature and painstakingly fit the individual into his montage of melody and rhythm.

I often wondered why Edward K. would so passionately assert that his music was American negro music, because, to me, jazz, swing, bop or what have you was all a part of the same thing, labels notwithstanding. But, there again, after years of thinking it out, I bow to the wisdom of the man. By his refusing to be placed in any particular category, he could stand above his contemporaries and feel free to give whatever he chose to give of his fertile imagination, not on a competitive basis but more in the manner of a god descending from Olympian heights. And why not? He had removed himself. Let the world catch up.

All of this is not to try and present a beautiful portrait of Duke Ellington as some godlike paragon of all the virtues. Not by any means. Here we have a man whose heart, mind and spirit may well soar in the clouds. But, at the same time, there's ample evidence that he walks the earth as any other man, with faults and weaknesses, which, upon scrutiny, would tend to be magnified by virtue of his stature in other directions.

I can't for the life of me remember seeing Ellington in Jelly Roll Morton's audience, but it is not important since time has proved that they thought alike, not only musically but also in the awareness of the necessity for creating an image. Let me compare them further. Jelly Roll was always resplendent in a tailor-made suit. His attire was gaudy but impeccable, and he was the first musician that I'd ever known who changed outfits three times a day – and every day! That included suit, shoes, shirt, and hats, which indicated to us all how much of a showoff he was. Added to this seeming peacock-flaunting there were his expensive cigars and the fact that he only drank French brandy (according to him everything else was for the peasants). Diamonds sparkled from his belt buckle and his shirt front, a big diamond was on his pinky finger, he had a diamond stick pin, and the picture would be completed by the smaller diamond that glistened in his gold tooth.

Duke, on the other hand, was the product of a more urban environment and set out to project a dual personality. His first line of strategy was to always present an immaculate appearance, both for himself and for his organization, which he accomplished with great care. His clothes were avant garde but not flashy or flamboyant. He knew full well that the audience will see you before they will hear you. I remember his favorite shirt, which he invented. It became known as a "Barrymore roll" because of the long rolled collar. We all were fascinated by his original wardrobe. Once he had a black satin jacket enhanced by a weskit of the same material, which he wore with houndstooth slacks and black suede Quaker-type shoes complete with silver buckles. And another exotic outfit was the peach-colored lounge coat with a tie of the same color over a chartreuse shirt and pearl gray slacks, with shoes to match. Along with the great facade, as a rule he managed to convey a sophisticated, knowledgeable hip attitude. One of Ellington's gimmicks, which reaffirms his position as a hipster, is "We love you madly," a remark that he sprinkles with sassy abandon throughout his performances. As a matter of fact, he has overdone this particular saying, which both manages to emerge as a part of the same old hash but also bolsters his image.

As for Jelly Roll, he proclaimed his opinions to all who would listen, and he always had a large audience of big-eared musicians. I don't recall that he ever had a good word to say about anyone unless they played in his band. When I first knew him he had the band at the Rose Danceland, which was located at the corner of 125th and Seventh Avenue. In this group I particularly remember Ward Pinkett and Omer Simeon. Although the policy of the dance hall was lily white at the time, I got to sit on the bandstand a few times through my buddy Ward, but this didn't happen often as Morton didn't encourage visitors.

His real name was Ferdinand La Menthe, a Creole, and part of his feelings of superiority stemmed from the southern practice of giving preference to the mulatto and the quadroon, who were hired for the better jobs. His theory concerning the white man was that they felt safer with their own offspring around them. Morton was a rather tall, well-built, apricot-colored person with features that reminded me of a Spanish grandee who had become a bit jaded with life. His eyes were the most fascinating, as they darted from face to face, emphasizing those sometimes disputatious monologues. His favorite topic, outside of dwelling on how great he was personally, would be to tell us what a bunch of hard-headed kids we were, that we had no sense running around copying one another, and that to get anyplace you had to be different, or we'd wind up digging ditches. The man was pompous, a braggart, but I can't deny that he had vision. Here's an instance. He was a rabid baseball fan and knew virtually everything about the subject. I remember his stating that some of us would live to see Negroes in organized baseball, which made all of the cats on the corner break into derisive hee-haws of laughter. But he was right about that as he was about many things. The man was truly a prophet!

Starting from Storyville in New Orleans, his career spanned several generations. He exemplified everything that I had ever heard about the glamorous piano players of the bordellos, where they reigned supreme. He started his upward climb from there, winding up as a respectable innovator and creator of jazz (although he didn't invent the music, as he claimed). He clung to the older concepts, and his image, when I met him, was diamond-studded flash. To me, Jelly Roll will forever be on my list of those I consider the indestructibles: Charlie Parker, Clifford Brown, Fletcher Henderson, Bix Beiderbecke, Frankie Trumbauer, Jimmie Noone, King Oliver, Jack Jenney, Chu Berry, Don Murray, Fats Waller, Art Tatum, Bunny Berigan, Jimmy Blanton, and oh so many more. And of course the boss, Duke Ellington.

Jelly Roll's favorite theme, to quote from memory, was that thousands upon thousands would try to play *his* jazz, but only a few would be able to because it was a gift from the soul, given by God, and all of the teachers in the world could not teach it. A person had to be born with it. He also said, "Me, I'm not a church-going man, but I do believe in a deity and my belief is bolstered by the fact that the true gift of music comes in its purest forms from the underprivileged, the crapshooters and the whores, the hungry poor. You just can't play my music until you've suffered, and even then maybe you still can't." Here, too, was a likeness to Duke, who had a religious side. I don't know that he ever went to services, but he read the Bible devoutly every day. It occurs to me that he probably also believed his talent was God-given.

Sometimes one of the guys would needle Jelly just for the fun of it. Then he would really perform, pulling out his clippings, his contracts and his photos of himself with the greats of that era. He always had an audience and, to our uninitiated ears, his pronouncements and declarations were way out. "You little pipsqueak," he would yell, "who the hell do you think you're talking to? I'm the 'Jelly Roll'. I *invented* this music." He talked about the meaning of jazz. "See these diamonds? My music bought 'em. There's enough dough in these stones to buy and sell your whole damn family! Don't you try to tell me nothing about my music, you little no-blowin', hardshirt-wearin' sapsucker." And the crowd would roar.

Another of his favorite subjects was music publishers. How he hated them! He said not only did they steal his music, but even after they gave him a contract he still had to hire lawyers to see that he was paid fairly. Although at that time there were only a few phonograph companies, he predicted with frightening accuracy the emergence of hundreds of record firms earning millions, and, "Your share," he said, "will be one tenth of 1 per cent." I remember his saying that a Negro had to be five times as talented and ten times as smart to get an even break in the business.

Today it seems like a dream, because during that period the only market for negro music was the negro population. Yet Jelly stood on that corner (his soapbox was a lamp post on the southeast corner of 132nd Street and Seventh Avenue) and told us that the time was very near when thousands of phonograph machines would be playing jazz all over the world. I'll never forget that statement, and Happy Caldwell, my buddy who was with me, laughed long and loud as he remarked, "Old Jelly is bughouse bound. Everybody knows there's only about ten record companies in the whole country, so where's all them machines going to come from? And how many cats can blow enough to play on all of them records he's talking about?"

One unforgettable evening he was really on fire, saying that "The publishers are no damn good, none of them, and you studs better listen to me. Learn these rules. Write your music out, send it to Washington to be copyrighted and then hire you a lawyer to get you a fair deal." Jelly Roll also said, "Watch and see if some of those characters don't come up with some so-called new kind of music to get in the act, 'cause I ain't never heard none of them that was able to play my kind of music yet. Except a couple of piano players way out West."

Let's face it. Both Duke and Morton had bad experiences with publishers. Duke really did create a new music. Both men were hip, but Jelly Roll fit the description perfectly of being "too hip to be happy." He was one of the most gifted but controversial showy figures of jazz that I have ever met, combining the talents of a sensitive visionary with the crudities of the sporting world. He was composer, gambler, philosopher and, last but not by any means least, a lover boy, which accounts for his nickname. Where he came from, "jelly roll" didn't refer to cake. His philosophy concerning the so-called weaker sex seemed like contradictory ideas to most of us, but his attitude was not new to me because it prevailed among other sporting-house piano players. I have known many of them, starting with Stick-A-Makum and Sam Taylor in DC to James P. Johnson and Fat Smitty in New York. Their credo was to treat a lady like a whore and a whore like a lady! I don't know how that worked out, but that's what they said.

To continue the parallel between these two men, Duke, who really was a Casanova with the ladies, used a far more subtle, elegant approach. His musical talents are legend but his enormous success with fair damsels is less well documented. He must have made each one feel really special, as we would overhear him tell the evening's prospect, "My, but you make that dress look lovely!" and "You light up the room with your presence," or "You make this evening beautiful." The ladies ate it up!

In Jelly Roll's day it was the fashion for piano players to transfix the audience with a hypnotic stare, thereby creating an image and also a way of communicating with the people. It's no wonder I remember his proclamations so well. Jelly, wherever you are, I salute you. Your many proclamations and prognostications have been proven right!

Jelly Roll was garrulous and talked about his ideas so you could feel that you knew the man. But to see Ellington and to be in his company did not necessarily mean that you understood him at all. I do not intend to imply or state that I really knew the Duke, either. The man was actually like an iceberg that has a few facets to be seen on the surface, but so much more than one could imagine was hidden beneath the exterior. As I tell my story, I'll include several instances and circumstances with the intention of creating word pictures that should give some clues to the personality of Edward Kennedy Ellington.

Returning to the visual side of Duke, there was his attention to his image which I mentioned. I remember the traumatic period we went through when we hustled out of Chicago *en route* to New York's Roxy Theater. This was to be a big show headlining Ella Logan, who was fresh from a Broadway triumph. Our schedule was so tight that we only had three or four days to rehearse the show and get new costumes. By the way, the necessity for new uniforms was beyond me, as we already had several trunks full of gear. I recall that the fellows grumbled about wasting time with tailors when we could be resting or rehearsing.

The mad scene started as we rushed from the train to the tailors. Then came the fittings and lunch – but eat quick, we're due at the theater to rehearse until dinner time. We had not yet been home to our wives, but back to the tailor we had to go. Finally the day ended, and you can believe we were tired. The next morning about 9 a.m. we began rehearsing again until noon, then back to the tailor for a final fitting, which lasted until 5 in the afternoon. Then we got a break. We had three whole hours to do whatever we'd like until rehearsal at the Roxy.

Next on the program was dress rehearsal, a real rundown with everything in, including stage lighting. How I grew to hate those words "stage lighting," because Duke took one look at the new uniforms and disaster struck. That was one of the few times I've ever seen Ellington lose his customary cool. He ran out into the audience (the theater being closed at this time) and then rushed back on stage, yelling, "Where's Jack Boyd?" Jack was band manager but did double duty as our stage manager and electrician as well. "Jonesy, get me Mr Soblisky. Jack, tell those people on the light board that this lighting will murder our entire color picture. This is a catastrophe!" Appearance was that important to the Duke.

Duke was also the fellow who was entranced by the laws of physics in, of all things, a yo-yo! For years I kept a picture of Dumpy standing on a train platform, enjoying play with his toy. In later years the gourmet and voracious eater of the past was supplanted by the hypochondriac who gulped pills and kept on a limited diet of mostly steak, grapefruit and ice cream.

By any criteria, those were fantastic days, and I do not delude myself with nostalgia. I'd been with other big and important groups, but never before or since has there been the cameraderie, the glamor, the excitement of creativity, and a time when so many new doors of experience were opened to us. We played music such as had never been heard before at the

Stevens Hotel in Chicago, the Adolphus Hotel in Dallas and the Ritz Roof in Boston .

Not too long after I became exposed to this new way of life and new visions of music, the caravan headed south. But this was a South with a difference from my previous visits with other bands. This was that beautiful big region which was all too often sullied by small ugly people, and now we met all of the nice people. Still, I couldn't help recollecting that this paradise was also the home of pellagra, rickets, the poll tax, and several vicious red-neck politicians. But it is not my function to moralize, so I'd rather dwell on the health-giving sunlight, the beautiful girls in Jacksonville, the lovely flora and the beautiful girls in Atlanta, the magnificent horses, the sleek cattle and the beautiful girls just everywhere in the South. And let me not forget to conjure up glorious memories of gracious hospitality. There were after-concert parties in Texas, moonshine parties in North Carolina, bundling parties in Birmingham, naughty but oh-so-nice parties in Nashville; the pace was so swift and constant that we felt like we were on a merry-go-round.

It was almost a relief to continue to California, where we found the basic motivational drives vastly different from those of the South. In the South there'd been a give and take attitude, a "let's have fun together" style which was not true in Southern California, which seemed to have a more subtle, intangible clutching, self-seeking atmosphere. But to me it also was brand new and therefore fun. We played Frank Sebastian's Cotton Club, recorded and made a movie, and all of this activity made the money roll in.

More and more my mind opened up to Ellington's music. When concerts came into vogue, we played concerts at New York University, Colgate, the University of Wisconsin, the University of Pittsburgh, etc., in swift succession. More and more concerts. We were spreading the word. And the word was Ellington, the Duke of American music. He was the shepherd but we were not sheep. No, we were also shepherds in our own right, but his little shepherds – all-star shepherds. The band also did jazz festivals, which were a new concept in the early 40s. The first one was held on Randall's Island off New

York City, which predated the famed Newport Festival, to the best of my knowledge. In later years, as there were more festivals, I led the Ellington alumni at Newport and was a co-producer at the Great South Bay Festival which was presented on Long Island. For that festival I led the Fletcher Henderson reunion.

Reluctantly, I have come to the conclusion that jazz festivals rarely fulfill their initial expecations. By that I mean that, with all of the best intentions, so many intangibles are involved in the production of a festival that, when one does really come off, the sighs of relief can be heard from all concerned in the promotion, booking and public relations. The problems are the weather, artistic temperament, and the carnival atmosphere which is always present when a large group of talented people get together. Someone has to contend with their egos, feuds and mutual admiration societies, their snobberies, posturings and the sad and lonely, barely concealed envy of the out-group of musicians who were not invited to play.

An unbelievable *esprit de corps* held the Ellington band together for those many years. In a way, this was phenomenal, especially when one considers that we came from such divergent backgrounds with disparate degrees of musical training, heritage, and cultural environment. But we all learned to cleave together, think alike and play together as Duke's band. I observed many instances of that while I was there.

A fascinating aspect of the Ellingtonians would be their apparent disdain for what they were supposed to be doing, such as playing music. I can see them now, sauntering to the stand; the time is 8:40 and the band was scheduled to start at 8:30. Harry Carney is trimming a reed, Greer is about to finish setting up his paraphernalia. Some others are tuning up while Tricky Sam is heatedly making a point with Toby. Johnny Hodges is contemplating the scene, unsmiling and bored. Barney Bigard is jiving with Ben Webster. As for me, I'm reading, oblivious to everything. 8:59, there are a few scattered hand claps and Himself enters.

Did anyone outside of me ever wonder why some toothpaste company didn't use Ellington in an ad? What a smile he flashed! There he is in all his splendor, a few arpeggios, a speculative glance at the keyboard and chord, chord, chord, then into foot tapping. The chords tell us what the song is to be and the tempo is from the tapping. Whammo! A certain sequence tells us, let's go, and the band starts playing. But wait a minute. You are wondering when do the fellows get out their music? Okay, I'll let you in on a secret. The Ellington men didn't require music, except when we were running through and getting a new composition down. Everyone had the ability to commit the arrangements to memory and could virtually play the entire book in their sleep. But that wasn't true of all musicians, and I am reminded of an episode in Detroit when Billy Taylor, the bass player, held McKinney's entire band library for ransom. And here's how it happened. At that time, Billy and I were inseparable, so when he learned that I was returning to New York and Henderson he wanted to quit also. But his two weeks' notice wouldn't be up until after I had left and, on top of that, McKinney refused to let Billy off. So he hijacked the music trunk and told Pop McKinney to let him leave or there'd be no library. PS: we left together!

The band was full of unforgettable characters. Duke kept people who no longer fit or who were outlandishly undisciplined through loyalty, I think. Besides, it seemed that he hated out-and-out confrontations and just couldn't fire anyone. At least, I don't recall that he ever did. He seemed to have a high tolerance for high jinks and outrageous behavior from the fellows. It's just possible that these doings amused him.

"Hardwicke, Otto James," affectionately known as Toby, can be found on page 154 of Leonard Feather's illustrious *Encyclopedia of Jazz*, which, by the way, I endorse as required reading for any jazz buff. The necessarily brief biography doesn't give one a hint of this erudite sophisticate of the Ellington saxophone section. Toby goes way back in the Ellington saga, back beyond my first memorable sight of his scramming out of Odd Fellows Hall, clutching that big bass fiddle for dear life. But whenever the old gang that used to hang around True Reformers Hall in Washington would meet anywhere in the world, the "remember whens" would always get around to Otto and the gang's adventures with the Dupadilly, as Toby's old wreck of an auto was called. Although that was kid stuff, it still was colorful enough to become part of the Hardwicke legend. And, try as I might to pass on to you the stories about the gang's doings with and in that jalopy, I regret that I was not a part of that scene and can't remember anything except that many tales were told about those times.

In writing anything about Toby, my thoughts first dwell on his beautiful alto saxophone tone. Over the years I have heard thousands of saxophone tones, but none like Toby's. Generally a person's tone on an instrument tends to be duplicated, but there have been some exceptions to the rule. To me, no one has reproduced the saxophone sounds of Hodges, Bechet or Otto Hardwicke. If all that I could speak of in reminiscing about Toby was his tone on that instrument, that would be unfair to the man, as Hardwicke led several colorful lives in one span. There was the gay boulevardier in Rome, Paris and London, with emphasis on Paris, and the linguist (French, German, Spanish). One aspect was as the debonair bandleader of Jack "Legs" Diamond's Black Cat Club in Greenwich Village, New York, where he became the intimate of people like the famous bootleggers of those days Texas Guinan, Dutch Schultz and other mobsters. To this background we'll add his important role as lead saxophone with his boyhood pal, Duke Ellington.

Among the multitude of funny incidents that I know about Otto (which was always pronounced Oh-Toe), there's one that stands out, and I'll pass it on despite its being out of context at this point, because I don't want to forget to include it. During our European tour we were in the diner having breakfast aboard a Swiss train. Our attention, logically, was centered on the marvelous quality of the food. Suddenly the train surged to a stop and the Swiss escort for that portion of the tour yelled, "Everybody out! Here's where we change trains!" With a lot of scuffling, everybody snatched horns and luggage and made it off the train okay. That is, everybody except Toby and Sonny, who gesticulated through the window wildly as the train sped on its way.

You'll get the picture better if I tell you how trains operate over there. In the first place, their timetable for railroad departures is in a 24 hours mode and will say something like 19:04. It takes time to translate that to 7:04 p.m. Another upsetting procedure to me was the way the trains take off the very second an attendant yells, "Departee," or whatever the word is. What I'm trying to say is that there's no pause or slow pulling out as we were accustomed to on American trains. In fact, if you weren't alert or already aboard, you could be standing on the platform and miss the train!

We'll pick up on Toby and Sonny right where we left them. They felt they couldn't leave the train like everybody else because they hadn't paid their check. And they hadn't paid for the very good reason that they had no money. In the middle of the confusion caused by the unexpected and sudden change of trains, they couldn't get to the band manager to draw any money. Later Greer told us that Toby shrugged his shoulders, sat down and started ordering highballs. They must have highballed for quite a while. Eventually the waiter asked to be paid. But, somehow, they didn't understand him, as he tried French, Italian, German and English. Finally he went away in disgust. Then a Canadian couple, who had been listening in amused amazement, spoke to them in English, saying, "Come on, now. We know that you are Americans. What's the story?" And when the facts were related, these people laughed merrily and offered to pick up the tab for Toby and Sonny. But our heroes gratefully refused, saying, "There'll be money and directions at the next stop." Whereupon the woman, trying to have a private conversation with her husband, spoke to him in rapid French, saying, "Who but an American Negro would have the nerve to travel in Europe without funds!" Toby terminated the conversation by apologizing for any embarrassment that he might have caused them – in his very good French!

We all knew that Ellington had earned a reputation for sartorial splendor and reigned in his own sphere. However, the Crown Prince was undoubtedly William Alexander Greer, always called Sonny. But one of his appropriate nicknames was the Baron. We never understood how he was always able to present such a striking appearance. We all bought lots of clothes, but Greer changed suits almost as often as Duke. We wondered where he kept all these clothes, and there was speculation that some of those drum trunks were really full of Greer's clothes – unknown to Duke, of course. Sonny would sit up behind the band, elevated high at his drums, an enormous array of blocks, bells, chimes, cymbals, snares and so on surrounding him, looking like the king of the band. At least, he always sat up high until one unfortunate occasion when he arrived for work having imbibed too much and fell from his lofty perch.

One side to Sonny was his phenomenal memory for people, places and events. Lots of times people would come up to him and say, "How are you, Sonny? I'll bet you don't remember me." And, without a moment's hesitation, he'd reply, "Why, of course I do. Your name is So and So, we met at such and such a place, and how's everybody back in Pittsburgh, Oshkosh or Paris, France? Greer's standard gag was, "Tell me your name and I've got your home-town paper." Another fascinating aspect of "Long Branch's gift to the world" was his claim that he spoke fluent Yiddish. I never heard him, but he had such a gift for gab this was probably true. Sonny was also known for the speedy quip and sometimes rather salty repartee. Under the influence of the convivial bowl, Sonny emphasized his conversations with language that tended toward the gamey side. And Sonny liked the sauce. Many is the time we'd listened and cracked up as Greer punctuated a tale with several of the most foul four-letter words, followed by, "Excuse me, lady," and, if the female looked upset, Sonny would say, "Oh, to hell with this place, let's go somewhere where we can talk. Excuse me, miss." Still, everybody had a good word for Sonny, and I've always told him he'd have made the world's greatest host for a nightclub.

Now here I was playing with these fabulous characters. Under the influence of this colorful pair and some of the other high-spirited fellows I had an adventure or two, as well. Here's one bad experience I had during my early years with the band.

A bunch of us decided to cross over to Canada from Detroit where we were playing. Our object was to have a ball on some wonderful Labatts beer, which was not exported into the States. After a mighty bout with the brew we started back, and, as was customary, paused at the border for the nominal questions. When the immigration man asked me where I was born, I told him, in hell! I suppose I was trying to be funny, but the potent brew had dulled my judgment. Ordinarily, I would have had more sense than to have gotten out of line. But, throughout the gaiety of the evening, I was feeling somber remembering the news of a recent lynching down South. Needless to say, the customs man didn't think my inappropriate answer was humorous at all and was startled at this uncalled-for venom. He reiterated, "C'mon fella, don't get smart! I asked you where you were born."

Trying to cover my *faux pas*, I then said, "Mister, I was born in Georgia, and if that isn't hell for a black man I don't know where the hell I was born. You think maybe I just grew like Topsy?" By now he was obviously irritated with me, and wanted some kind of ID. Did I have a driver's license? Negative, I answered. Well, did I belong to a lodge like the Elks or the Masons with a card that would identify me? Nope. Finally he grew exasperated and said, "You must have a passport or other means of identification or I can't let you through." At that point I showed him my union card, Musicians Local 802 AF of M, New York. But by now he was in no mood to be lenient, and imperturbably took me to the pokey, saying I could damn well cool my heels until someone identified me. My smart-assed attitude resulted in my being held in jail until somebody did come down and identify me. It could have been worse. I only spent about two hours in custody, but that was another lesson I learned the hard way. It wasn't a smart move to get tanked up on beer when I was so steamed up about the lynching!

Since *Go-Get-It* I'd always loved playing for shows, and now we were about to do our first Cotton Club opening in New York since I had joined the band. I'd heard about the club but had never played the spot before, so I anticipated this event with great big eyes. The governor, as Duke was called by the guys in the band, had out-done himself in outfitting the band for this one. When we appeared on stage the audience gasped and applauded. We wore white mess jackets, boiled tuxedo shirts with wing collars, white bow-ties above crimson trousers and crimson shoes. That orchestra made a picture – a delight to behold! And of course the Duke personified elegance and contrast in his somber midnight tails. But, since nothing can be perfect, I inadvertently added the right touch with my battered beat-up silver derby hat that I used over my horn. At least, that's what I was told by Charles Addams the cartoonist many years later.

In speaking about the unforgettable group with Ellington, let me not forget to mention Ivie Anderson, the little girl from Gilroy, California, who was queen of the flock. Our Ivie wasn't a classic beauty, but how lovely she was to behold as she sparkled through every scene, her small, shy smile unexpectedly quickening into an impish bump or dance step. And this always made the audiences take her into their hearts. In later years she wore only white evening gowns, but what gowns they were! Ivie was another one of our group whose gorgeous wardrobe made a big impression. When she sang a melancholy refrain such as *Solitude* or *Mood Indigo*, oft times the fellows in the band would get caught up in the tide of her emotional portrayal and look sheepishly at one another in wonder at her artistry. The magic of Ivie was in her personality. Her voice wasn't great, but the moods she projected were fantastic. She did the serious songs in a way to make you weep. And she also did serio-comedy duets with the Great Greer (another of Sonny Greer's nicknames) which she carried off with all the aplomb of a grand duchess, making fans for her all over the world. Off stage our Miss Anderson was another person entirely, bossing the poker game, cussing out Ellington, playing practical jokes or giving some girl advice about love and life. Then sometimes she would sit very quietly, stoically battling the asthma which took her from us.

Ivie told us that she started dancing in small clubs in the San Francisco area, then toured up and down the California coast with a dance act. She finally married the boss of the act.

Together they went to Australia as part of a revue in which Sonny Clay's band was featured. I think she also told me that Buck Clayton, the great trumpet man, was in the troupe. After they had finished the Down Under tour they next hit the Windy City, Chicago. They played at the Grand Terrace Cafe, I believe. Then something broke up the marriage, and the early 30s found Ivie in New York, in the chorus line. The story continues that Ivie strong-armed Ellington into giving her the vocal spot with his band. This account may not be completely factual but it's the way I remember what she told us.

Ivie was also a great cook. About the time we did *Jump for Joy* and Los Angeles became home base, she opened a restaurant, Ivie's Chicken Shack. It was on Vernon, just east of Central Avenue, in the heart of the action. Needless to say, the Shack featured some very good fried chicken, long before the Colonel.

Ivie fit Duke's band to perfection, so much so that her spot has never been filled adequately by anyone else in my opinion. Sonny Greer, who was Ivie's stage partner, was one of the wittiest impromptu jesters in music. Together, Ivie and Sonny were a great team. Whenever I think of "Nasty," I am reminded of Eddie Condon, for whom I worked many years later, because he too had that same sort of spontaneous ebulliance that is so rarely evident.

Duke was much given to introducing a tune by telling a little story which described what he had been thinking when he wrote it, especially the ones without lyrics. There was *Harlem Air-Shaft*, which tried to reproduce the sounds a person living in a Harlem tenement might hear. He loved unusual sounds and was also a dyed-in-the-wool train buff. Consider, if you will, how frequently the names of tunes reflected his conception of being on a train. There was *Daybreak Express, Take the "A" Train, Happy Go Lucky Local*, etc. And, as much as we traveled by that Pullman train, it's no wonder.

When most jazz buffs think about Duke, they regard him as an orchestra leader, musician and composer. What is not common knowledge is that he also was also a lyric writer of no mean ability. Of all the things he has written, the greatest, to my way of thinking, was the blues from *Black Brown and Beige*. It goes "The blues . . . the blues ain't . . . the blues ain't nothin'. . . the blues ain't nothin' but a cold grey day," adding a new word each time. This was a most unusual construction, one I've never heard before or since. It was a real innovation and another instance of Duke's creativity.

I believe that the lyrics are a critical link in the chain of musical communication. A melody may evoke different moods to different listeners, just as viewing a picture will remind people of scenes and circumstances that the artist never thought of. But when there's a successful molding of music to lyric (or vice versa), a perfect medium of communication has been created. Hear the tune, you recall the lyric. Hear a few lines of the lyric, you know the tune. There's no question that the Duke and his many compositions have become a part of the common vernacular.

17

We Go Abroad

My first trip to the Continent almost didn't come off, for a few reasons. This was in 1939 and the newspapers were full of impending doom and the threat of war. "France Mobilizes, Will Hitler March?" ran the headlines. Mussolini sat in Italy licking his chops like a jackal over his unprovoked rape of Ethiopia. Chamberlain, umbrella at the ready, stood poised on the other side of the English Channel, confident that English diplomacy would make everything all right. And Hitler was angry with the world, threatening to spank it – like a naughty child. I thought to myself that if this bastard was small enough to publicly snub Jesse Owens, then what better indication was needed to discover what Hitler thought of Negroes? I didn't want to get any closer to that maniac than I had to.

The next reason I was not enthusiastic was that, having had no experience with the ocean, I didn't relish the idea of being cooped up on a boat for several days way out there on the high seas. Then there was the question of money. Everyone wanted more salary for a European jaunt, but Ellington became increasingly irritated whenever I broached the subject. So I told Duke, "I'll sit this one out and, when you get back, if you want me to rejoin you, okay." But he never could accept the idea that anyone didn't want to be with him. He pulled out all the stops being persuasive. The money that he offered began to rise like it had yeast in it. Finally I paid less attention to the newspaper headlines and began packing my trunk.

The gaiety of a bon voyage party can best be described as a combination Mardi Gras and New Year's Eve revelry. The Ellington entourage and fans really got into a festive mood for our departure. This was enhanced by the fact that we were sailing on the French liner *Champlain*, which resulted in many quips and toasts about "champagne on the *Champlain*." Joe Nanton took honors as "chief jester" that day. As he strode briskly down the gangplank, a full quart of whiskey dropped out of his pocket, crashed into pieces and sprayed liquor all around. But Tricky was apparently oblivious and continued walking without breaking his stride. The whole crowd of onlookers howled with laughter. Tricky's mishap provided the lighter side. Almost at the same moment, five nuns in their habits stood at the bow of the ship singing a hymn, as they gazed toward the Statue of Liberty. The scene was beautiful and fitting. I'll always treasure that special occasion which I remember so clearly.

Eight hours and a hangover later found me groggy but ravenous and eager to explore everything about the good ship *Champlain*. First things first. Shower, shave, shine. Billy Taylor, my roomie, had evidently been up and around for hours as there was no sign of him in our cabin. "I guess he's putting dents in the ship's provisions by now," I thought. He'd have no problem communicating with the French staff as he had thoughtfully cut out magazine pictures of ham and eggs, pie, steak and his other favorite foods!

The voyage was not boring in the least. As a matter of record, I had the time of my life enjoying the beautiful cuisine, the gay times at the various bars in first, in second and in tourist classes – and we tried them all. There was more fun in tourist than anywhere else, including our own second. Actually, I was quite amazed when it dawned on me how much I really enjoyed the sea, especially on those rare occasions when I was able to tear myself away from that soothing berth in time to see the sunrise. Often I'd run into Dumpy, as he communed with nature a lot more than people would surmise from his "I love you madly" routine.

After the first day out I gave my supply of dramamine to Freddie Guy, who needed it. I was having a ball, loving every minute of lurching on the lady *Champlain*. One thing I have noticed, starting with this crossing, is that the motion is different depending on whether you are eastbound or westbound. Now I realize this is due to several factors such as the course of the vessel, the prevailing winds and the ocean currents themselves. But, coming from Georgetown, this was all new to me. I became familiar with the ship's movement, which was from side to side on the New York to Europe crossing. I was surprised when we returned that the motion was an entirely different dipping and bobbing one. What did I care? Let her rip! Let her roll! Sailing is for me.

Prior to leaving New York, that eminent doyen of foreign critics Hugues Panassié was a dinner guest in our apartment. He told me at great length about the European attitude toward American jazz musicians. But having it happen to you personally is definitely more rewarding than being told. In any case, I wasn't at all prepared for the kind of reception that we received on our arrival at Le Havre. As I remember, there were a lot of people from all over France to meet us, members of the various "hot clubs," both fans and musicians, who all greeted us with such absolute adoration and genuine joy that for the first time in my life I had the feeling of being accepted as an artist, a gentleman and a member of the human race. My eyes were opened when I saw the special boat train that we rode from Le Havre to Paris because it was unlike anything I had seen before. Even as I write these lines, the closest resemblance I can think of is the monorail at Disneyland in California. The boat train, however, was not on a suspended rail, but the way it was built was similar – and don't forget: this was 1939. This unusual vehicle held about 50 people and was low to the ground. The big speedometer was plainly visible from all over the train. We erased our nervous tensions by chewing gum frantically as the instrument registered 80, 90, 100, 110, 140, etc. It went all the way to 200 before Toby, displaying his knowledge of things European, ostentatiously remarked, "The speed is calculated in kilometers, not miles." 200 kilometers is plenty fast, well over 100 miles an hour. We sat back, hanging on to our hats and hearts as this demon crashed on through time and space. Paris, here we come!

The arrival scene was like rush hour in New York's Grand

Central station, but magnified twice over. To meet and greet us there was a big contingent of jazz buffs and oh, so many pretty girls. One covey of beauties had the specific assignment of presenting bouquets to each fellow, starting with Duke and ending with Jonesey. I still marvel at the French fans' thoroughness and kindness. Everyone was made to feel a part of the welcome. Even Irving Mills (Duke's partner) and Jack Boyd, our road manager, were a part of the tumultuous welcome. Many other jazz aficionados and writers were on hand who had come from England, Spain, Belgium, Italy and Sweden. For the first time I realized the tremendous scope of this music and the general acceptance throughout the world from a cultural standpoint.

To continue, we first were taken to a sumptuous banquet, then to our hotel. By that time we were all as limp as a rag from fatigue. But la belle France, in the form of some of its beautiful daughters, was keen to project friendship. These girls wanted to know us personally. The telephones rang constantly with invitations for a *tête-à-tête*, luncheons, dinners or suggestions for a personally escorted tour of Paris. Some of these conversations were in quite good English and frankly alluded to an *affaire d'amour*, but, to a man, we politely begged off, as the spirit may have been willing but the flesh was weak and tired.

It was about noon the next day when Toby knocked on my door, saying, "Let's go. We're off to Montmartre. We're going to Boudons, Madame Blanchard's place in the rue Pigalle, where only Frenchmen and us musicians or artists and so on are welcome." What he told us was reminiscent of the Sphinx club. You entered a room which had a bar and you could get anything you needed from anybody. The sky was the limit. That included shirts, money, a meal, an instrument or whatever. The famous example I remember during the New York days was that of the fellow who borrowed a trumpet from week to week for about a year. And when he finally hit the numbers and bought his own horn, we celebrated our buddy mightily.

Returning to Le Club, as Boudons was called, it was the same kind of place. I guess we'd have spent the afternoon there with our chums, and why not? The drinks were flowing but the visit was broken up by a telephone call. Mme Blanchard summoned M Otto to her place of business. So regretfully we all lurched out and headed for more adventure – our first excursion into the city of Paris. As we passed down the dingy streets *en route*, I wondered, were we really in the famous Montmartre section of Paris? Could this be the scene that I had read so much about? The haunts of the talented, the weak and wise, the gilded lair of the players at life and lust? Habitat of the infamous Apache? If this was it, then it had been over-glamorized. Why, this looked just like Harlem slums! Then I recalled that the major difference between them was language, because both places are meccas for fun seekers and, at the same time, their drabness symbolized the decay of society. At least, that's the way it seemed to me.

And I wondered, why it is that this normal appetite (sex) is not recognized for what it is, right out in the open, as a natural part of life? Always it is hidden away in some dark corner of a city. The question I am raising is, why can't sex share an acknowledged position in society, in bright, clean surroundings, in a supervised atmosphere that would erase all graft and sordidness from this essential human urge? There would be a hell of a lot less neurotics, I'll bet. Don Quixote, that's me. But these thoughts faded as we stood in front of Mme Blanchard's, which looked like any other ordinary house on the street. However, inside it was something to behold, exquisite but subdued in decay. The walls were spectacular, covered with tapestries interspersed with mirrors and gorgeous paintings of beautiful women. Later I found out these were original oils by some of France's outstanding painters of courtesans. There were works by Vincent Van Gogh, Gustave Courbet and others.

Mme Blanchard turned out to be a short, dumpy female who greeted Toby with shrieks of delight. Servants came running with champagne for everyone. The fellows were wondering, where were the girls? Meanwhile, Toby and Madame had a long, lively conversation in French, until finally Otto realized that we hadn't been introduced to her. He apologized and explained his *faux pas* was due to their not having seen one another for so long. And we were presented.

At that very moment action arrived, as les girls turned up

seemingly from everywhere. As gassed as I was by that time from the pernod and champagne, I couldn't begin to describe this group of females. But I do know that soon we were all paired off, including the fellows who had resolved to remain faithful. Yes, I succumbed, too. But this was Paris. Besides, my wife of those times will never know unless she reads these pages. Anyway, this belated revelation is of no importance as the beautiful mother of my three wonderful offspring divorced me many years ago, telling me that nobody could compete with my love affair with my horn. Maybe the lady was right?

Our first concert in Paris was on the right bank, in the Palais de Chaillot. I believe it was then Paris's newest theater, only a year or two old, and I heard that it was built on the very site of the old Trocadero. As we were driven up, what a thrill to pass that Paris landmark, the Eiffel Tower! What also made this concert so out of the ordinary was the fact that the theater was two-thirds underground. The building also housed a couple of museums and another, smaller, underground theater.

Every so often I come across the rather tired cliché "truth is stranger than fiction," but I no longer scoff because one of my unforgettable experiences in Paris bore out this adage. It started when I wrote several tunes for a record session with the great Django Reinhardt. This effort won me the Grand Prix for the best composition in France for 1939. It was awarded for a tune I titled *Finesse*. We entered the studio – me, Billy Taylor, Barney Bigard, Panassié and Reinhardt. Actually, there was no written music. I had all of the tunes in my head – *Low Cotton*, *Montmartre* and *Finesse*.

I had jammed with Django the second night in town. A few of us were in a small nightclub being captivated by a battle of guitars – Henri Salvadore, as I recall, from Martinique, Oscar Alemán from Argentina, and Reinhardt. The air was electric, the champagne flowed and the magic of the moment is firmly etched in my memory. In retrospect, in some ways Django reminded me of Jimmy Blanton. The two of them had a way of smelling out a session and being there. I was so overawed by his virtuosity that it never occurred to me that there would be any communication problem at a record session, despite his not speaking English. And I was never so right. The gypsy picked up on the harmonies just as though he had written the music. A gesture towards the brandy bottle was all that we needed and everybody understood everything.

The world had heard him on record as an important member of the Quintette du Hot Club de France with violinist Stephane Grappelli. When Django played, his savage rhythmical impulses and tender romantic nuances were underscored by his driving, rock-steady beat. Django, in my opinion, was to the guitar about what Louis Armstrong was to the trumpet or Art Tatum to the piano. He inspired the playing and thinking of countless hundreds of guitar players all over the world. But he confounded the critics, who couldn't exactly label his work and were antagonistic toward this gypsy with a song in his soul. He was born in a small Belgian town and wandered the world in a gypsy caravan before winding up in his adopted country, France. In many ways this 6-foot guitar genius was his own worst enemy and a maze of contradictions. He insulted the wealthy and adored the poor. Women in droves threw themselves at his feet; society matrons and ballerinas adored him but he preferred the poulettes of the pavements. He married twice and sired two sons, one by each wife. Yet his allegiance was always with the cocottes. He was arrogant, yet humble; imperious yet kindly. He was elegant in his attire, but only if or when someone was permitted to guide him; normally, his inclination was to look like a left bank Apache.

Django doted on big, flashy cars which seldom ran. The French gendarmes respected and admired Django despite his getting besotted with wine and lashing out at the world with his fists. This happened rather frequently and resulted in his severing all relationships for the moment. He had a way of disappearing for weeks or months. It was speculated that he went roaming with his Romany tribesmen. When he finally chose to reappear, he'd smile like a guilty schoolboy who trusts he'll be forgiven. And the jazz world always did understand and welcomed him back into the fold because there was only one Django.

When we left Paris, it was the same tender scene as when we

had entered the city. We were sent off with a brass band, pretty girls, touching farewells – "Hurry back." As I review that departure, we were all glad for a rest from the constant galas and at the same time eager for the next stop – and their pretty girls.

Brussels, The Hague and other capital cities all offered scenic delights and old world culture. But they weren't Paris. The French had presented an enigma because their response ran the gamut from cheers to catcalls, as well as conventional hand-clapping. But, after leaving Paris, there was an amazing change in national customs. I, for one, was greatly surprised at the way we were greeted by the audience in Belgium. When we appeared on stage, there was a brief second of silence, then there was pandemonium in the form of hissing! I had never heard anything like it. After that I began to notice how each country had its own method of showing their delight. For the most part, however, hand-clapping was the thing. But I do recall several other manifestations in other places. For instance, in Holland, I think it was, the fans again created something special when they stomped their feet in unison. And I can't figure how, but they'd start in cadence, at first slowly, and I will try to indicate how this went. Each number represents a foot beat: 1+2+3+4 – 1+2+3+4 – 12345678910, etc. It was very noisy and thrilling. In Norway, it was still different because they whistled. This in itself was confusing, as in France whistling was a definite sign of disapproval.

En route to Norway, we had an unforgettable experience as we changed trains in Hamburg, Germany. All of the fears that we had had concerning the onset of war returned with a vengeance as we saw many hundreds of sailors, soldiers and other types of military in the station, all apparently on the ready for the inevitable dance with death. On disembarking from the ferry we were screened by the customs officials and those infamous lethal appearing SS guards. They were frightening to see in their jet-black regalia embellished with silver death heads on their caps. Even their attitude, their steely glinted, non-smiling frozen glances, said, "Here's death *à la carte*." But once we had passed the frontier, the atmosphere changed into the customary speculation, curiosity and even friendliness.

The most unexpected happening was after we boarded the train. Our coach was next to many cars filled with air and naval cadets, who tried to attract our attention by playing Ellington records on their portable phonographs. We ignored these efforts at first because of the many well-publicized statements the Führer had made condemning jazz in particular and Negroes in general. After a while, one youngster shyly crept into our car and, in very nice English, asked for autographs. Then the ice was broken. One, ten, 40 or more soldiers crowded in, and then their officers competed with the cadets in asking questions about jazz. I recall that one fellow had a record of McKinney's Cotton Pickers and wanted to know when the group found time to play such fine music and also pick cotton. He was crestfallen when I explained that they didn't pick cotton and that was just a name.

They also asked all about America, and was there really going to be a war, did we think? There was no way to answer this question that was on everybody's lips at the time. The war didn't start yet, but there was one event that evidently caused Duke to curtail the tour. I think this was on the way back to Paris. We were staying in Malmö, which is a large sea port in Sweden, when we were rudely awakened by several bursts of machine-gun fire. This caused all of us to get up, dress, and go from room to room asking one another, "Is this war? And if so, what do we do?" Joe Nanton, perhaps, was the most unperturbed, as he discoursed at length on the beauty of the porcelain stove in the lobby of the hotel. And I don't suppose he ever knew how close he came to being the victim of our wrath at a time like that when we were all worried sick.

I've witnessed many celebrations, but I doubt that I'll ever again capture such a rare moment as the Duke's birthday, April 29th, in Stockholm. After another triumphant concert and much schnapps with friends, we bedded down for the night and I started dreaming. It seemed I was in heaven, a heaven with angels singing oh, so sweetly. The sky was lovely and blue; even the air was perfumed with the beautiful scent of flowers. And just as I was about to kiss the most beautiful angel that I had ever seen, I woke up to discover it really was no dream. What I heard was the voices of 1500 school children, who were grouped in a garden surrounding the hotel, holding bouquets, serenading Duke Ellington on his birthday. What a night! What a soul-shaking demonstration of the love Sweden bore for Ellington! For once, a guy received flowers when he could smell them and enjoy being honored.

After our very successful European jaunt, the band started hitting on all cylinders like a wondrous musical juggernaut. Virtually everything we did turned out to be something of value, especially on records, where we were represented by the splinter groups of the Ellington organization, most given a fanciful descriptive name, such as, Ivie Anderson and her Boys from Dixie or Cootie Williams and his Rug Cutters. Johnny Hodges and Barney Bigard did sessions and my group was dubbed Rex Stewart and his 52nd Street Stompers. We all made contributions to the mighty musical empire of Duke's repertoire and I don't mean to imply that there was anything unusual in this because there wasn't. Long before this, Bubber Miley, Otto and Barney had added to the Ellington tune catalog, as had Harry Carney, Juan Tizol, Johnny Hodges and others.

That reminds me of the strange quirks of fate involved in writing a hit song. I am thinking of the tune *Caravan*, which was a throwaway melody that accidentally was born at the end of a record date. The scene, as I remember, was at the studio during the closing moments of a Barney Bigard session. They had put three numbers in the can and needed one more to complete the schedule of four tunes. In the frantic consultation it was decided to forego the blues and play some kind of melody. But before continuing, I had better explain that a lot of times a leader would be so painstaking with music that he considered important to the date that the allotted time would be almost up. Then, for the last side, out would trot "the blues." This time, however, Juan Tizol was johnny-on-the-spot with a melody which evolved from another tune, *Alabamy Home*. I can't forget this occasion because Sonny Greer made one of his rare vocal appearances singing it. *Caravan* was the obbligato strain.

Another familiar example of this type of happenstance, or what came from what, would be the tunes *I Let a Song Go out of my Heart*, which was originally a riff which Johnny played behind the melody of the song *Once in a While*. The lyric to this was written by Henry Nemo for a Cotton Club review and he claimed that he had the idea for the title while sitting on the toilet! I understand that this tune was supposed to go out of the show and be replaced by another, but it had been played so much on the remote broadcasts that it had become popular. So it stayed in. After some years of success as *I let a Song . . .*, it then reappeared, with slight modifications, even bigger as *Never No Lament*, later known as *Don't Get Around Much Anymore*. I hasten to point out that this type of creativity is common in the music business. For example, *Night Train*, a national hit, was a direct steal from Ellington's *Happy Go Lucky Local*. Then there's a thing called *Robin's Nest*, the main structure of which is from a tune I wrote called *Morning Glory*. And, while we're on the subject, the old standard *Moon Glow* is almost identical with an earlier Ellington tune *Lazy Rhapsody*.

Getting back to that record session we had with Django in Paris, that particular session was such a happy combination of musical inspiration and understanding, such a thoroughly happy blending of talents, that in later years it was hard to reconcile it with the events that ensued. I couldn't understand how my music caused me to lose so many friends. And this is where truth is stranger than fiction. The chain of events started on the band's return to New York. Naturally, one of the first persons I got together with was my old buddy Brick Fleagle, who was not only a good friend but also the arranger on most of my record dates. So I loaned my copies of the Paris date to Brick, because he was also a guitar man and I knew he would really enjoyed Django's artistry. So far, so good. That is, until he loaned my records to Steve Smith, who at the time operated a label, HRS. The next thing I knew, HRS had my Paris date on the market – only it had been retitled *Ellingtonia*! Well, you can bet I was furious at this type of double dealing. But, exactly as I had done in the case of *Stompin' at the Savoy* and the other tunes that earned dough for somebody else, I bitched, sputtered and did nothing about it. Subsequently my friendship with Brick was never the same. Then, farther down the line, after my pal Billy Taylor had left the band, Johnny Hodges made a record of my tune *Finesse*, but this time it was called *Night Wind* and credited to my boyhood buddy Billy Taylor! And that is why truth may well be stranger than fiction. Aside from commenting on these deals and regretting the loss of revenue which I could have derived from the above-mentioned music, I guess it's just as well that I was "taken" by my friends, because, if they hadn't, someone else probably would have wound up with credit for my compositions.

That reminds me, the one composition that I really liked, *Morning Glory*, I sold for 50 bucks – 50 bucks-worth at a time when I really needed the dough. I think it's a pretty fair tune. Ellington thought so also. I guess this reads like a fellow crying over spilt milk, and I am crying, but not because I was all too often sold down the river. No, it's because I was stupid enough to be vulnerable again and again.

18

Back Home

Home again, the war had not broken out yet but there was an almost imperceptible tightening of the nation's economic belt, and, while I make no pretense of being knowledgeable about such specialized matters, still I couldn't help but notice our theater and dance dates began to show a slow but certain decline in attendance. And our jumps grew longer (we made one such trek in an unheard-of fashion – Indianapolis to New York in a day coach). Everybody started bitching, "What the hell happened to our Pullmans?" We were told that there were none available. So, as our activities slowed down a lot, we also were laid off more than ever before. We played only some scattered dances and theaters. Then things got really tough; the phonograph record ban started and there was no recording. We were always paid extra for these dates, so everybody began casting about for more dough in order to maintain the standard of living to which we had become accustomed.

I started creating more songs and trying to sell them anywhere, Juan put in a lot of time copying music for Duke, and Johnny asked to be paid extra for playing soprano saxophone (request denied, and that golden tone exited from Ellington's band forever). Cootie joined Benny Goodman for more money, and, considering the small amount involved, to this day I just don't see how Duke could have lost this giant. But it was his band, not mine.

In any case, these rough circumstance drew the fellows closer together for a while. It seems to me that there had been a lot of friction between the guys and even a couple of feuds. Barney wasn't speaking to Lawrence Brown, who was not on speaking terms with Ellington. Wallace Jones, who had replaced Whetsol in the first trumpet chair, tried to be the peacemaker between Cootie and me, but to no avail. We didn't speak to each other for at least two years. These were the major feuds within the band, and not to be included among the minor beefs the guys had with each other and the Duke from time to time. I won't bother to name the other guys who were involved in occasional feuds because it is of no importance. But there were frictions among us and especially when things were rough. Over and above any personal feelings, no one wanted to see Cootie leave Ellington despite the certainty that he'd be bettering himself financially. All white musicians in name bands earned more than we did and Cootie would move into the white pay schedule with Benny Goodman. Neverthess, I especially prayed that Coots and Duke would come to terms, especially as we had heard that the amount involved was only 25 dollars a week.

Some time back, Cootie and I had forgiven and forgotten our old antagonism and for more than a year we had footstomped that band into a swinger. By that, I mean Cootie and I always sat near the drums and, whenever Greer wasn't putting down the beat hard enough, we would both whip his flagging rhythm until it moved and swung like Chick Webb. This is how we used to spur Kaiser Marshall on when we were with Fletcher Henderson. I'm sure that anyone who heard us stomping and grunting and exhorting, "Sonny, come on, umph, grab it! Umph! Whip 'em, Nasty, umph," etc., would have thought we were crazy. But it worked, and over the years I doubt if Duke's band ever moved like we had it moving during that period. And I also bet that Duke never realized the influence we had over his rhythm section.

It appeared that the whole *esprit de corps* was in tatters and was exacerbated along with everything else when Christmas came and we didn't even receive a card from Duke or Irving Mills. Previous years, *lagniappe* was the rule rather than the exception. The year before I joined, the fellows received 500 bucks each as a bonus. And the wives were delighted with flagons of French perfume. My first Christmas loot was a crisp 100-dollar bill plus a wallet with a replica of my signature on it in raised gold. Presents varied from year to year, but as a rule everyone was remembered during the holiday season with a watch or money or something tangible, until this particular year when the bottom dropped out of everything.

When we returned from abroad, something big and important did happen and that was the addition of Jimmy Blanton to the band in 1939. In my opinion he connotes genius for the simple reason that no other adjective would be fitting for that young man. In my time I have had the good fortune of knowing several people whose talents have placed them in a special rarified, in-front-of-everybody-else, stratospheric category. In that group I'd place Don Redman, Jelly Roll Morton, Benny Carter, Ellington and only a few others. Jimmy is quite apart from the aforementioned, as the others were writers primarily and instrumentalists second. What indicates how tremendous the artistry of Blanton actually was, is that he influenced the entire profession and forever changed how the bass was played.

Going back to the early days, another stringed instrument, the violin, was then the most popular instrument. It was dethroned as the leader of musical ensembles by its natural successor, the cornet. As we know, jazz started out with humble origins. We nurtured, fostered and sponsored it and watched as its myriad offshoots soared and waned into the present complexity. From the work songs, the ring-shouts, into ragtime and foxtrot, these were the dances which led to the imaginative explorations of our musicians who then created the many forms of swing, bop, progressive, cool and so on. As jazz progressed the trumpet became the dominant instrument, and the story of modern jazz trumpet starts with two words: Louis Armstrong. In other words, if you play a horn, somewhere along the line you play something that Louis has created. Armstrong is the sturdy trunk of the tree and all of those fellows that followed, disciples or not, became the offshoots and branches.

There are people who say I belong to this select company. Yes, I admired him mightily and tried to imitate him, but I rather doubt that I came close, despite Louie's having chosen me as his successor in the Henderson band. But I do accept the role of link between Louie and Roy Eldridge, as I first developed a style that Roy liked and he told me that he had followed it. Then Roy developed another dimension of his own, which was faster and better than mine, incidentally. My style was a combination of my hero, Satch, and a guy named Reuben Reeves. I haven't spoken of Reuben before, so right now I want to give credit to this outstanding man whose name and talents I have not seen mentioned anywhere. More about him later. From Roy, the popular style of trumpet playing continued on to John Birks Gillespie, commonly known as Dizzy, who made his musical personality a part of the idiom. By taking the velocity of Eldridge and adding another harmonic concept, Dizzy imparted impetus that left nowhere for the instrument to go except to return to simplicity, which Miles Davis did with great success. Consequently, Miles Davis is currently considered the man in this day and age. To my mind, that would just about sum up the direct line of succession. However, there are other giants who for one reason or another do not quite fit in with my theory that each one stemmed from another, but their crowns shine ever bright because, by and large, these talents transcend styles.

I speak now of Clifford Brown, the late genius who had to be heard to be believed. There's Clark Terry who can play any and everybody's style but also has a distinctive style of his own; Wild Bill Davison who plays dixieland the way it should be played; Bobby Hackett, a real reincarnation of the great Joe Smith, he of the velvet tone; and last, but not least, that unbelievable brace of trumpeters Harold Baker, Adolphus Cheatham and Taft Jordan. These are trumpet players that most trumpet players (like Manny Klein and Sweets Edison) consider "real" players. I am forced to save one fellow for a special category. I consider him the best that I've ever heard doing what he does. That's Cat Anderson, whose command of outer space on the trumpet has to be heard to be believed. So the tree grows on and on, ever dependent on its roots for sustenance and propagation.

To follow this thought, it has occurred to me that if one were to chronicle musicians as they give pedigrees to race horses, you might conclude that Benny Goodman owed a lot to Thornton Blue and Jimmy Dorsey might give a vote of thanks to Benny Carter. Bix Beiderbecke stemmed from Joe Smith, with overtones of Red Nichols. In going through a line of succssion, it is not my intention to denigrate any of the above gentlemen, only to comment on who influenced whom. I have freely admitted how much Louis was responsible for what I became. There are these parallels and it is significant that, among the tens of thousands of musicians, only a few made an enduring mark.

I have often been asked about the early days and who influenced whom on the trombone, such as specifically between Jimmy Harrison and Jack Teagarden. The main difference between them would be money, as negro musicians were never paid the same kind of salary then nor at the time Cootie left Duke, and I doubt if they are equal even today. Both men were great. I couldn't say one was better than the other nor their styles that distinctive.

On the bass fiddle, Jimmy Blanton has to be considered a genius. He was one of these rare indivuals who appeared to be made of finer clay than his fellow musicians. His amazing talent sparked the entire band. Despite his youth, there was a certain calm assurance which vibrated visibly, and you could sense this permeating his public and private life. When he spoke, which was rarely, people listened, feeling, truthfully, that he was wise beyond his years. Curiously, his greatest fans were people like Charles Münch and Sergei Koussevitzky, conductor of the Boston Symphony. One night, while we were playing in downtown New York, Stravinsky spent the entire evening enjoying Blanton. And, when Duke introduced them, Jimmy amazed us by talking with great composers as easily as if Igor Stravinsky was just one of the fellows on the corner. Actually, Blanton's sudden fame didn't change his attitude in any sense. He remained a beautiful human being. It was funny to compare Jim with his road buddy, Ben Webster, who was older, a pure extrovert and always into some escapade. Somehow, Blanton had a quietening effect on Ben. And it certainly seemed as if Ben felt responsible for Jimmy.

As I remember, it was Ben who was the first one to hear Jimmy play in St Louis and brought him to Duke's attention. In any case, the paternal instinct really emerged after they met. Ben would watch over the kid he nicknamed Bear like a mother hen. And Blanton didn't seem to mind too much. However, one thing Ben couldn't influence was when Jimmy went to bed. Many is the time Frog, as Jimmy nicknamed Ben, thought he had the Bear safely tucked away for the night, only to walk into some club and there the kid would be, whaling away to the delight of the musicians. Jimmy loved his instrument, holding it close like it was a woman, playing with his face near the strings, listening to every sound. Maybe if he had minded Ben and if he had quit smoking when he discovered that he had TB, we would still have this wonderful musician with us.

Looking after Jimmy was an odd role for my old friend, Benjamin Francis Webster. He is a very complex individual, in some ways a throwback, a twentieth-century shadow of Piney Brown and other noted sporting-house characters of the bygone days of Kansas City. As I see it, Ben was never able to be merely "Ben Webster, the musician." In his youth he became infamous as the hoodlum swingster. Actually, he was one of my oldest chums, and over many drinks we have argued over where and when we met. I recall the scene on campus at Wilberforce when he chose to play saxophone for the welcoming committee instead of getting the customary paddling. Sometimes Frog agrees and sometimes he denies being that fellow.

Ben and I got to be real buddies later at the Lido pool in Harlem along with some other fellows who hung out there. Ben had a Buick in those days and drove us all home when the sun went down. I admired his playing a lot. In my opinion, he is one of the greatest creators on the tenor sax who ever lived and truly must be considered in the same category with Coleman Hawkins and Lester Young. And there the creative line stops, as far as I am concerned. Actually, Frog was modest and doubtless would never agree with me. But he would like to accept acclaim as a stomp piano player! Now admitted that he does play a pretty good barrelhouse-type piano, but on his horn and in his composing (when he chooses to settle down and write) is where he displays his tremendous imagination.

Like the other Ellingtonians, there were many sides to Ben. I only mention some happenings to help gain insight into this very remarkable man. Ben was generous and would give you the shirt off his back. Actually, he did just that for me when, early one morning in Detroit, my Margie got her dander up and decided to carve a totem out of me. I guess I wouldn't have panicked if I hadn't been asleep at the time and groggy from drinking. Plus that I always slept in the raw and didn't have a stitch on. She and I waltzed around that room for ten or so minutes. Then, when the room clerk came to see what all of the commotion was about, I broke for the door, went to Ben's room at the other end of the hall and borrowed money, underwear, suit, hat, coat, shoes and overcoat! Within a few hours, I was in Chicago, thanks to Ben.

I know I must have presented a strange sight in these ill-fitting garments, as Ben was a burly fellow about four inches taller than me. But then, we entertainers must often present an exotic image to the guy who works from 9 to 5 at a mundane job. I think of some of the outstanding eccentrics in the music fraternity. There was Jelly Roll Morton, flashing all those real diamonds. Later, there was Liberace with his brocade and lamé coats, ruffled shirts and fingers laden with rings. These were the flamboyant dressers.

There's another side to the coin, and I think of Junior Raglin, the bass player who was hired after Jimmy Blanton became too ill to continue. I couldn't say if his feet hurt, if he didn't know any better or was a bit zany. Whenever he could get away with it, he played performances in his ordinary felt bedroom slippers. Now remember, this band had Duke in the vanguard wearing his hand-made, square-toed shoes, and most of the fellows followed his lead with some very classy footwear. Junior also differed from the norm, and I can still see the scene. The fellows would be scattered all over our Pullman, some in a poker game, Toby Hardwicke and Sonny Greer running their black jack operation. But Junior left all of these activities to us, as he sat quietly in a seat by himself, enthralled with stacks of comic books.

In the 60s, when I came to Los Angeles to live, Ben was also here sharing a house with his mother and his grandmother. He again came to my rescue several times with loot. However, our friendship was not a one-sided affair, and many a time I stuck my chin out for him, mostly in the role of peacemaker. Ben managed to get himself into all kinds of messes. Once he ran into Joe Louis in an elevator, when Joe was world boxing champ. Ben greeted him with a little "hello" punch. Ben got a little punch back, which rendered his arm useless for a week. When Ben drank he got somewhat out of hand and into various jams. One time he went after the toughest policeman in Chicago. A phone call alerted me of the impending problem so I rushed over to the Club DeLisa where he had started the confrontation and looked all over for him. But it turned out he had left for "the church," a gambling spot. And there, I found him with the cop, sitting and drinking side by side like old buddies!

Don't misunderstand: I'm not throwing stones at Ben for drinking nor for gambling, because in those years we all did a lot of both. I remember well the occasion that cured me forever of playing craps. We were doing a theater in Dayton, Ohio, and there was a game going backstage, but I was only a spectator. For a change, I had been in luck the entire week. I'd been a winner in black jack, tonk and poker games. So when I was challenged by Pops Whitman of the team of Pops and Louis to a little crap game, I didn't hesitate. Now, usually, craps was not my game and I didn't usually play. But this time I figured the luck was running with me, so why not? I made a few passes with the galloping dominoes, adding about 50 bucks to my already fat bankroll, and was all set to quit when Pops raised the ante from 10 dollars to 25. Then the roof fell in, as I watched him make ten consecutive passes at 25 dollars a pass! Then I lost my head – not over 250 dollars he'd already won from me. No: I refused to believe those damn cubes would continue to hit for him and not for me. Long after the theater had closed, Pops and I battled. Dawn found me weary, hungry and $537.86 poorer – and I never played craps again.

During the period from 1934 to 1940, Chicago was like a second home to us. We played the Stevens Hotel, the Blackstone

Hotel, the Oriental Theater, the Regal, and the State and Lake theaters, among other spots. Yes, the Windy City with its combination of western hospitality and northern drive was a mecca after our necessarily far-flung tours into the hinterlands. It was always wonderful to return to civilization, and I'd like to explain here that tooters, artists, etc. really don't differ from other people. Professionals work to entertain you during your hours for recreation. And then our playtime comes when you are sleeping or working. Somehow, the non-pro never seems to understand that entertainers are people also, and as such require relaxing from their jobs just as others escape from the day-to-day routine. Oftentimes, while the public may enjoy our offerings, they look at us as a breed apart. We cannot and do not lead normal lives, as we must create, dream, execute and combat life's pressures living on a different clock. I have often had people tell me that they envy me, getting to see the world, meeting new experiences and sleeping all day. This is really another case of the grass growing greener on the other side of the street, because no one takes into consideration the drawbacks of the life we lead. For instance, we must always be on call for whatever the occasion may be, be it weddings, wakes, bar mitzvahs, dances or whatever. This means we must be ready to make the scene by plane, train, bus or car, and despite the weather or physical ailment, marital disruption or anything else. I have first-hand knowledge of the pressures which being a musician places on a marriage, since I have lost wives twice on account of the economic and sociological stresses involved.

One particular gig I'll never forget points up the travel discomfort. It happened when Ellington was booked into some small town in Wisconsin out of Chicago. Now bear in mind this was an important musical group, not some impoverished fly-by-night combo. First we took a bus to another town in Wisconsin, then a ferry boat, two street cars and private autos before we finally arrived. We had left Chicago at the crack of dawn with almost no sleep and it was dusk when we reached the job. No time to rest, bathe or shave. Just like the bad old days! Usually, of course, the Ellington band traveled by Pullman with our own car.

A certain musician in the band was, perhaps, the most socially motivated person that I've ever known. He possessed a fabulous gift of the gab and was known far and wide as a "hail fellow, well met" sport. He was also famous for his ready wit, his *savoir faire* and his generosity. Essentially he was a man's man, but when some girl was attracted to him his *modus operandi* remained the same. He always poured plenty of whiskey. Once, however, his largesse backfired and, if he is still living, I'll bet that he never knew what happened. On this particular occasion, the combination of his wisecracks and happy grins succeeded in captivating one of the prettiest little pheasants in the dance hall. And, as we watched the scene with undisguised envy, he proceeded to charm her like an Indian fakir putting a hooded cobra through its paces. Afterwards we returned to our Pullman, which was parked right in the station, and saw that Little Joe (not his real name) had beaten us back again. He was all set for a gala *affaire d'amour* with the fine damsel and a fifth of Scotch. He pressed drink after drink upon his fair guest, but she soon began to show how unaccustomed she was to such heavy imbibing. His eyes, too, began to glaze, and their conversation became mumbles. Then, when the booze took over completely, they both sat stupified, clutching each other. The ever-present vultures among us gently separated them, placing Joe in his berth and taking the lady to the drawing room on this Pullman, offering complete privacy. Now don't get me wrong. There were only two fellows involved in this caper. But they both proceeded to score and the loud female sighs of pleasure left no doubt as to the successful conclusion of their diabolical girlnapping.

Actually, the little lamb had been thrown to the wolves and maybe she knew it. But maybe she didn't. From the sounds of enjoyment, it would appear that everyone had a ball. As I look back, I can still hear her moaning, "Joe, oh Joe, you're so good to me." Sometime during the evening the two culprits took the girl back to Joe's berth. And, as the train began to pull out of the station, the various overnight guests said fond farewells. This little cutie was heard to say, "Well, goodbye Joe. I really enjoyed myself and you sure know how to treat a girl right!"

At this point, I'd like to say a few words in defense of the morals of artists in general and musicians in particular. The lives we lead are not conducive to our being like others. Therefore one of the most rewarding aspects of being a musician would be the opportunity the profession affords for contact with virtually the entire spectrum of people. They get to know us and we get to know them. This gives us a wide view of the variation in mores around the world. The point that I'm making is that a musician can be and usually is a very competent observer of his fellows. People sense that and somehow tend to place a musician in the role of reporter, psychiatrist, critic and, strangely enough, father confessor. At one time I was almost tempted to put out a sign "Advice, Ltd," because so many people sought solace from me on so many subjects, such as how to kick the habit; should she have the child?; how much did I think the house was worth?; was she true to him?, etc. And the more I'd protest, saying that I was merely a tooter with little knowledge of anything outside my own trade, the more often somebody would seek me out. And there I'd be, straining to pontificate on some problem that I had only a vague experience with.

This was particularly common concerning politics and in that field, for many years, I knew less than a babe in arms, except being aware of our two-party system. I guess I started being aware sometime during the early 30s, when most of the Harlems all over the country began being exposed to the stratagems of various shades of political thought. So I started reading Spengler, Karl Marx and anything else I could lay my hands on that concerned the economic causes and effects of politics. I read, digested and made up my own mind, and thus was not influenced by the blandishments of the far left which concluded that the American system was unworkable. And so it seemed, during those dark Depression days. Still I came to the conclusion that our way best represented a road to the dreams and aspirations of men living in our society.

There was one fellow in the Ellington band who used to offer me sound advice, and this was strange because he was three years younger than I was. That was Harry Carney, as nice a fellow as you would ever want to meet, and a great contrast to some of the others because he displayed no strange behavior at all. He was the epitome of the nice guy next door that the neighbors point out to their sons as an example to be followed. He would also be the ideal example for present day tooters to emulate in public relations. Harry was a past master of the art, with his ready broad smile and the warm graciousness that emanated from him. I have watched him snatch his horn from his mouth to inform a questioning fan about the tune we had just played. The other musicians in the front line just ignored the question. Harry had a memory like Sonny's and could remember a huge number of fans' names, the circumstances and even the place they had met. It was also Harry who had the most enormous address book crammed with entries of practically every Ellington fan and friend all around the world. And each of them was on his gigantic Christmas card list, not to mention that many of them were also on his regular long-distance call schedule.

Besides being nice, Harry was also a past master on his instrument, the baritone sax. His range surpassed credibility because he could play the higher octaves in tune and with a tenderness mindful of the upper register of the cello. At the bottom of the horn he could get some other wonderful growling effects, and it is small wonder that he was the anchor man in Ellington's orchestra from the time he joined Duke, which was 1927. Harry was so steady that, even though he never was band manager, I have often seen him act as straw boss for the Ellington crew, stomping off the beat. Also, in a crisis, his word was accepted by all the fellows. In later years, long after I had left the band, he acted as Ellington's chauffeur. The rest of the band went by bus or train or whatever, but Harry drove Duke from gig to gig in his perfectly kept-up car and was an easy relaxed companion for the boss.

If it is true that the formative years develop character, then Harry came by his likeable personality quite naturally. He was the product of the most harmonious household, and I well remember how both his parents always extended themselves in making Harry's band buddies welcome every time we played Boston. His mother was a beautiful cook and would graciously put out a feast that makes my mouth water even now, as I think about it. This was typical Bostonian fare with codfish balls, hot rolls and Boston baked beans, winding up with chocolate layer cake or strawberry shortcake, in summer.

I first met Harry at a dance in Boston and neither of us was ever positive of the date or the year, but we both recall the circumstances. At the time I was playing with Leon Abbey's Savoy Bearcats, and I remember coming up from New York to play a few nights at this swanky ballroom, right in the heart of town. Our clarinet man, Carmelito Jejo, was the real star of our group, and from our opening number there was a second line of fans and musicians in front of him. Carney was quite recognizable due to his baby face and the way he clutched his clarinet case as if he was afraid that it was going to jump out of his arm. The interplay of emotions on Harry's face as he watched and listened to Jejo made me remember him.

When Harry joined Duke in 1927, the saxophone section consisted of Otto Hardwicke on first alto, Rudy Jackson on tenor sax and Harry playing alto and clarinet. I've wondered if perhaps Harry was hired to replace Toby on one of the sudden self-declared vacations Toby had a tendency to take? And then, when Toby returned, Harry switched over to baritone? Whatever the case, Harry became Mr Baritone, the definitive sound on his instrument, another consistent *Downbeat* award winner and one of the all-stars. I've often suspected that he was probably influential in getting Johny Hodges, a fellow Bostonian, to join Duke way back when.

Well, maybe Harry wasn't always so perfect. There was the year that he took up photography. He teamed up with the mischievous Otto Hardwicke and together they accumulated trunks full of equipment and at least several thousand dollars' worth of enlarging cameras. The equipment was real but their company was mythical. Nevertheless, they had cards printed for this venture, which read:

Hardwick and Carney, We aim to Tease
or Pick a Flick of Pickled Pictures.

PS Bring your own pickles.
We're pickled enough already!

They didn't make much money (if any), but they had a lot of fun.

19

Los Angeles

Chicago had been fun in many ways, but California was a new world to me, so clean, so sparkling – and particularly Los Angeles. The houses fascinated most of us Easterners who had never been west of the Rockies. The city was a contrast to the dull, dingy atmosphere of eastern cities. To see the beautiful multicolored homes, the clean, broad streets, the orange groves and the huge vistas of shimmering lights from a mountain top was a treat. But, for all of its beauty, Los Angeles never was a good area for music. I can quote many great artists on that. Fellows like Jack Teagarden, Roy Eldridge, Sidney Bechet, Bill Harris, Wild Bill Davison and so on have all commented and agreed that Los Angeles is a cemetery surrounded by pockets of Iowans, Okies and Texans. But I didn't believe them because I did quite well in the town, perhaps riding on the prestige of Ellington.

On my first trip to Los Angeles we were busy and made a movie, my first. We played several dances plus a theater engagement, and between these activities we sandwiched in record dates. Life was good. I thought the town was jumping, especially on Central Avenue, where the Club Alabam was the big-time spot among six or seven other smaller clubs, all on the Avenue. There was Alex Lovejoy's club, which was a gathering place, as was a club in Watts, where Wynonie Harris was shouting the blues. And there were after-hours spots running full blast. We went to different pads for different things.

From that time on we were in Los Angeles often, so I may confuse the years that certain clubs were our favorite hangouts. I do remember one popular spot, Helen's, which was just an ordinary frame house in the colored area, on, as I recall, Hooper Street. This was a favorite with piano players because she had a good grand piano which she kept tuned. Art Tatum prefered Helen's, so naturally his admirers could be found there, too, after hours. Teddy Wilson, Jess Stacy, Fats Waller, Jimmy Rowles and Rozelle Gayle were other top-rank pianists who headquartered at Helen's or one of the other local after-hours places.

By now, to unwind after the gig, we would go out to listen to other musicians blow. Most of us no longer thought jamming was as great fun as we had in previous years. I guess the fellows were getting older. But over the span of years there were unforgettable forget-me-nots of jam sessions and cutting sessions which remain in my memory. An example is the night Thornton Blue carved Benny Goodman to ribbons playing *Sweet Georgia Brown* – on clarinet, of course. And one morning in Buffalo, New York, Buster Bailey held one note for four minutes then played 15 choruses on *Tiger Rag*. Thornton Blue packed up his horn and left. Then that unsung master trumpet player Reuben Reeves once challenged Jabbo Smith to a trumpet battle to see which one could play faster – but Roy Eldridge cut them both. Roy had a way of lurking in the doorway while two other men were vying for the championship, and he'd come in blowing. He didn't always win with this ploy. One night of glory I screamed an altissimo B flat to end the meeting between Sid De Paris, Ward Pinkett, Cuban Bennett and Roy. Another occasion I won't forget is when Chu Berry held court on tenor for Dick Wilson, Herschel Evans, Elmer Williams and so on. PS: Coleman Hawkins was there that night. Later Hawk decided to show Lester Young how he played tenor after being in Europe for a long time.

Yes, there were some sessions with Ellington men. Jimmy Blanton, for one, who was still a youngster, never missed a chance to jam. At one point we and the Lunceford band were both in Los Angeles at the same time – they were booked at Sebastian's Cotton Club and we were doing *Jump for Joy*. I heard about a great session: Willie Smith, Lunceford's swinging alto player, playing against our Johnny Hodges, who was in my opinion possibly the world's greatest alto player ever, with Nat Cole on piano and I don't know who all else. That's one I'm sorry I missed.

I have known Hodges for so long that I've forgotten exactly where and when we met, but I do recall that it was in Boston prior to his coming to New York. If memory serves me correctly, we met in a little bistro around the corner from Shag Taylor's drug store. Incidentally, this was a common meeting place for all musicians during those times, principally because Shag sold the best whiskey in town, never mind that we still had Prohibition. This was my first visit to Beantown and I was playing with Leon Abbey's Savoy Bluesicians. Later Johnny came to New York with a pianist named Bobby Sawyer, I believe, and it was not long after that I next saw him in the Henri Sayres Orchestra and also at the jam sessions which were held nightly at the old Hoofer's Club. I figure that it was about that time when Johnny came to the attention of Sidney Bechet, who sort of adopted him. Harlem had some giants playing alto saxophone then, and I recall Eugene Fields, who was greased lightning (and I never knew what became of him), and others who have disappeared from public notice.

Johnny once told an interviewer that he started lessons on saxophone when he was a lad, and after about eight or ten sessions the teacher asked, "Show me how you do this," and "How did you do that?" So Johnny figured he knew more than the teacher and stopped taking lessons. This may or may not be true. He was a very good reader and you don't learn that without studying.

He played with Chick Webb for a while in New York, and it was a sight to see and hear him and young Johnny arguing about how a saxophone riff should be played. This happened frequently up at the old Savoy Ballroom and it amused us because they were both so serious. Verbally, they would square off at each other like a pair of bantam cocks. However, they were really pals. Chick always had definite ideas about how his arrangements should be played despite his not being able to read a note. But since he possessed a phenomenal ear and a very retentive memory, he would sing, whistle or hum his

arrangmeents, note for note. At rehearsals Chick took full
charge and told his arrangers how the routines should go.
Johnny, who read well, really enjoyed baiting Chick by telling
him that he was wrong, which would make the little king of the
Savoy furious.

He didn't stay with Chick too long. It was in the late 20s
when the still very young Johnny joined Ellington. Early on
somehow he acquired the nickname Rabbit, which was usually
shortened to Rab. But that all happened before I came along, so,
although I've heard a lot of speculation about how he got the
name, let me presume it was because, straight on, he did look
a little like a rabbit.

One way and another Johnny was involved in several songs
which later were attributed to Duke, such as *I Let a Song Go out
of my Heart*. Actually, we all brought bits and pieces of songs to
the boss, maybe 16 bars, maybe only four, and then Duke
added, changed or embellished, so really the finished product
bore his stamp. For whatever reason, Johnny had a strange way
of airing his grievances. He was very visible in his front-row
saxophone chair near the piano, from where he directed remarks
and questions to Ellington, out of the side of his mouth. It was
hard for Duke to ignore him, but he always put on that wide,
phony smile and did his best.

Hodges, perhaps unknown to himself, I surmised was a
direct descendant of an ancient Indian heritage, and I choose
that particular lineage deliberately because, within my frame
of reference, there's no other racial stock that can control
emotions so completely or present such a stoic exterior to the
world. Johnny had that kind of impassive face, with a skin color
like coffee with a lot of cream. Since so little of his personality
emerged from the cocoon of his imperturbability, any scrutiny
of this talented man must lean heavily on his music. And he
was one of the most gifted musicians it has ever been my
privilege to work with. He was among the short musicians of
our era, about my height, and by this time was slowly giving
way to middle-age spread. However, we couldn't help noticing
that he had a special something which was irresistible to the
ladies. They oohed and aahed when he played and would have

willingly gone home with him if he had beckoned.

While we were in California, this time, I had the pleasure of doing a musical sequence in a movie called *Hellzapoppin'* with Oleson and Johnson and fellow musicians Slim Gaillard and Slam Stewart. Slim and Slam, as they were called, were a very popular act, having just achieved fame with their hit songs *Flat Foot Floogie*, *Cement Mixer* and others. Their bit in the movie was typical of the time. Slim played a gas station attendant, Slam was a butler and I felt lucky to be given a chef's outfit. This was right up my alley, since I had always had the desire to be a cook. Many years later I did something about that inclination.

There were other small parts. I was in an alligator scene for some picture which I never saw and in a jazz extravaganza for which I was required to play one note. For this I was not photographed at all. I sat in the section for two days counting bars with no music until my head reeled. Then I was supposed to scream a high F on the end of the music. I have Rafael Mendez to thank for cuing me in for that one. Here's what happened. As a jazz man, my forte was building up tension as I proceeded with my solos, so it was new for me to have to count and then scream only one note. Rafael dug my insecurity and said, "Don't bother counting, just watch me until I nod my head and that will indicate the beginning of 16 bars before you scream. And, to make sure, I'll kick you. Then go ahead and make your horn scream!" And that's how we did it. He kicked me in the shins so hard that I really screamed in pain and the F rang out loud and clear. One take and that was it.

Hollywood was good to me, and over a period of years I remember making a few movies. There was *A Day at the Races*, starring the Marx brothers, and, with the Ellington band, *Hellzapoppin'*, *Reveille with Beverly* and *Cabin in the Sky*. The big one for me was *Syncopation*, which starred Jackie Cooper. In this, I had lines. I was an actor! I took the script home and had it letter perfect. I grimaced in front of a mirror and went over and over my part. You'd have thought I had the lead. But the next day I froze at rehearsal, which made me want to cut my throat. Here I was on the payroll at 175 dollars a day and about to goof the deal. And I didn't feel any better when I heard one kid remark to another lad, "Damn, he sure is dumb. He's only got one page of dialogue and he can't even remember that!" Overhearing this made me feel terrible, but at the same time I resolved to show myself, the kid and everybody else that I could do it. And I did. What a glorious feeling at the end of the day to walk up to the payroll window and be handed my check for 175 dollars!

On one trip I worked 11 days, and bought my first house with the loot after it looked like California was going to be where we'd spent a lot of time. It was just a cottage in Southwest Los Angeles, but that was a big deal for Margie and me. Shortly I persuaded her to make Los Angeles home, and by that time baby Helena made us three.

This was about the time we were doing the revue *Jump for Joy*, which was a sprightly dream of a show, a joy-studded avant-garde revue. It starred Dorothy Dandridge, plus our two vocalists with the band, Herb Jeffries and Ivie Anderson. And there was the blues shouter Big Joe Turner and the comedians Pot Pan and Skillet, along with a big cast of 60. Highlights of the show which I remember were the bit done by dancer-singer Marie Bryant with our Ray Nance (who was very talented, and sang and danced besides playing violin and trumpet) and the dancing of Pete Nugent and Al Guster. There were clever blackouts written by Sid Kuller and a classic bit called "In a 5 and 10¢ Store," written by Langston Hughes. We all liked the show and enjoyed doing it. It was projected that *Jump for Joy* would play Los Angeles for several months and then go to New York. It never happened. The show ran for about three months to fairly good houses and then folded. Shortly after *Jump for Joy* closed we moved into a big ballroom in South Gate called the Trianon and stayed there for several months. We did nightly broadcasts from this site and this brought out all our fans for miles around. Then we were back on the road again.

Gradually we were in LA more and more. When we went on the road we seemed to wind up at a pretty regular string of cities where we were most popular. We made these dates in the Midwest and back East plus up and down the West Coast mostly by Pullman. It is rumored, and indeed it is a fact, that band musicians who were on the road tended to have a special girl in each frequently visited town, just like sailors do. I recall a comical incident. One of the younger men in the band had a steady, a cute little chick named Eleanor, in St Louis. We had all seen him with her several times. As we were leaving St Louis for Los Angeles, we saw our Lothario tenderly bidding Ellie goodbye. After the train rolled away he said something to me about he'd sure miss her, but then he'd have Gladys to keep him company in LA. And, the way he said it, I gathered that Gladys was pretty special.

A couple of days later we pulled into the big new Los Angeles Union station. He pointed out Gladys, a stunning brownskin gal in a big hat. But, to his horror and everyone's surprise, standing there big as life and only a few feet away in the waiting area, there was Eleanor! How was this possible? How could this be? (The time was, of course, long before the days of easy, available plane travel.) Our young Romeo persuaded the porter to stash him away in the luggage compartment. I was delegated to tell Gladys he'd been taken sick the day before and had been left behind, but would get in touch with her as soon as he got to town. Then he had Sonny Greer tell Eleanor some other concocted story. She must have been too smart to buy it. We never saw him with Ellie again, but he hung out in Los Angeles with Gladys for several years.

There was a lot of competition for those Los Angeles area engagements because just being there meant the possibility of getting cast in a movie, not to mention the big attraction of the climate. Every orchestra in the country vied for a gig at one of the plush hotels, the theaters or a ballroom. Actually, at one time or another, all of the giants of the big-band era played the city, from Paul Whiteman to Boots and his Buddies. When we were there, besides the major spots, there was a lot of talent appearing around the clubs in the western part of the city. Nat Cole's trio at the 331 Club (where we were not welcome) and Billy Berg's Capri, with a great combo of mostly local musicians, where we were. But you might see all the big names, such as Coleman Hawkins, Chu Berry or Lester Young, sitting alongside Erskine Hawkins, Roy Eldridge or Dizzy Gillespie.

Actually, once, by chance, Erskine, Diz, Roy and I were all in LA at the same time and decided to start a trumpet club. The idea was that we would find and encourage youngsters, give them horns and promote them with the big-band leaders. But the dream died when I asked the King, Louis Armstrong, to be honorary president and he told me I'd have to see Joe Glazer. Not that I blame him for looking to his manager for advice. Anyway, it wouldn't have worked, as most of the time we tooters were hundreds of miles apart from one another. It's hard to plan to be at a special place at a certain time when your life is not your own.

20

Postscript: Jazz faux pas

The war years were both difficult and tragic for practically everyone, world wide. Among the Ellingtonians, there were our personal sorrows and disappointments. Our wonderful bassist Jimmy Blanton never rejoined the band. We all mourned when he died at the sanitarium in Duarte, outside Los Angeles. That was 1942 and he was only in his early 20s. About the same time, Barney Bigard left Duke for Freddie Slack's group (and a lot more loot I'm sure). Wallace Jones, my trumpet mate after Cootie left, was drafted. Several different men sat in the trumpet section including, for a few quick weeks, Dizzy Gillespie. Both our regular vocalists left. Ivie Anderson became ill and went home to Los Angeles. Herb Jeffries, the handsome male singer, didn't go on the road with us but stayed in California to do movies. Ben Webster checked out a year or so later. About 1945, Jonesy our band boy died. Adding to these disruptions, because of Musicians Union strikes or battles between the music societies (ASCAP and BMI), there was little or no recording either. This cut down on our income. Then the record companies weren't even pressing the hits because shellac was hard to come by. Food rationing meant that the fare was even worse in the greasy spoons that catered to us. Going on the road was tough. Trains were commandeered; the armed forces, of course, took precedence, while we scrambled to get to our gigs however possible.

During this time of travail, suddenly we were spending a lot of time in New York. I got restless and took a six-month hiatus from the band when my friend Brick Fleagle persuaded me that a trip would do me good. I'd get to Los Angeles to see my family and I could make some much-needed extra money on the way. We first played a gig in New Mexico with Dick Ballou, then went on to Mexico City and environs and wound up for several weeks in Los Angeles. That was in 1943.

By the time the war ended a few years later I realized that taking another holiday from the Duke would not eliminate a current nemesis of mine. Once, many years before, Big Green drove me out of the Fletcher Henderson band. Now I had a similar but different problem with a new member of the Ellington organization who was harassing me. This time I was in no mood to stick it out, especially since there were a lot of other opportunities being dangled before me. The best one was my selection by Hugues Panassié to be the second American band to play in postwar Paris. I was both proud and happy. The late great Don Redman had led the first group to go overseas and I felt myself to be in exalted company.

In 1947 I left the United States to tour the Continent with my six-man combo. We were to tour the Hot Clubs, about 45 of them, which were devoted to the study and understanding of United States jazz. Most of the scheduled concerts had been arranged by the Hot Club of France. I wasn't able to lay my hands on any big-name musicians – the money wasn't good enough to attract them – but I found several younger men who were eager to go. We had a seven-man group with a rhythm section of Ted Curry on drums, Don Gais on piano and Bill Houston on bass; John Harris played alto and clarinet, Sandy Williams was on trombone, 25 year-old Vernon Story was our tenor sax man, and I played cornet.

We landed in Paris, where the atmosphere was gay and festive. Imagine my surprise when we were met at the Gare du Nord by a band of young French musicians playing a tune that I'd composed and recorded years earlier. Note for note it was faithfully duplicated! After a mad succession of dinners, luncheons and other social expressions of goodwill and appreciation, we settled down to the business at hand, which was to set French feet tapping to American jazz. They had been craving our music all during the long war. Incidentally, next to nylon hose the most valued export which was sneaked past the

German noses was American jazz discs. One of my proudest possessions is a snapshot of Monsieur Panassié and company secretly having a session, listening to records in a cellar right under the German noses. The picture was smuggled out of France into Lisbon and delivered to a dear friend to pass on to me. It seems unbelievable but it is a fact that many French people were hauled off to prison for the crime of playing jazz records.

After playing the Salle Pleyel, an important concert hall in Paris, we toured the major cities Marseilles, Bordeaux and Toulouse. It was here that we first enjoyed the miracle of French fried soft-boiled eggs. On to Lyon, Lille and more cities. In Limoges I was delighted to be made honorary chairman of the Hot Club, which I still am to this day. We also did many smaller French towns such as Montauban, Carcassonne, Bezier and so on – about 45 Hot Clubs in all. Though rewarding, it was a long and arduous trip.

By June of 1948 we had finished our booking of the French Hot Clubs. Meanwhile the Special Services of the American Army had invited me to do a two-month tour in Germany leading a mixed outfit of fellows, not my own group. The musicians were to be selected for me in England "of dark people" from Ceylon and Trinidad. I sent the fellows in my group back home as there was nothing else happening to keep them overseas. The German tour was arranged by the Hot Club of Berlin, who had the notion that some of their local jazzmen would sit in with us for a jam session or two. Now these fellows hadn't played any jazz in years and were, I was informed, "somewhat rusty." Needless to say, I didn't hold high hopes for this venture. But I wasn't going to turn down the American Special Services, even though it didn't sound as if this was going to be an especially agreeable tour.

My worst anxieties became more certain when I was told that my first concert was at 2 a.m. in the practically deserted Delphi Palast located on a ruined Berlin street, and would be lit only by two carbide lamps. The invitation to the event read, "In view of the power cuts, each guest is requested to bring a candle." To my surprise, the lack of lighting turned out to be an asset. It was a stunning sight to look out into the pinpoints of fluttering candle light. Furthermore, the big crowd of jazz buffs, both German civilians and American soldiers, greeted us with tumultuous applause. Because I had expected so little, this concert is one I will never forget – an outstanding page in my book of memories.

A few days later I recorded with some of the German jazz musicians. We did *Blue Lou*, *Muskrat Ramble* and a couple of my original tunes. I've often wondered if any of these records still exist. From Berlin we went on to play concerts in Munich, Wiesbaden, Frankfurt and Cologne. All did not go as smoothly as one could wish. One of the two cardinal rules in the business is to keep the music going whenever there is any disturbance. I was taught this when I started playing, but I found out personally that this rule, like all others, was sometimes better broken. While playing for US troops in Germany, a few American GIs included me and my band in a fracas. The music stopped. I returned to Paris to relax a bit before returning home myself.

On my previous visit to France with Ellington, there had been no chance to see the country. This time I took the opportunity to make side trips to the Champagne wine country, the legendary cathedral in Rouen and, in Paris, Notre Dame, the catacombs, to walk along the Seine and, most important of all, indulge myself in something I had longed to do – attend class at the famed Cordon Bleu cooking school. Now I was a tourist, too, and did all these and more. Although I considered myself on holiday, besides the classes at Cordon Bleu, I found time to keep in touch with my fans by lecturing at the Cité Université in Paris. I also had a daily radio show and made some nightclub appearances, as well as appearing at the Théâtre Edouard VII as a soloist from time to time. This was the theater where I once observed a most unusual phenomenon when the late Sidney Bechet came on stage and received a roaring, standing ovation which lasted a full three minutes or more. I found myself spending my time off quite happily.

One morning, shortly before noon, the telephone rang and a charming female voice, in good English but slightly accented, introduced herself as Mme —. I recognized the name immediately because I had followed her election with great interest in the Paris edition of the *Herald Tribune* newspaper, which had given her considerable coverage. At the time she was the only negro woman who was a senator in the chamber of deputies. The lady invited me to have lunch with her, saying that she had some business to discuss. I couldn't imagine what sort of business such a highly placed political personage would have to talk over with me. She reassured me when she explained that she had attended one of my concerts, where, as it happened, I had done one of my rare vocals. It was agreed that I was to be picked up at my hotel at 1 o'clock the following afternoon, and I came downstairs at ten to, making certain to be prompt. Mme — arrived in a long black limousine and I was pleasantly surprised to observe how elegant and chic the lady was. She was a symbol, representative of millions of people of color which were at that time in the French empire.

Her business, it turned out, was to ask me to provide a small group of my people to sing spirituals at the premiere of an African picture. As my only other commitment for that evening was to appear at a club at 11 p.m. for a half-hour turn, I figured that I had plenty of time to do both. But that was not allowing for the pomp and ceremony that evidently accompanied such openings. Anyway, I got some pretty good singers together, four women and three other males, besides myself. We rehearsed and all was set for *Deep River* and two other typical spirituals. The dawn broke on this eventful day.

During the previous hours, Pierre, that legendary "Great French Lover," held court next door to me and continued his efforts for what seemed like hours. After the sounds of *l'amour* had subsided, some chance acquaintance phoned me and asked if I wanted to buy a diamond. This was at 7 a.m! I snarled, "Hell, no," and was just falling asleep when an expatriate piano player fell into my pad. He was *en route* to Egypt or someplace and needed money. It was obvious that the cards were stacked against me as far as getting any sleep was concerned, so I got up, had coffee with brandy to give me strength and gazed moodily out the window. My dear wife started bugging me with questions like, "Can you depend on the singers to show up on time?" and "How do you think they'll look in their costumes?" and Did I think we could all stay in tune? – adding that nothing was so terrible as a vocal group singing out of tune. Ordinarily, I would have dismissed these remarks as being the usual helpmate's concern.

It is no coincidence that so many fine musicians also wound up abroad after World War II. Everybody in the industry knows full well why the quota of expatriates keeps growing. This is not a new phenomenon. It has been going on for years and has more than one cause. It is a big draw to find work someplace where we are treated like human beings in an unsegregated atmosphere. Then television dealt a crushing blow to the music industry in the United States by virtually closing its studios to music except as background. And much of that is canned. Those splendid orchestras which used to play for important radio shows were no longer needed. Added to that, nightclub jobs dried up, too.

By contrast, all over the world American jazz is admired and the people throng to hear it. As time goes by, sometimes I wonder when, if ever, my country will relinquish its traditional posture of ignoring the obvious, this self-conscious dissociation from its most significant exportable art form, which by virtue of its singular appeal has done more to pave the way for international goodwill between the nations than the Marshall Plan. Further, I view with deep concern and genuine alarm the catastrophic decline of jazz music in the country of its origin. The scene is bad and probably will get worse before it gets better. This is due to many factors, unfortunately most of them resulting from a lack of foresight and its accompanying evil, greed.

Living in Europe, I had the time to compare and realize that the European who plays jazz as a professional often has a different day-time job that pays the bills. An examination into musicians' lives, in depth, shows the great contrast between Europe and the United States. For instance, some of these fine part-time musicians whom I knew included an Icelandic consul, a famous Parisian philosopher and left-wing writer, a very wealthy and important South American industrialist, and a Swiss locomotive engineer who arranged his work schedule so that it would not interfere with playing engagements with Henri Chaix, the Swiss bandleader. In the US, although regrettably the interest in dixieland is far less obvious, the layman would no doubt be puzzled and intrigued by the diversity of the individuals who enjoy and are emotionally involved with two-beat jazz, either as a record collector or sometime player.

In my opinion, the music of a civilization, to a definable degree, mirrors the tempos and sociological attitudes that exist within the framework of that particular period. Therefore the professional musician occupies a highly sensitive position in any society. This has been true down through the ages. Paradoxically, it has also been customary for the masses to regard people who play for money as some kind of sub-human species, forgetting that most kinds of relaxation or fun are aided and abetted by music. Actually, the musician enjoys a dual and privileged position by virtue of being able to see behind the scenes, with its myriad nuances, causes and effects there for him to observe. And, at the same time, in his capacity as entertainer, he is able to a large degree to set and sustain the mood.

Nevertheless, it seems to me that, for the negro musician, the color prejudice added to this undeserved suspicion about musicians has made the scuffle tough for a long time. A few people have done their part to break the color barriers. Norman Granz, for one, was a shining example of integration in American music. I personally have witnessed Norman walking out of a hotel when the negro members of his troupe were denied accommodations.

This is a good opportunity to talk about another group of musicians who have been discriminated against – the ladies. One of the most subtle and vicious forms of segregation continues to be perpetuated against the women, particularly within the myriad spectrum of jazz music. I realize that to some degree this attitude results from a simultaneous conscious and subconscious rejection by the males of the considerable talents of the ladies. The female artist, composer, arranger and instrumentalist, no matter her skill, ranks far below her male counterpart and is for the most part denied the acclaim and, even more important, the monetary rewards that men receive. Actually, there's an existing parallel between the Negro and the female. The Negro still remains the fertile fountain, the true source of creativity, but when his bread is being passed around, monetarily speaking, the brother's slice of same (if and when it reaches him) is cut thinnest because his place at the table of worldly goods is below the salt. The female's position at the bounteous board is even more obscure. She sits below the pepper and is rewarded only by crumbs.

I refer to talented ladies like Della Sutton who, as a trombonist, arranger and orchestra leader in Washington DC's Howard Theater and later at New York's Lafayette Theater, was many years ahead of her time. There was Valaida Snow, trumpet player, singer, songwriter; Margie Gibson, arranger, composer, artist; Irene Higginbottom, composer. Margie Pettiford (Oscar's sister) was a talent, as were Lil Armstrong, Margie Hyams on vibes, Vi Redd on saxophone and Melba Liston on trombone. Wilder Hobson's wife was an amateur bassist who was such a little bit of a thing that he had to carry her bass to her gigs. And of course there is that wonderful pianist and arranger Mary Lou Williams.

Having arrived at the venerable, and I might add dubious, position in life when the youngsters ask for advice and how to succeed in the music business, I normally discourage the question by asking the neophyte, "What makes you think I am qualified to counsel anyone on such an undertaking?" And I usually pause before delivering the *coup de grace*, which is explaining exactly how remote the chances are for any modicum of fame, stability, yes, or even monetary compensation worthy of the effort that you must put in to become a pro. Today, the scene is no longer conducive nor is the public climate such that there is a demand for musical talent. That is, unless you plunk a guitar or honk on a tenor sax, because by and large these instruments are the ones that are making it. Violins, trumpets, trombones and the rest of the musical family are sort of out in limbo, waiting for their turn to regain popularity. Who knows, someday maybe they will all be back in vogue. However, here are some of the obstacles that exist today. First of all, and assuming that you have real talent, where do you go to present that talent? The local high school or college? They will love you but there's little money, if any, there. The jazz clubs will let you play, but only on an off-night and for free. And then the Musician's Union will start breathing down your neck, wanting you to join up, thereby enabling them to continue the fiction that they are protecting the swarms of fellows and gals that fight tooth and nail for what few jobs there are around.

But to keep this on a constructive, impersonal level, OK, you've got the talent plus "stars in your eyes," and you are determined to make it – but big. You'll show them. But first, and don't let it scare you, if you make it big, it will be over the corpses of the ten or fifteen thousand youngsters who have been emerging from our high schools, colleges and music schools yearly for the last 30 years. Here you are, a lad or lass fresh out of music school or whatever, who arrives at a point where a choice must be made: either get a job in something that will provide a living or stay with the horn that gives so much pleasure. If the dilemma is solved by the person's forsaking everything for his instrument, there's a psychological reason for this, as the music provides the most rewarding outlet for one's ego. No matter how badly the kid plays in comparison with his betters, when he plays there is always someone around to marvel at his skill. So our hero breaks the sad news to the family that he's through with school and plunges headlong into being a tooter for better or worse. Once he's in the world of professionals it is not long before he realizes how little he knows, as he finds out that most of the theories that he has been taught in school are just that – theories. Now he must learn how to apply the knowledge to the practicality of communication. Otherwise it will prove to be tough scuffling.

There are more hurdles. The boys just happened to mention that the system works something like this: in order for a have-not to crack the sound barrier and get a gig in this select club of haves, first you have to be related to someone. All right, you are at the post being related, but your relative has to have a big "in" with either the executive's secretary's secretary or, maybe, know where a body or two is buried. And, after all that, where is there for a musician to play? Perhaps it is time for a complete reappraisal of music's value, because back over the years I've seen vanish from the New York scene the neighborhood theaters, the burlesque houses, the ballrooms, the dance halls, the taxi-dance halls and all those spots where musicians used to play. So what opportunities are left for the professionals to make their living in music? Radio? TV with its clique? Musicals with their contractors' syndicates? These bands are ignored by the federal government despite the tremendous impact of music as a propaganda medium.

Or musicians are being asked to work gratis. They are placed in the same category as the underworld by the New York city police department, fingerprinted in a rogue's gallery and forced to pay for the privilege. It seems to me that the musician is the last to be hired and the first to be fired. A fledgling club owner will spend much thought, time and money over his lease, his bar and decor. He will devote hours deciding upon a chef and the policy of his place, the dishwashing equipment and the proper lighting. Once this has all been taken care of, then next comes the bandstand, if he intends to have music. Does he seek the advice of a professional musician about how large a stand should be? Of course not! He decides to stick it in the corner, out of the waiters' way – never mind the acoustics, the musicians' comfort or anything else.

I can't believe that the average musician of status is enthralled at the frenzied sounds of the past few years or that the cacophony extant will really become a permanent part of American jazz music. I recall the earlier revolution led by such stalwarts as Monk, Diz and Charlie Parker, all of whom were innovators once. But, as success beckoned, these gentlemen, without so much as a glance over their shoulders, gradually matured into more than a semblance of good taste. Surprisingly, most of the aforementioned are no longer looked upon as daring by their younger compatriots, who prefer to chase the illusion of newer sounds. For these lads, I have news. The same tones that you are struggling with now are the very ones that Johnny Dunn, Kid Ory, Joe Oliver and Louie and a lot of your older brothers created beautiful music with, long, long ago. Today, the avant garde, the young and the would-be sophisticate embrace various cults that spring up whenever a youngster discovers a set of musical clichés that baffles description. The professional musician and the person who reveres jazz as an inspirational source find it hard to relate these efforts to what has gone on before. Of course, it is understandable that neophytes have to try and spread their fledgling wings and prove that they, too, have something to say in music, and I am all for that. But it seems such a pity that music should be forced to pay the price of extinction as an art form merely to justify one's open-mindedness.

In my opinion, the very structure and communication of American jazz depends on identifiable rhythm and a melody that establishes some rapport with the listener. Personally, I empathize with the lads who are valiantly trying to make their voices heard above the mob. And I also feel that encouragement should be accorded them more frequently, considering the basic fact that, although evolution is a constant ebb and flow, still the immutable laws of jazz as a communication must abide by attention to its integral elements – that is, melody and beat. For without a definitive rhythmic cohesive impulse, the resulting effort actually emerges as chamber music, not jazz.

As an American musician, my protest stems from the conflicting attitudes which, on the one hand, produce inertia from the American people and on the other, are counter-balanced by the greedy parasites who prostitute the music for their own ends, leaving the musician in the middle. The musicians' national body, the AF of M, which is supposed to help us, is also guilty of short-sighted leadership when they attempt to keep in step with the labor movement by raising their scale every time the economy takes a spurt. Frankly, I am not an economist, but I'll be damned if I can see how a musician expects to compete with the essentials like steel, bread, etc. This is not to suggest a return to the age of non-unionism for the musician but rather to ask the question, "Are we not being deprived of work due to the expense of hiring live music?" There used to be hundreds of song pluggers trying to get the new songs played so John Q. Public could hear them and decide to buy or not. We musicians do wonder how the fine songwriters feel with no market for their creativity. Now big business has taken over and proved that one disc jockey is equivalent to the former mass effort. Is music being made obsolete even before it has attained popularity?

It is true that nobody forced me into the music profession, if you don't count my dad's razor strap. But whoever thought it would get to the point where we would be told, "Your music is great but we want a younger-looking group, because youth attracts youth." It does seem as if this is the only so-called profession wherein one is penalized for the years of study, preparation and experience that you've put into the business. How Jelly Roll would have responded to that! And then they tell us how styles have changed and we're not playing what's "in." And just in case you think this is all abstract, it could be that your milkman or elevator operator or cabbie used to sit in a great big orchestra just a few years ago, resplendent in a tuxedo, surrounded by beautiful musical instruments and wafting beautiful music your way. Sadly, lots of important musicians have wound up like this. Friends are marking time trying to make a living at whatever, praying for that all too infrequent weekend gig. Nevertheless, as a rule it pays so little in comparison to what the fellow was accustomed to earning in his salad days that most of it is considered only as reaffirmation that once we were musicians.

This emotional outburst may seem like a gripe, which it is. Selfishly, I am obeying the first laws of nature because the gigs have been few and I like to eat, too. Finding myself with time on my hands these days, I thought that I would jot down my various experiences, joys and sorrows, having a little fun by doing so and maybe making a little loot, too. Well, I was never so wrong, as this writing business is harder than blowing a horn while some character is sucking a lemon in front of you. But if anyone prints this, there will be some honest money coming my way. Then I, too, can pass that old folding stuff on to my butcher and baker and even a small taste to my tailor, never mind the candlestick maker. Secondly, I hope to be doing a service for my fellow tooters, some of whom are too shy to cry or are great at reading music but perhaps not so hot at writing.

Anyway, I blithely started out making dozens of notes on bits of paper about incidents and happenings that I could recall over the years, only to discover that that was the wrong approach for me. After getting a bunch of recollections on paper, invariably, when I got around to looking for them, they had disappeared. Gremlins or carelessness? So I had to start all over again, grumpily asking myself how the hell I could write when I couldn't remember where I had hidden my notes? By this time, I was intrigued and hooked and I damn well had to write. Not particularly because I thought there would be any great interest in my collection of reminiscences, but by writing I figured to kill two birds with one stone. I'd get rid of my boredom and at the same time get even with society for my being unemployed by boring any casual reader. What a revenge! And a pox on obsolescence.

Even if I and my kind of music have become obsolete, music continues. To me, jazz music is valuable when it plays the role that inspired its creation – that of bringing happiness and joy. Along with that, there are the other levels of blues and sexual musical connotations. All of this is really the secret of the music and explains why jazz has such universal appeal throughout the world. By definition, it is the creation of sounds that are pleasant to the human ear. By application it is a true source of expression and relaxation which mirrors the mores at any given point of a civilization. And I conclude that, if it is true that love makes the world go round, then of course there'll always be music to spark the romance of life.

(A. R. W. Johnson, Dec. 31 1880)

Star of Bethlehem

All hail thou bright and glorious Star,
Thou precious messenger to men,
By faith we see its gleam afar.
Thou beautiful Star of Bethlehem.

When Shepherds saw its wondrous glow;
This Star like some rare diadem
. . . .
To greet the Babe of Bethlehem.

Who in a manger lowly bed
Reclined in calm & faithful ease
While cattle rude kept quiet for
Beside the babe the Prince of Peace.

Oh Star of joy of Hope, and Love;
Oh radiant glowing Star of light;
Thy beams shall guide us through faith alone
To find the God of truth and might.

Autograph of a poem by Rex Stewart's grandmother

Notice!!!

The Johnson Family will appear for the first time this season at _____ , evening, _____ , 1904.

They are wellknown in the Musical World of Philadelphia, Newport, Jamestown, Rhode Island, Atlantic City and Lakewood N.J. Etc. ...

...Program...

1.
2.
3.
4.
5.
6.
7.
8.
9.
10.
12.

ADMISSION

A program showing that the Johnson family gave concerts together in 1904.

RESPECTFULLY DEDICATED TO
MISS. M. BOOTH
THE MOST ESTEEMED SUNDAY SCHOOL TEACHER
OF MY TWO DECEASED CHILDREN
FLORENCE. R. AND CHARLES L. JOHNSON.
by MOTHER.

BE NOT FAITHLESS.

HYMN
for Mixed Voices.
WORDS BY
MRS. A.R.D. JOHNSON
MUSIC BY
EDWIN HILL.
PRICE 10¢

PUBLISHED AND FOR SALE BY
EDWIN HILL
1614 CHANCELLOR ST.
PHILADELPHIA. PA.

Copyright. 1905. by Edwin Hill.

Title page of one of the hymns for which Rex's grandmother wrote the words

le cordon bleu

revue mensuelle illustrée de cuisine pratique

ÉCOLES DE CUISINE & DE PATISSERIE

129, Rue du Faub. St-Honoré

Tél. : ÉLY. 35-39

71, Rue de la Pompe, 71

Tél. : TRO. 32-69

Rex's cordon bleu certificate

Index